Day Hiker's
GUIDE
to Vermont

Green Mountain Club

Day Hiker's

GUIDE

Vermont Hiking Trails Series

Volume 2

Fourth Edition

Edited by Sylvia L. Plumb
with Scott K. Christiansen

Green Mountain Club
Waterbury Center, Vermont 05677

Editions
First Edition 1978
Second Edition 1983
Third Edition 1987
Fourth Edition 2002

The Green Mountain Club, Inc.
4711 Waterbury-Stowe Road
Waterbury Center, Vermont 05677
(802) 244-7037
gmc@greenmountainclub.org
www.greenmountainclub.org

Information in this guide is based on the best efforts of the
publisher, using information available at the time of printing.
Changes resulting from maintenance, relocations, natural
disturbance, etc. occur over time, and use of the information in
this book is at the sole risk of the user.

Cover and book design by The Laughing Bear Associates,
Montpelier, Vermont

Watercolor painting by Helmut Siber, ca. 1955. Collection of
Fairbanks Museum and Planetarium, St. Johnsbury, Vermont.
Information about Helmut Siber, and more of his paintings,
may be found at the Fairbanks Museum and Planetarium Web site:
www.fairbanksmuseum.com/htm/weather_gallery.shtml.

Text illustrations by Ed Epstein

Format by Electric Dragon Productions, Montpelier, Vermont

Copyedited by Kate Mueller,
Electric Dragon Productions

Maps edited and revised by Map Adventures
Maps compiled and digitized by
Middlebury College Geography Department

Printed in Canada on recycled paper.

Fourth Edition 2002
Second Printing 2003
ISBN 1-888021-07-1

Dedication

George Pearlstein

This fourth edition of the *Day Hiker's Guide to Vermont* is dedicated to George Pearlstein, a longtime member of the Green Mountain Club. Recognition for George's work to create the first edition of the *Day Hiker's Guide to Vermont* is long overdue. George almost singlehandedly field checked trails and prepared and edited the first edition of the book published in 1978. While George's attention to detail is legendary, he did miss one important detail in that first edition — a credit to himself as editor. It gives the GMC great pleasure to finally recognize George for his contributions.

An avid outdoorsman, George completed his first of seven Long Trail end-to-ends in 1961, and was the first person to hike the Long Trail end-to-end in winter. By 1998, George had climbed to the high point in every town in Vermont, perhaps a record held by him alone.

In addition to his guidebook efforts, George served as GMC president from 1971 to 1973 and chaired the Trails and Shelter Committee and Guidebook Committee. George also was editor of the *Long Trail Guide*.

Thank you, George, for your work for GMC, your passion for trails, and for creating the first *Day Hiker's Guide to Vermont*.

Contributors

Editors

Sylvia L. Plumb with Scott K. Christiansen

Champions

Several people deserve special recognition for the work they put into this guide: Joe Frank for getting the ball rolling; George Pearlstein for sharing his passion for trails; Rick White for so happily helping us out; Keri Foster for cheerfully tracking down missing pieces; Ben Rose for helping us keep it moving; Katy Klutznick for her way with words; Dave Hardy for his advice; Mason Singer, Kate Mueller, and Steve Bushey for being such wonderful consultants; John Carl for helping with the introduction; Mark Haughwout for providing fire tower history; Jeff Nugent for making draft maps of the West River Trail; Cat Eich for those last helpful errands; and Scot Applegate for counting topo lines, researching trails, testing the index—and for his many kindnesses.

Contributors

It is impossible to list every person who assisted in the production of this edition of the guidebook, but many deserve recognition. Thank you for your creativity, patience, and enthusiasm for the *Day Hiker's Guide to Vermont*.

Pam Ahlen, Peter Alden, Glenn Andersen, Rolf Anderson, Pete Antos-Ketcham, Kim Armstrong, Kathy Astrauckas, Brian Aust, Paul Austin, Christine Barnes, Philip Becker, Paul Benoit, Geoff Beyer,

Lawrence Blood, Lars Botzojorns, Jerry Bourque, Stephen Brill, Brenda Brown, Farley Brown, Joseph Camardo, Nicole Carpenter, Peter Chapin, Michael Chernick, Brenda Clarkson, Jane Coffey, Seth Coffey, Carolyn Cooke, Kit Davidson, Jean Davies, Rod Davis, Stephen Dickey, Kate Donaghue, Bob Drachman, Beth Dugger, Jane Dudley, Russ Eastwood, Smith Edwards, Greg Epler-Wood, Harry Fisher, B. T. Fitzgerald, Cathy Frank, Diana Frederick, Arthur Gilbert, Jr., Pam Gillis, Robert Gillis, Steve Gladstone, Arthur Goldsweig, David Goodman, Reed Goossen, Carolyn Grodinsky, Don Groll, Malcolm Guild, Mark Guilmette, Paul Hannan, Theresa Hoffman, Tim Hoopes, Anne Hoover, Lisa Hughes, Allen Jacobs, Dick Johnson, Joan Kahn, Paul Kendall, Peter Kenney, John Keough, Maeve Kim, Peter Kim, Gale Lawrence, Marty Lawthers, Leo Leach, Ed Leary, Pete Ledwith, Bob Lincoln, Chris Lloyd, Virginia Lopez, Jay Maciejowski, Andrew Marks, Wilhelm Merck, Bill Morison, Malcolm Moore, Matt Moore, Tom Mulcahey, Dorothy Myer, Bob Northrop, Andrew Nuquist, Reidun Nuquist, Luke O'Brien, Herbert G. Ogden, Jr., Bill Osgood, Tina Palmerio, Rose Paul, Gregory Pedrick, Sandy Moore Pedrick, Pirk Pirkanen, George Plumb, Sharon Plumb, Connie Plunkett, Walter Pomroy, Pat Pranger, David Prescott, Mary Lou Recor, Roderick Rice, Wally Rogers, Gary Salmon, Gary Sawyer, Eric Scharnberg, Jeff Schoellkopf, Dennis Shaffer, Susan Shea, David Skidmore, Scott Smalley, Bob Spear, Kimball Simpson, Chapin Spencer, Julie Sperling, Shaun Stephens, Sandy Tarburton, Carl Taylor, Tim Tierney, Heinz Trebitz, Inge Trebitz, Jennifer Waite, Doris Washurn, Barbara Brown Watts, Thomas Weiss, Greg Western, Arthur Westing, Carol Westing, Dave Willard, Richard Windish, Kara Wires, Katharine Wolfe, Joan Woodward, Paul Woodward, John Zaber, and Samuel Zaber.

Many thanks to Professor Bob Churchill's geography students at Middlebury College who created the initial digitized maps, with a special thanks to Adam Sobek for seeing the project through. Thanks to Steve Bushey of Map Adventures for making final edits to the maps. The original maps were created by students working with Professor H. Gardiner Barnum at the University of Vermont and later edits by Theresa McCoy who worked with Professor Bob Churchill.

GMC thanks the state of Vermont, the Green Mountain National Forest, and the private landowners who allow the trails to cross their land. Lastly, the GMC acknowledges the invaluable efforts and contributions of the many organizations and agencies and their volunteers and staff who maintain hiking trails in the state. These organizations are mentioned throughout the book. Vermont's trails are a precious resource that contribute to our sense of community.

Contents

Celebrating Vermont's Trails

Much has happened in the world of trails since the third edition of the *Day Hiker's Guide to Vermont* was published fifteen years ago. Trails have come and gone. New recreation paths have been built (many utilizing old railroad beds), and trails long grown over have been reopened. A recent resurgence of trail building has led to the creation of small trail organizations throughout Vermont. A grassroots trail movement is afoot that harkens to when GMC founders envisioned and built the Long Trail.

In this fourth edition of the *Day Hiker's Guide to Vermont*, we have worked to include trails of many types, from well-loved footpaths that make their way to scenic summits, to new recreation paths that travel in populated areas, to short paths in state parks that lead to a nice overlook. In all, the book includes more than two hundred trails totaling 420 miles. Our goal was to create a guidebook that would provide the most comprehensive coverage of Vermont's trails outside the Long Trail system. The result, we hope, is that the *Day Hiker's Guide* and the *Long Trail Guide* provide nearly complete coverage of the state's varied trails. More than seventy volunteers field checked trails for this new edition.

Because most of the trails in this guidebook are not maintained by the GMC, we rely on hikers' feedback to help us update future editions. Your comments are most welcome—and requested! And please, let us know if there is a trail in your community that should be added to the next edition. We give our heartfelt thanks to everyone who contributed in some way to the publication of this guidebook.

Trails play an important role in our lives. Traditionally, they helped us get from one place to another; today this function is served by roads. Trails offer us a means to get away from our busy lives and allow us to connect with the natural world. Many communities are working to reestablish the importance of trails in our everyday lives by linking our homes to places we frequent, like markets and schools. We hope we have succeeded in providing you with a book that offers trails for escape and for your everyday travels. Happy hiking!

—*Sylvia L. Plumb*
and Scott K. Christiansen

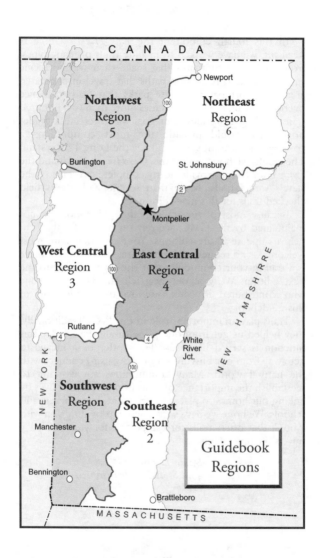

Using This Guide

The Six Regions

For guidebook purposes, the state of Vermont has been divided into six regions, roughly divided from west to east by Vt. 100, and from north to south by U.S. 4 and U.S. 2. In a few instances, trails are included in neighboring regions for geographic reasons; however, this happens rarely. Region boundaries are indicated on the map on the opposite page. The six regions are:

- Region 1: Southwest

- Region 2: Southeast

- Region 3: West Central

- Region 4: East Central

- Region 5: Northwest

- Region 6: Northeast

Region Components

Each region has three components: (1) a region map (2) a map locator key, and (3) trail descriptions and maps.

1. Region Map

The region map depicts the location of the trails that are described in the region. It is meant as a quick reference, not as an exact locator of trails.

2. Map Locator Key

The map locator key lists the trails indicated on the region maps and the page numbers where they are found in the guide.

3. Trail Descriptions and Maps

Within each region, trails are grouped by (1) trails in general (2) rambles. Some trails are only described and not depicted on a map.

Trails are described from trailhead to destination or terminus. Hiking distance, elevation change, and estimated hiking time are given. If an exact elevation gain is not provided, the elevation gain is described as minor, moderate, or difficult. Departures from this norm are noted.

The scales of the maps vary as shown on each map. The contour interval is 200 feet. Trails are shown as dotted lines. Dashed lines distinguish roads that are not driveable. In Vermont, the compass points about 15 degrees west of true north.

Abbreviations

AMC . . . Appalachian Mountain Club
AT . . . . Appalachian Trail
ATC . . . Appalachian Trail Conference
CCC . . . Civilian Conservation Corps
CVT . . . Cross Vermont Trail
DOC . . . Dartmouth Outing Club
ft. . . . . feet
GMC . . . Green Mountain Club
GMNF . . Green Mountain National Forest
hr. . . . . hour(s)
km . . . . kilometer(s)
LT . . . . Long Trail
mi. . . . . mile(s)
min. . . . minutes
Mt. . . . Mount
Mtn. . . . Mountain
NEPCO . New England Power Company
USFS . . . U.S. Forest Service
WHPA . . Windmill Hill Pinnacle Association
WMA . . Wildlife Management Area

Welcome to the Mountains of Vermont

A day spent in the outdoors is one of the great pleasures in life—and hiking is one of the best ways to spend a day out of doors. Vermont has more than 900 miles of hiking trails of varying length and difficulty.

The *Day Hiker's Guide to Vermont* describes the many trails scattered about the state that are suitable for day hikes. A companion to the *Long Trail Guide*, which concentrates on Vermont's largest hiking network, the *Day Hiker's Guide to Vermont* explores trails beyond the Long Trail System.

More than 200 trails are presented here; they include high peaks, natural areas, state parks, nature centers, and multiuse recreation paths. Many of the spots in this book are old favorites, while others are less well known. There are hikes that are perfect for half-day outings; others will take a day to complete.

Many of the trails lead to ecosystems rare to Vermont, with oak or mountain laurel, pitch pines, and bogs with rare plants. There are trails to suit most anyone—from the outdoor athlete to the casual walker. While concentrating on footpaths, this guide also describes many of the recreation paths in the state.

Together, the *Day Hiker's Guide* and the *Long Trail Guide*, the official guide to the Long Trail, describe the majority of the publicly accessible hiking trails in Vermont.

Vermont's Hiking Trails

Long Trail

Known as the "Footpath in the Wilderness," the Long Trail follows the main ridge of the Green Mountains for more than 270 miles from the Massachusetts line to the Canadian border. Along the way, the trail passes more than forty of Vermont's highest peaks, follows streams, skirts ponds, and passes through areas of aesthetic or historical interest. More than 175 miles of side trails complete the 445-mile Long Trail System.

Built by the Green Mountain Club (GMC) between 1910 and 1930, the Long Trail is the oldest long-distance hiking trail in the country. It was the inspiration for the Appalachian Trail, which coincides with the Long Trail for 100 miles. As the protector, manager, and maintainer of the Long Trail, the Green Mountain Club works to ensure that the trail—one of Vermont's most significant natural and recreational features—is protected and maintained for the enjoyment of future generations.

Appalachian National Scenic Trail

Vermont and the Long Trail hold a prominent place in the history of the Appalachian Trail (AT); it was on the summit of Stratton Mountain that the idea of an extended footpath linking the scenic ridges of the East crystallized in the mind of AT visionary Benton MacKaye.

The Appalachian Trail extends 2,150 miles from Katahdin in Maine to northern Georgia's Springer Mountain. The Appalachian Trail Conference, founded in 1925, works with its member clubs and federal and state agencies to preserve and maintain the Appalachian Trail, the world's longest linear national park.

More than 145 miles of the Appalachian Trail pass through Vermont. The AT coincides with the LT from the Massachusetts border to Maine Junction, north of Sherburne Pass at Route 4, and then swings easterly to cross the Connecticut River near Hanover, New Hampshire. The Appalachian Trail in Vermont is described in GMC's *Long Trail Guide*. For more information about the Appalachian Trail, contact the Appalachian Trail Conference, P.O. Box 807, Harpers Ferry, West Virginia 25425; (304) 535-6331; www.atconf.org.

Trails Beyond the Long Trail

Although the Long Trail System is the largest trail network in Vermont, there are other wonderful hiking opportunities throughout the state. These trails are the subject of this guide.

Vermont's trails are scattered throughout the state on private, state, and federal land. Many of these trails are of obscure origin and receive minimal maintenance. Elsewhere, organizations such as the Ascutney Trails Association, the Taconic Hiking Club, the Westmore Association, and various summer camps are active in maintaining and restoring abandoned trails and constructing new routes.

Although this guide includes large trail networks and trails leading to summits, it also describes some nature trails and recreation paths that are perfect for novice hikers, families with small children, or those seeking a moderate walk. Maintained by private organizations and public agencies, these trails provide satisfying outdoor experiences, educational opportunities, and fascinating insights. Nearly all the trails are self-guiding. Several of the state parks and a few of the private organizations provide resident naturalists, nature museums, and various field programs in addition to the nature trails.

Please contact the GMC with any changes, corrections, or additions to this guide.

Support Vermont's Trail Organizations

Many of the trails in this guide are cared for by small, local trail organizations. Like the GMC, these organizations need monetary and volunteer support to ensure the continued existence of these trails. To learn more, contact the organizations mentioned throughout the text and the listing on pages 345 to 348.

Guidelines for Hiking in Vermont

With proper care, most of the trails described in this book can be used with confidence, even by inexperienced hikers. Before using any of these trails, however, carefully study the information provided and determine whether a proposed trip is suitable for your experience and capabilities.

Trail Markings

Because the trails in this guide are maintained by many different agencies, trail markings vary. The Long Trail and Appalachian Trail are marked with white rectangular blazes, and their side trails are marked with blue blazes. Other trail markers run the gamut from yellow paint to blue metal disks and from scarce to abundant.

Staying Found

Many of the trails in this guide are minimally maintained and used and have marginal trail markings. A well-defined trail bed and indications of past clearing and blowdown removal will usually be apparent to an observant traveler. Occasionally, trails are neglected for so long that they become difficult to follow. Only reasonably experienced hikers accustomed to route finding should use obscure trails.

Should you have difficulty spotting the next blaze within a reasonable distance, stop, look, and backtrack if necessary. It is better to lose a moment looking for the correct route than to forge ahead on the wrong one. If, by chance, you do lose the trail, a compass and map—and the knowledge to use them—will help you get back on the trail or to the nearest road. The guidebook maps serve only for reference and should not be considered suitable for map and compass work.

Trip Planning and Safety

Planning a hike can be almost as much fun as the hike itself—and is probably the most important step in any hike. Good planning, common sense, proper gear and clothing, food, and water should provide for a safe and enjoyable trip. Precautions may prevent a small problem from quickly escalating to a dangerous situation. It is always safer to hike with others.

When planning a hike, consider the experience and conditioning of all members of your group, the terrain you plan to cover, the season, the weather, and the hours of daylight. Leave a copy of your itinerary with a reliable person.

Try out your equipment, new or old. Know how to deal with emergencies. Become familiar with the area you are visiting, particularly for winter trips. Determine where roads and towns are located in relation to the trail. Learn basic first aid. Most important, use your judgment to prevent problems. During periods of high water, streams may be impassable. Hikers may need to wait, backtrack, or detour.

Please, be safe, but most important, enjoy your hike!

Hiking Gear Checklist

Even experienced hikers forget something they wish they had remembered to bring. The following checklist is recommended for a safe and enjoyable day hike:

- ❑ guidebook and/or map
- ❑ lunch and snacks
- ❑ water—and plenty of it!
- ❑ sturdy boots or hiking shoes
- ❑ wind jacket or rain gear with breathable shell (remember it is considerably colder at higher elevations)
- ❑ warm layer (wool or synthetic fleece)
- ❑ hats and mittens (even in summer)
- ❑ flashlight or headlamp (extra bulb and batteries)
- ❑ compass
- ❑ first-aid kit
- ❑ waterproof matches
- ❑ insect repellent and sunscreen
- ❑ toilet paper and trowel
- ❑ whistle

Mileages and Hiking Times

Mileages used in the summaries and trail descriptions are actual hiking distances, including twists and turns. Hiking times given in the book are based on the age-old formula: a half-hour for each mile plus a half-hour for each 1,000 feet of ascent. These figures are for actual walking time; allowances should be made for lunch breaks, viewing and resting, ruggedness of terrain, hiking experience, and also for trips to summits and other viewpoints reached via side trails. Everybody has his or her own pace; actual times are likely to differ from "book times."

Climate and Weather

Although summers in Vermont's mountains are often cool and pleasant, hot, humid days are quite frequent. Never underestimate the variability of Vermont weather. Conditions on mountain summits are rarely the same as in the lowlands; temperatures often vary dramatically, sometimes as much as 5 degrees Fahrenheit per 1,000 feet. There is also a marked increase in the amount of precipitation at higher elevations. The annual average precipitation in Vermont is thirty-eight inches. Other conditions such as rain, fog, and sudden drops in temperature can occur at any time, even in the summer. Summer nights are usually cool, and hikers should always be prepared for rain.

Hypothermia

The threat of hypothermia, a dangerous and potentially deadly condition, exists year-round. Hypothermia is the cooling of the body's core temperature caused by heat loss and the body's inability to keep its internal temperature constant. This condition is not limited to winter. In fact, what is often referred to as hypothermia weather is not minus 20 degrees Fahrenheit, but those rainy, windy 40- to 50-degree or even 60-degree Fahrenheit days that occur in Vermont's mountains at any time of the year.

Symptoms of hypothermia include poor judgment, forgetfulness, and confusion. Motor control may suffer, leading to problems with coordination (such as being unable to fasten one's clothing), an unsteady gait, or even slurred speech. Other warning signs include being unable to keep one's fingers and toes warm, uncontrollable shivering, or extreme unexpected fatigue. If untreated, hypothermia can result in coma and even death.

Prevention is the key to avoiding hypothermia. Body heat is lost by heat radiating from uncovered surfaces such as a bare head; from direct contact, such as sitting on frozen ground; from wind blowing away the warm air in clothing; and from evaporation through breathing or sweating. Always be sure to eat and drink plenty. Dress in layers, including, as needed, wicking underwear, an insulating layer, and a wind- and waterproof shell. Wear wool or synthetics like polypropylene or pile or, if it's warm, keep some of these in your pack, just in case. Be sure to regulate body temperature by adding and removing layers as needed. Wet clothing will not keep you warm.

When spotted early, hypothermia is easy to treat. Immediately get the chilled person out of the wind and into dry and warm clothing, including a hat. Give him food and water and get moving again. This is usually all it takes to warm up. Once the person is walking, keep him walking. If the person can no longer walk, then you must try to rewarm him. Put him in a prewarmed sleeping bag. Place either hot packs or bottles filled with warm water around the person's neck, armpits, and groin. If the person becomes unconscious, he must be handled extremely gently and evacuated as quickly as possible. For more information about hypothermia or other backcountry emergencies, consult *Medicine for the Backcountry*, by Buck Tilton and Frank Hubbell.

Lightning

Injury from lightning, although fortunately rare, is a serious risk to hikers. Don't provide a tempting target. Whenever you feel there is a threat:

- avoid open summits, ridges, and fields,
- if in the forest, seek an area amid shorter trees,
- avoid wet gullies and crevices, and stay out of small depressions where ground currents may travel,
- also stay out of small caves (large, dry ones are usually good, however),
- sit or crouch on insulating objects, such as a dry sleeping bag or mattress, making yourself as small as possible, and

• set aside exposed metal objects (things inside a pack are usually all right).

About 70 percent of people hit by lightning survive. If a person is still conscious and breathing after being struck, the chance of survival is excellent. Even if a lightning victim is not breathing or has no pulse, prompt and effective CPR may save him or her. Continue CPR as long as possible—there is a much greater chance of survival in this situation than in most other cases of cardiac arrest.

Hunting

Most trails in this guide cross land that is open to hunting, a time-honored Vermont tradition. Hunting seasons are underway from September 1 through mid-December. Deer rifle season occurs from mid- to late November.

Late fall offers some of the best hiking of the year, with no bugs and with leafless trees affording greater long-range visibility, but it is necessary to take precautions. Wear bright, visible colors, preferably fluorescent orange.

During hunting season, avoid wearing brown, tan, black, or patches of white that might be mistaken for the white tail of a deer. For information on hunting in Vermont, contact the Department of Fish and Wildlife, 103 South Main Street, Waterbury, Vermont, 05671-0501; (802) 241-3700; www.anr.state.vt.us/fw/fwhome/index.htm.

Leave No Trace

You can help preserve Vermont's backcountry and wilderness by practicing Leave No Trace. The seven Leave No Trace principles are:

• **Plan Ahead and Prepare.** Prepare for extreme weather, hazards, and emergencies; bring appropriate clothing; carry and know how to use a map and compass; purify drinking water; know local regulations.

- **Travel on Durable Surfaces.** Travel only on foot and stay on the trail—shortcuts erode soil and damage vegetation; walk single file in the middle of the trail, even when it is wet or muddy; stay on rocks above tree line, to avoid fragile vegetation.
- **Dispose of Waste Properly.** If you packed it in, pack it out; pick up trash others have left behind; when provided, use toilets; otherwise, bury human and pet waste in six- to eight-inch cat holes at least seventy steps from water sources. Pack out toilet paper and sanitary products.
- **Leave What You Find.** Take only pictures, leave only footprints; do not disturb plants, flowers, rocks, and wildlife; leave natural objects and cultural artifacts.
- **Minimize Campfire Impacts.** Build fires only where permitted and only in established fire rings; use a portable stove instead of fire.
- **Respect Wildlife.** Don't feed or disturb wildlife; if you bring a pet, keep it leashed.
- **Be Considerate of Others.** Travel quietly, allowing nature's sounds to prevail; take breaks on durable surfaces away from the trail and other visitors.

Leave No Trace, Inc. is a national program dedicated to promoting responsible recreation by teaching minimum-impact practices and wildland ethics. For more information about Leave No Trace, contact GMC.

Water

The quality and quantity of drinking water cannot be guaranteed. All water sources should be treated. During dry weather, water sources may fail.

Contamination of water supplies is a problem, even in remote areas. Water may look and taste clean but still be unsafe to drink. Giardiasis, caused by the intestinal parasite *Giardia lamblia*, is just one of many illnesses caused by drinking contaminated water. Other bacteria and viruses may also be present in water sources. If giardiasis symptoms such as severe cramping and diarrhea occur, consult your physician.

The best way to prevent illness is to treat all drinking water. To kill *Giardia*, water must be boiled for one minute, filtered with a water purifier guaranteed to remove the *Giardia* parasite (filters may not remove all contaminants, such as viruses), or treated with an iodine-based chemical purifier (follow the directions on the bottle). To kill all viruses and bacteria, water must be chemically treated or boiled for ten minutes.

Spring and Fall Mud Seasons

The Green Mountain Club and the state of Vermont encourage hikers to avoid higher elevation trails during the spring and late fall mud seasons (usually late March through the end of May and late October until snowpack). Snow melt creates extremely muddy trails and makes them vulnerable to damage from foot traffic, which is often compounded when hikers walk beside the trail to avoid the mud.

• If a trail is so muddy that you need to walk on the vegetation beside it, turn back and seek another area in which to hike.

• Whenever you hike, walk through the mud rather than around it.

• Plan hikes in the hardwood forest at lower elevations.

• Avoid the spruce-fir (conifer) forests at higher elevations.

Camping

While this guide mostly focuses on day hikes, camping is usually allowed on state and national forestlands. Guidelines for each type of land ownership are described below. Unless you know you are on federal or state land and in an area where primitive camping is permitted, camp only at designated sites. For more information, contact the appropriate state or federal agency listed on pages 345 to 348.

STATE LANDS. With the exception of state lands north of Mount Mansfield State Forest, and some areas on Camel's Hump and Mount Mansfield, primitive camping is permitted below 2,500 feet if Leave No Trace practices are followed. Groups larger than ten require a state primitive camping permit. For more information, contact the state regional offices of the Department of Forests, Parks, and Recreation listed on page 347.

FEDERAL LANDS. Camping is permitted in the Green Mountain National Forest if Leave No Trace practices are followed.

PRIVATE LANDS. Always seek permission if planning to camp on private land.

Group Hiking Guidelines

More groups are heading for the woods. To help your group minimize negative impacts on the land and the experiences of other hikers, follow these guidelines:

• **Keep Groups Small.** The maximum group size for day use is twenty people (including leaders); for areas above tree line, fragile areas, and popular destinations, groups should be no larger than ten. Overnight camping should always be limited to no more than ten. Be considerate of other hikers.

• **Experienced Leaders Are Essential.** Groups should include one leader for every four hikers.

- **Avoid Overcrowding.** If possible, plan your trip for weekdays instead of weekends and holidays.
- **Obtain Necessary Permits.** Organized groups hiking in the Green Mountain National Forest may need an Outfitter Guide Special Use permit. Groups of eleven or more planning to camp on state land should contact the Department of Forests, Parks, and Recreation to obtain a primitive camping permit. (See page 346 for phone and address information.)

Natural Areas and Wildlife

Many of the trails in this guide pass through natural areas with sensitive ecosystems. Please follow the guidelines described here or posted at trailheads.

WILDERNESS AREAS. Parts of the Green Mountain National Forest are federally designated as wilderness. The United States Congress established these areas as places where human impact must be minimal. Appropriate recreation and scientific research are encouraged. Hunting and fishing are allowed, but logging, roads, and mechanical equipment (including mountain bikes) are not.

Restricting day and overnight group sizes to fewer than ten people is particularly important in wilderness areas. Trail blazing and brushing are limited. Signs are less frequent, and they often omit mileage figures. There may be more downed trees across the trail, reflecting the reduced intensity of trail maintenance. Bridges are rare, and some streams will require fording.

PEREGRINE FALCONS. After almost a thirty-year absence, peregrine falcons have returned to nest in Vermont. But they are still rare, with only twenty-three nesting sites reported in 2001. Peregrines prefer high cliffs and outcrops. They are easily disturbed, especially by hikers above their cliff-side nests. During the nesting season, from mid-March to mid-August, hikers may encounter trails that have been closed or relocated. Please give these areas a wide berth until the young have fledged.

For information, call the Vermont Department of Fish and Wildlife at 103 South Main Street, Waterbury, Vermont 05671-0501; (802) 241-3700; www.anr.state.vt.us/fw/fwhome/index.htm.

BLACK BEARS. Although black bears exist in Vermont, they are generally not a problem, being shy and seldom seen. Don't feed them and please follow Leave No Trace practices so bears do not become a problem.

INSECTS. Black flies and mosquitoes can make hiking in the Green Mountains very uncomfortable and at times unbearable. Black flies are most abundant in early summer. They usually disappear by mid-July. Mosquitoes are around most of the summer. Wearing head nets is helpful. Almost nothing works against black flies, except long-sleeved shirts and pants.

Rabies

Like other areas in the Northeast, rabies is present in Vermont. Although human cases are rare, and the danger of contracting the disease remains greater at home than on the trail, it is best to take precautions. Hang your food, keep your campsite clean to avoid attracting animals, carry out food wastes and trash, refrain from feeding animals, and stay away from any wild animal that is acting strangely, such as too tame or unafraid or too aggressive. Leave dead animals alone.

If bitten by a wild animal, wash the wound thoroughly with soap and water and get to a doctor as soon as possible. Rabies today is preventable—as long as medical treatment is received soon after contact; otherwise it is 100 percent fatal.

Winter Use

The winter hiking experience can be rewarding, filled with solitude, challenge, clear skies, and breathtaking views, but it can also be dangerous. A winter trip must be planned and conducted with caution. The margin for error on a winter hike is small.

Following a trail in winter can be difficult; blazes are often only four to five feet from the ground, a height that could be at knee level or even completely buried under snow during winter. Overhanging branches, well out of reach during summer, may obstruct the winter hiker's way.

Vermont winters are severe and prolonged, with abrupt temperature changes. Unpredictable and changing weather conditions, deep snow, and the weight of extra warm clothing and safety gear will add time and effort to your hike. Shorter daylight hours compound the situation. Breaking trail is strenuous and exhausting. Conditions at higher elevations will be much more severe, and wind may make winter travel impossible. On open ridges and summits, hikers may encounter icy, windswept conditions. Hypothermia, always a threat, is especially dangerous in winter. (See more about hypothermia on pages 8 to 9.)

Always give yourself extra time; the estimated hiking times in the guidebook do not apply during the winter months. Be prepared to get lost—but try not to. Carry a map and compass and know how to use them. Be prepared to spend a night in the woods, if necessary.

Winter conditions occur from October to May in Vermont's mountains, with snow lasting until early June at higher elevations just below tree line. At 3,800 feet snow lingers for eight to twelve weeks longer than at 1,800 feet. Maximum snow depth usually occurs in March.

If you are new to winter outings, gain some experience before you set out. Go on outings with friends who have experience, take a class, or join a guided hike. GMC sections offer winter trips, as do outing-goods stores. Several good books on the subject of winter hiking and camping are available (see pages 351 to 352). The GMC sells cross-country skiing guidebooks and maps at the GMC headquarters, (802) 244-7037 or at www.greenmountainclub.org.

USE SKIS OR SNOWSHOES. Please think of your fellow hikers and those who come after you. Avoid post-holing through the snow. These knee-deep holes can make it unpleasant, unenjoyable, and even dangerous for the person who comes next. Wear snowshoes or skis on all winter treks.

WINTER SANITATION. Carry a shovel and dig out the outhouse whenever possible. Be aware of where streams are and avoid making a pit stop near them.

CATAMOUNT TRAIL. The Catamount Trail provides the full range of skiing opportunities. Fashioned after the Long Trail, it traverses the length of Vermont from Massachusetts to Canada, linking cross-country areas with long stretches of backcountry trail. For more information about the Catamount Trail, contact Catamount Trail Association, P.O. Box 1235, Burlington, Vermont 05402; (802) 864-5794.

Trail Access

Although directions to all the trails are given in this guide, hikers should refer to road maps to find their way to trailheads. Hikers may request the official highway map of Vermont from the Vermont Department of Travel and Tourism, P.O. Box 1471, 134 State Street, Montpelier, Vermont, 05601-1471; (802) 828-3236 or (800) VERMONT. Vermont road atlases are critical for finding one's way to trailheads. Northern Cartographic's *The Vermont Road Atlas and Guide* and DeLorme's *Vermont Atlas & Gazetteer* are excellent resources.

The advent of E-911 added or changed road names throughout Vermont. There are some places in the text where two names are given for the same road. Please send any updates on road names to the GMC.

Parking and Fees

Trailhead parking varies from large lots to roadside pull-offs. Wherever you park, avoid obstructing traffic or blocking access to homes, farms, or woodlots.

To prevent trailhead vandalism, try not to leave your car at trailheads overnight. Leave valuables at home, or, at the very least, keep them locked in the trunk or otherwise hidden. Remove or hide your stereo, if possible. Don't leave a note on the car advising of your plans. Leave the glove compartment open and empty and park in the open and parallel to the highway if possible. If you have a problem at a trailhead, call the local or state police.

Although most hiking trails in Vermont are free to the public, some state parks and nature centers do charge a nominal fee for hiking on their trails.

Public Campgrounds Near the Trail

State and U.S. Forest Service campgrounds make ideal base camps for hikers. They are inexpensive and near many trailheads. Many are situated near lakes or ponds with excellent swimming. Many campgrounds are described in this guide. For a listing of Vermont campgrounds, contact the Vermont Department of Travel and Tourism.

Green Mountain Club

Protecting and Maintaining
Vermont's Hiking Trails Since 1910

I n 1910 the Green Mountain Club (GMC), declaring a mission "to make the Vermont mountains play a larger part in the life of the people," began building the Long Trail. Although the GMC's mission philosophically remains the same as when the club was founded, its responsibilities have grown. Entering the twenty-first century, the club faces modern-day pressures of encroaching development and damage to natural resources from overuse. Providing hiking opportunities now involves much more than building and maintaining trails. Today, the GMC and its 9,000 members are involved in all aspects of protecting and managing the trails and facilities of the Long Trail System in coordination with the state of Vermont, the Green Mountain National Forest, and the Appalachian Trail Conference.

Membership and Volunteers

Membership in the GMC is an important way to support hiking opportunities in Vermont and is open to anyone with an interest in hiking and the preservation of Vermont's backcountry. Annual membership dues support trail maintenance, trail protection, education, and publications.

Those wishing to participate in outings and organized trail maintenance activities may choose to join a GMC section. Sections provide four-season schedules of outings, including hiking, biking, cross-country skiing, and canoeing. They also maintain portions of the Long Trail and its shelters. Often GMC sections maintain trails in their geographic areas that are not part of the Long Trail System.

The club offers an at-large membership for those who wish to support the work of the GMC but are not interested in affiliating with a local section. Both section and at-large members enjoy the same benefits including a subscription to the club's quarterly newsletter, the *Long Trail News*, which provides up-to-date information on trail and shelter conditions, hiking, statewide trails, club history, and a club activities calendar. Members receive discounts on club publications and items carried in the GMC bookstore, reduced fees at some overnight sites served by GMC caretakers, opportunities to participate in a wide range of club activities, and discounts on admission to most GMC events. Section members also receive their section's newsletter and activity schedule.

There are fourteen GMC sections. Twelve are based in Vermont: Bennington, Brattleboro, Bread Loaf (Middlebury), Burlington, Killington (Rutland), Laraway (Northwestern Vermont), Manchester, Montpelier, Northeast Kingdom, Northern Frontier (Montgomery), Ottauquechee (Woodstock), and Sterling (Stowe-Morrisville). Two sections are based out of state: Connecticut and Worcester (eastern Massachusetts).

To join the GMC, send payment for dues ($30 individual, $40 family, $20 student/volunteer/limited income) to the Green Mountain Club, 4711 Waterbury-Stowe Road, Waterbury Center, Vermont 05677 or call the GMC with your VISA or MasterCard number at (802) 244-7037. Memberships can also be purchased online at www.greenmountainclub.org.

Volunteers are the backbone of the GMC and the Long Trail. They serve on committees and blaze and maintain not only the trail itself but the club's spirit as well. To volunteer, contact the GMC.

Publications

The GMC publishes books, maps, and brochures. In addition to the *Day Hiker's Guide to Vermont*, the club publishes the *Long Trail Guide*. A comprehensive list of GMC publications is on pages 349 to 350.

Headquarters

Information and Education Services

The Green Mountain Club headquarters are on Route 100 in Waterbury Center, Vermont, midway between Waterbury and Stowe. To reach the GMC from I-89 in Waterbury (exit 10), take Vt. 100 north four miles. The headquarters are in the red barn and office building on the west (left) side of Vt. 100. From the intersection of Vt. 108 and 100 in Stowe, the GMC is six miles south on Vt. 100.

The Marvin B. Gameroff Hiker Center houses the club's information services and bookstore. The hiker center is open seven days a week (9:00 A.M. to 5:00 P.M.) from Memorial Day to Columbus Day. During the colder months, information services are located in the GMC administrative offices in the Herrick Office Building across the driveway from the Gameroff Hiker Center. Business hours are Monday through Friday from 9:00 A.M. to 5:00 P.M. year-round.

GMC staff will respond to telephone, written, or e-mail inquiries about hiking in Vermont. Hikers are encouraged to stop by the center for trail information.

Protecting Vermont's Mountain Lands

In 1986, the GMC launched the Long Trail Protection Campaign in an ambitious effort to acquire land or easements where the trail crossed private land. By 2002 the GMC had protected 51 miles of the Long Trail and 14 miles of side trails. More than 21,000 acres of back-country land with wildlife habitat and recreational value have been safeguarded. This effort has been made possible in large part through state legislative appropriations for Long Trail acquisitions. Much of the acquired land has gone into state ownership. Help preserve the trail for future generations with a donation to the Long Trail Protection Campaign.

A Brief History of the Green Mountain Club

The Green Mountain Club was established in Burlington on March 11, 1910 as a first step toward turning the dream of a Long Trail into a reality. Originally conceived by James P. Taylor as he waited for the mist to clear from Stratton Mountain, the Long Trail is the oldest long-distance hiking trail in the United States.

Taylor, associate principal of Vermont Academy in Saxtons River, had been frustrated by the lack of suitable hiking trails in the state. He promised that the new organization would "make the Vermont mountains play a larger part in the life of the people."

The club's first objective, unprecedented in concept and magnitude, was to fulfill Taylor's dream of a Long Trail—a continuous footpath that would follow the length of the Green Mountains from Massachusetts to Canada.

In the first decade members built 209 miles of trail and provided forty-four overnight facilities, fourteen of which were raised by the GMC.

Completion of the Long Trail

The next decade saw the extension of the Long Trail north from Johnson, culminating at Jay Peak in 1927. Many club members felt Jay was "almost" to Canada and far enough, but Bruce Buchanan of Brattleboro vowed, "We better get rid of the 'almost'." Two years later Roy O. Buchanan, professor of electrical engineering at the University of Vermont, and his brother, Bruce, marked the remaining ten-odd miles to the Canadian border. In 1930 Charles G. Doll and Phillips D. Carleton cut the final link to Canada. On its twenty-first birthday, the GMC could celebrate the completion of Taylor's footpath from Massachusetts to Canada.

Well before the Long Trail was completed, the club had made progress in several other areas. Members organized several sections (local chapters), both within and outside Vermont, to maintain and improve the trail system.

The year after the final segment of the trail was completed, the club established its salaried trail crew, the Long Trail Patrol. Since then, the LTP has spent summers assisting the volunteer members and friends of the Green Mountain Club with trail and shelter maintenance and construction. For its first thirty-six years, the patrol was led by its founder, the late Professor Roy O. Buchanan of the University of Vermont.

Between 1966 and 1975, responding to heavy trail traffic, the club launched a variety of initiatives, including promotion of a "carry-in, carry-out" policy; dissemination of information on responsible trail and camping practices; stationing of caretakers at the most popular shelters and ranger-naturalists (now called summit caretakers) on the summits of Mount Mansfield and Camel's Hump.

Founder, Sponsor, Defender, Protector

In 1971 the Vermont General Assembly passed a resolution recognizing the club as "the founder, sponsor, defender, and protector" of the Long Trail System and delegating to it responsibility for developing policies and programs for "the preservation, maintenance, and proper use of hiking trails for the benefit of the people of Vermont."

Although the General Assembly's recognition has meant very different challenges to different generations of GMCers—from pioneer trail blazing to environmental concerns and land acquisition—the club's main responsibility remains the same: to maintain and protect the Long Trail for all Vermonters, now and in the future.

A Place of Our Own

When the GMC adopted its first vision statement in 1990, it could not foresee that one goal, owning its own headquarters, would become reality within two years. In 1992 the club bought the former 1836 May Farm on Route 100, a popular tourist avenue into the Green Mountains, in Waterbury Center. After renting office space for many years, first in Rutland, then in downtown Montpelier, the GMC was at last its own landlord.

Wide support for the Long Trail Protection Campaign and continued public interest in outdoor recreation have contributed to a steady increase in club membership. The club's activities today reaffirm GMC's original mission and call for GMC to play a leadership role in protecting, managing, and maintaining hiking trails throughout Vermont.

REGION 1
Southwest Vermont

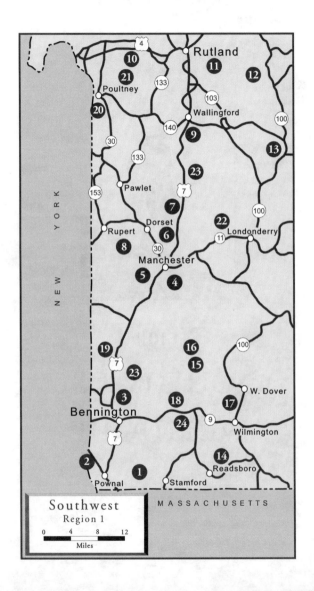

Rutland

10

21
Poultney

4

11

12

133

20

103

Wallingford

140

30

9

100

133

153

Pawlet

23

7

13

Rupert

7

Dorset

6

8

30

22

100

Londonderry

11

Manchester

5

4

NEW YORK

19

7

16

100

23

15

3

18

17

W. Dover

Bennington

24

9

Wilmington

7

2

14

1

Readsboro

Pownal

Stamford

Southwest
Region 1

MASSACHUSETTS

0   4   8   12
Miles

REGION 1
Southwest Vermont

The geography of southwestern Vermont is largely defined by the Taconic Mountains on the west and the Green Mountains on the east. In between, the Valley of Vermont, which originates in northwest Massachusetts, extends north 85 mi. to Brandon. This lowland distinctly separates the two mountain ranges and is several miles wide in the Bennington area, narrowing dramatically to a few hundred yards near Emerald Lake in Dorset. Within this valley lie Otter Creek, the longest river entirely within Vermont, and the Batten Kill, a world-famous trout stream.

Of uncertain geologic origin, the Taconic Mountains rise steeply from the Valley of Vermont. Beginning as low hills in northwest Connecticut, the Taconics reach their greatest height at Mt. Equinox in Manchester before dwindling to insignificant hills north of Brandon.

A part of the Appalachian Mountains that extend from the southeastern United States to Canada, the Green Mountains run the length of Vermont. East of the Valley of Vermont, they continue southward into Massachusetts, where, together with the Taconics, they are known as the Berkshire Hills. Unlike northern Vermont, where the

Green Mountains form two or three parallel ranges, in southern Vermont the mountains spread out in an irregular manner to form a highland plateau. Much of the area has been relatively inaccessible and unsuitable for permanent settlement. As a result, more wild country is found in southern Vermont than anywhere else in the state except the Northeast Kingdom (see Region 6).

POWNAL AREA

Lying in the southwest corner of Vermont and the northwest corner of Massachusetts, this large trail network offers many loop hikes. Maintained by the Williams Outing Club and the Green Mountain Club, the Pownal trails (USGS Williamstown, Pownal) climb several peaks with wonderful views across Vermont's southern Green Mountains, New York's Taconics, and Massachusetts's Mt. Greylock, and the Berkshires.

Most of these trails lie within a watershed area owned by the city of North Adams, Massachusetts. Camping is allowed only at Seth Warner Shelter on the Long Trail and at Sherman Brook Primitive Campsite on the Appalachian Trail in Massachusetts.

BROAD BROOK TRAIL

Distance: 3.9 mi. (6.3 km)
Elevation Change: 1,210 ft. ascent
Hiking Time: 2¾ hr. (reverse 2 hr.)

ABOUT THE TRAIL: Starting in Pownal at the Massachusetts-Vermont state line, this blue-blazed trail follows Broad Brook up the hollow between the Dome and East Mtn. to the Long Trail just south of County Road. The trail forms a loop to the Dome with the Agawon and Dome Trails and provides access to Seth Warner Shelter on the Long Trail. The Broad Brook Trail is maintained by the GMC.

THE DOME

Distance: 2.6 mi. (4.2 km)
Elevation Change: 1,650 ft. ascent
Hiking Time: 2½ hr. (reverse 1¼ hr.)

ABOUT THE TRAIL: Although most of the broad ridge of this aptly named mountain has a dense cover of spruce and balsam, an exposed rock area on the summit (2,748 ft.) offers views of the southern Green Mountains, the Hoosic Range to the east, Mt. Greylock and the Berkshires to the south, and the Taconic Range to the west. The trail is maintained by the Williams Outing Club.

TO THE TRAIL: Continue 0.3 mi. beyond the parking lot for the Broad Brook Trail (page 29) to a logging road, which enters from the right where White Oaks Road veers left. Parking is available along the apron of the logging road. A trail sign is posted on a tree set back from the road.

DESCRIPTION: From White Oaks Road (0.0 mi.), the trail follows the logging road past a chain barring motor vehicles, through a large log landing, and into the hardwood forest. After following the log road for a distance along a moderate ascent, the trail veers left into the woods (0.5 mi.) following yellow blazes. (The log road continues straight ahead onto posted land.) The trail eventually reaches a junction on the right with the Agawon Trail, a few feet below Meeting House Rock (1.2 mi.). (The Agawon Trail leads 0.7 mi. southeast to the Broad Brook Trail.)

Bearing left at the junction, the trail climbs easily for some distance, and then descends gradually to a shallow sag (1.7 mi.), where it turns to the right and follows an occasionally muddy woods road. (No trespassing signs in this area are intended to keep out unauthorized hunters.) The trail follows the woods road past a spur road to the left, then within 50 ft. bears left itself, leaving the woods.

The trail climbs out of the hardwoods into a spruce-fir forest before beginning a steep and circuitous climb over a series of quartzite outcrops to a false summit on a narrow ridge with a limited view through the trees (2.4 mi.). The trail then passes through a heavily wooded wet area before swinging to the east side of the ridge and climbing easily through scrub growth to the open summit (2.6 mi.).

AGAWON TRAIL

Distance: 0.7 mi. (1.1 km)
Elevation Change: 880 ft. descent
Hiking Time: 20 min. (reverse 45 min.)

ABOUT THE TRAIL: This yellow-blazed trail connects the Dome Trail with the Broad Brook Trail.
TO THE TRAIL: This trail leaves the Dome Trail just below Meeting House Rock, 1.4 mi. below the Dome summit.
DESCRIPTION: From the Dome Trail junction (0.0 mi.), the Agawon Trail ascends gradually toward the northeast on an old woods road. Soon turning sharply to the right (0.1 mi.), the trail makes a steep and winding descent, crosses a small stream, which later disappears underground (0.2 mi.), and continues its steady winding descent to a wooded knoll overlooking Broad Brook (0.6 mi.). Here the trail turns to the right and continues on easier grades to a junction with the Broad Brook Trail (0.7 mi.). Via the Broad Brook Trail, it is 1.4 mi. to White Oaks Road, 0.3 mi. south of the Dome trailhead.

PINE COBBLE TRAIL

Distance: 2.0 mi. (3.2 km)
Elevation Change: 1,240 ft. ascent
Hiking Time: 1 hr. (reverse 1 hr. 40 min.)

ABOUT THE TRAIL: One of two access routes to the southern terminus of the Long Trail, the Pine Cobble Trail is enjoyed by hikers for the fine views from the cobble, an outcrop of exposed quartzite with excellent views of the Hoosic Valley, Mt. Greylock, the Dome, and the Taconic Range.

TO THE TRAIL: From its junction with U.S. 7 in Williamstown, follow Mass. 2 (0.0 mi.) east to the first stoplight (0.6 mi.), and then turn left (north) onto Cole Avenue. Just after crossing a bridge over the Hoosic River and railroad tracks, turn right onto North Hoosic Road (1.4 mi.). Turn left on Pine Cobble Road (1.7 mi.) and continue to a parking area (1.9 mi.) on the left. The trailhead is on the right.

DESCRIPTION: From Pine Cobble Road (0.0 mi.), the blue-blazed Pine Cobble Trail slabs the hillside and shortly enters the woods. After passing a side trail on the right (0.8 mi.), which leads downhill 350 ft. to Bear Spring in a hollow, the trail rises steeply to the ridge where an orange-triangle-blazed spur trail (1.4 mi.) on the right leads 0.1 mi. to the quartzite outcrops of Pine Cobble (1,894 ft.).

Continuing from its junction with the spur trail, the Pine Cobble Trail follows gentle grades through scrub oak, pitch pine, and stunted white pines to a rocky knob where the trail ends at its junction with the Appalachian Trail (2.0 mi.). From here the Appalachian Trail (see below) leads north (left) 1.2 mi. to the southern terminus of the Long Trail at the Massachusetts-Vermont state line, or south (right) 2.6 mi. to Mass. 2 in Williamstown.

APPALACHIAN TRAIL

Distance: 3.8 mi. (6.1 km)
Elevation Change: 1,790 ft. ascent
Hiking Time: 2⅔ hr. (reverse 2 hr)

ABOUT THE TRAIL: This section of the 2,100-mi. Appalachian Trail (AT) intersects the Pine Cobble Trail, and then further north, where it coincides with the Long Trail, it reaches the Broad Brook Trail and Seth Warner Shelter beyond. See page 36 for the LT/AT description from the Massachusetts-Vermont state line to Seth Warner Shelter.

TO THE TRAIL: This section of the AT begins on Mass. 2 opposite Phelps Avenue at a traffic light 3.0 mi. east of the U.S. 7/Mass. 2 traffic circle in Williamstown, and 2.4 mi. west of the center of North Adams. There is no parking at the trailhead, so hikers should obtain permission to park at the Greylock Community Club 0.1 mi. east of the trail on Mass. 2 or at the Holy Family Catholic Church adjacent to the AT.

DESCRIPTION: The white-blazed AT proceeds north from Mass. 2 (0.0 mi.), opposite Phelps Avenue east of the church, and crosses over the railroad and Hoosic River on a footbridge. From the Appalachian Trail footbridge, the AT follows Massachusetts Avenue east. Just before reaching a stone bridge, the trail turns left off the road and crosses two footbridges before reaching a small reservoir on Sherman Brook (0.2 mi.). After following Sherman Brook upstream, the trail makes a short, steep ascent away from the brook. Descending, the trail soon reaches Pete's Spring (1.4 mi.) on the right and a spur trail to the left. The spur leads 0.1 mi. to Sherman Brook Primitive Campsite and continues another 0.1 mi. to rejoin the AT.

The AT continues and shortly returns to Sherman Brook at some old bridge abutments. From this point, the trail bears northwest and reaches the north end of the campsite spur trail. Ascending, the trail joins an old woods road (1.7 mi.), which it follows for some distance before swinging to the west and making a steep climb through an old rock slide from which there are good views to the south and east (2.3 mi.). There is a bad weather alternate route around the rockfall to the west. The trail then skirts a boggy pond and rises to a rocky knoll where the Pine Cobble Trail (2.6 mi.) enters from the left.

This junction is near the southern end of an extensive area on East Mtn. that is recovering from old forest fires. There are limited views of the Berkshire Hills to the south, including the Hoosic Range (left), the Taconics (right), and, between them, Mt. Greylock (3,491 ft.). Turning right at the Pine Cobble junction, the AT ascends north along the ridge, and soon reaches Eph's Lookout (3.0 mi.), named after Ephraim Williams, founder of Williams College. Just beyond, the trail enters the woods and finally comes to the southern terminus of the Long Trail (3.8 mi.) at the Massachusetts-Vermont state line.

LONG TRAIL

Distance: 2.8 mi. (4.5 km)
Elevation Change: 390 ft. ascent
Hiking Time: 1½ hr. (reverse 1½ hr.)

ABOUT THE TRAIL: The Long Trail (LT) extends 270 mi. along the main ridge of the Green Mountains from the Massachusetts-Vermont state line to Canada. A 2.8-mi. section of the trail from the border to Seth Warner Shelter is described here.

TO THE TRAIL: The start of the LT lies in the woods at the Massachusetts-Vermont state line. It may be reached from Massachusetts via the Pine Cobble Trail or the Appalachian Trail. See Pine Cobble and Appalachian Trail descriptions (pages 33 to 36) for access to the LT.

DESCRIPTION: From the Massachusetts-Vermont state line (0.0 mi.), the white-blazed Long Trail/Appalachian Trail descends to a brook crossing (0.4 mi.). It then climbs to the east side of a low ridge, passes over a bedrock ridge (1.7 mi.), and continues to a woods road (2.4 mi.). Crossing the road, the trail proceeds to a dirt road, which is the Broad Brook Trail (2.6 mi.). The Broad Brook Trail leads southwest 3.9 mi. to White Oaks Road in Williamstown.

The LT crosses the road and rises to a junction with a spur trail (2.8 mi.), which leads 300 yds. west to Seth Warner Shelter. This frame lean-to has space for eight. A brook, which may fail in dry seasons, is 150 yds. to the west. A primitive tenting area is located 400 ft. south of the shelter on a spur trail.

• • • • • • • • • • • • • • • •

TACONIC CREST TRAIL

1

Distance: 7.8 mi. 12.5 (km)
Elevation Change: 2,520 ft. ascent
Hiking Time: 5¼ hr. (reverse 4½ hr.)

ABOUT THE TRAIL: The Taconic Mountains extend from northwestern Connecticut until they dwindle to small hills near Brandon, Vermont. The Taconic Crest Trail, maintained by the Taconic Hiking Club of Troy, New York, follows the west and central ridges of the Taconic Range southward for about 30 mi. from Route 346 in Petersburg, New York, to Berry Pond in the Pittsfield Massachusetts State Forest. While there are few trail signs, the route is well marked with metal diamonds and white-paint blazes. A trail guide with maps is available from the Taconic Hiking Club (see page 347 for contact information). A new map and guide will be printed in 2002.

The only Vermont portions of the trail are two short sections leading south to N.Y. 2 at Petersburg Pass, which is just west of the New York–Massachusetts line (USGS North Pownal, Berlin). A blue-blazed approach trail once led to the ridge from North Pownal, but until landowner issues are resolved, the trail is closed.

Never far from the ridgeline, this section of the Taconic Crest Trail generally remains in mature hardwoods, but several large clearings and other vantage points offer wide views of the Adirondacks, Catskills, Taconics, and Berkshires. Water sources are scarce along the ridge. Camping is permitted off trail on lands belonging to, and marked by, the New York Department of Environmental Conservation.

TO THE TRAIL: From North Pownal, travel west on Route 346 to the New York–Vermont border. A large Department of Conservation sign on the south side of Route 346 marks the northern end of the Taconic Crest Trail, approximately 200 meters west of the bridge over the Hoosic River. There is a parking lot for ten cars and a kiosk.

DESCRIPTION: The trail begins at the southwest corner of the lot (0.0 mi.), west of the kiosk. (Do not take the jeep trail on the east side.) The trail ascends steeply for approximately 0.25 mi. on an old woods road, then breaks sharply left (south), still climbing, to emerge into a brushy open area marked by small evergreens.

The trail then reenters the trees, curves to the west, and crosses the earlier mentioned jeep trail at right angles. Steadily climbing through the woods, it crosses wet sections to emerge on a ridge where it turns left, crosses over a small knoll, and descends, on the far side, to a woods road that continues to the true Taconic Ridge crest (1.5 mi.).

From here, the trail travels along the broad and meandering ridge. After passing over two minor knobs (2.3 mi. and 3.3 mi.), the trail briefly returns to the Vermont side of the state line in the vicinity of a wooded knob (3.9 mi.) and descends into the saddle north of Bald Mtn. (4.1 mi.). The trail then begins a steady climb to the wooded summit (4.4 mi.) and then continues around its east shoulder to a spur, which leads 250 ft. to a lookout, where there are views of the Pownal Valley, the Dome, and Mt. Greylock. The main trail descends past two other lookouts to a sag (4.7 mi.) and follows an old road uphill to a junction (4.9 mi.). To the left (east), a spur descends about 250 ft. to the Snow Hole, a deep fissure in the rocks where tradition holds that snow and ice may be found year-round.

From the Snow Hole spur, the trail continues uphill along the old road, eventually crossing to the west side of the ridge, bypassing the wooded summit of White Rock, and passing through two large clearings (5.4 mi. and 5.5 mi.), both offering good views to the west and south. Returning to the woods after passing through two smaller clearings, the trail continues with minor elevation changes to a nameless peak (2,485 ft.) on the Vermont side of the state line (5.8 mi.). The trail then descends across the boundary into a wet sag (6.1 mi.) and climbs easily to the east of a wooded peak (6.4 mi.). Descending to a junc-

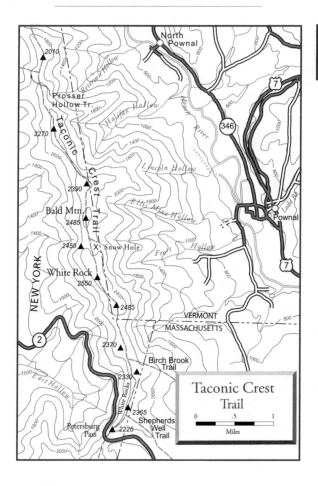

1

Taconic Crest Trail

0   .5   1

Miles

39

tion on the left with the red-blazed Birch Brook Trail
(6.5 mi.), the trail continues through an overgrown clearing (6.6 mi.) before reaching the north end of the extensive White Rocks clearing (6.8 mi.). The open summit of
Jim Smith Hill (2,330 ft.), a few yards east of the trail, offers extensive views to the south and west. Soon returning
to the woods (7.2 mi.), the trail descends steadily on a
woods road to two small springs on the left (7.4 mi.). A
short distance beyond, the trail turns to the right off the
road and rises to a large open area (7.7 mi.). Descending
in the open, the trail soon reaches N.Y. 2 at the summit of
Petersburg Pass, opposite the Taconic Trails Ski Area
(7.8 mi.). The trail continues through the ski area.

From Petersburg Pass, the highway descends about 4.0
mi. east to U.S. 7, south of Williamstown, Massachusetts.
To the west, it is about 5.0 mi. to N.Y. 22 at Petersburg.

• • • • • • • • • • • • • • • • •

BALD MOUNTAIN, WOODFORD

Reputed to be as old as any hiking trail in Vermont, the
blue-blazed trail (USGS Bennington) up Bald Mtn.
is maintained by the Bennington Section of the GMC. The
trail provides two access points to Bald Mtn., one from the
southwest (Branch Street Approach) and one from the
southeast (Harbor Road Approach).

Along the upper western slope are several areas of rock-
slides and ledges, known locally as the white rocks, which
offer excellent views west to the Bennington area, the
Taconic Range, and on a clear day, the Hudson Valley. The
summit provides a wide view to the north, noteworthy for
the expanse of wild country beyond, as well as views to the
east and south. The summit area is marked by krummholz
and scrub unique to the region, due, at least in part, to a
large fire on the summit in the 1920s. Note: The lower
portion of the trail is crisscrossed with woods roads and

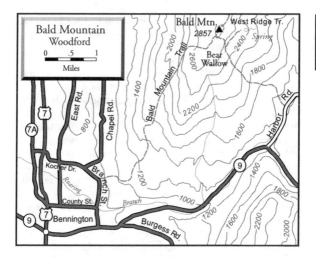

Bald Mountain
Woodford

0   .5   1
Miles

Bald Mtn. West Ridge Tr.
2857
Spring
Bear
Wallow

has been disturbed by logging activity, so special attention should be taken to follow the blazes.

The Bald Mountain Trail connects with the West Ridge Trail, which travels northward 8.0 mi. to the Long Trail near Goddard Shelter and Glastenbury Mtn. The GMC's *Long Trail Guide* describes this lengthy route.

BRANCH STREET APPROACH

Distance: 4.1 mi. (6.6 km)
Elevation Change: 2,150 ft. ascent
Hiking Time: 3 hr. (reverse 2 hr.)

TO THE TRAIL: The western trailhead, located on Branch Street in the northeast corner of Bennington, is unmarked but obvious. From Vt. 9 (East Main Street), about 0.8 mi. east of U.S. 7, turn north onto North Branch Street. Where it meets County Street, Branch Street Extension bears to the right and crosses Roaring Branch before continuing north. The trailhead is on the right side of the road at a sharp left turn and a power line crossing.

To reach the trailhead from the north end of town, follow Kocher Drive east from the junction of U.S. 7, Vt. 7A, and Northside Drive, through a traffic light, and past Chapel Road on the left. The trailhead is on the left, past a trailer park on the right. Parking is available along the roadside.

DESCRIPTION: From Branch Street (0.0 mi.), the trail ascends a woods road, roughly parallel to the power line but just to the left of it. After crossing two smaller lines, the trail crosses the wide clearing of a much larger power line (0.3 mi.), where there are views north and south. Following the road on easy grades and soon swinging to the north, the trail crosses a brook (0.6 mi.), either on the flimsy remains of a bridge or across a ford about 30 ft. downstream created by recent logging operations. The trail continues straight ahead from the bridge crossing for a short distance before curving to the left and eventually meeting a woods road. Arriving at a fork in the road (0.9 mi.), the trail bears to the left, and in another 50 yds. veers left off the woods road altogether. After some distance, the trail crosses two small spring brooks (1.3 mi.) and ascends through a "rock garden" between two diverging streams. The trail then crosses the stream at the point of diversion (1.7 mi.) and continues to an open rock area deep in the woods beside the brook (1.9 mi.).

Returning to the woods, the trail recrosses the brook (2.1 mi.) and soon begins a steady climb to the right out of the hollow. After reaching a spur, which leads 75 ft. left to a view of the Bennington area (2.7 mi.), the trail continues its steady climb to cross the first of a series of old rock slides (2.9 mi.), marked infrequently by blazes and cairns. From here there are views of Bennington, Mt. Anthony, Lake Paran, Mt. Greylock, and the Taconics. Eventually returning to the woods (3.2 mi.), the trail continues on easy grades, turns left at the site of a well-established fireplace, and climbs steadily, for the most part, toward the ridge. Soon after entering scrub growth, the trail continues in the open to a junction on the ridgeline (4.0 mi.).

To the left, the West Ridge Trail rises gradually to the summit of Bald Mtn. (2,857 ft.) (4.1 mi.), where there are views to the north of Glastenbury Mtn., Mt. Equinox, and Dorset Peak.

HARBOR ROAD APPROACH

Distance: 2.0 mi. (3.2 km)
Elevation Change: 1,580 ft. ascent
Hiking Time: 2 hr. (reverse 1¼ hr.)

TO THE TRAIL: From Bennington, follow Vt. 9 4.0 mi. east to the Woodford Hollow town office. At the church follow the gravel Harbor Road north 0.8 mi. to limited parking in the field next to a water tower on the left. Take care not to block any of the nearby woods roads.
DESCRIPTION: The blue-blazed trail follows an old woods road to the left of the private driveway (0.0 mi.). After passing a camp on the left (0.4 mi.), the trail reaches the red blazes of the national forest boundary. The trail soon veers off the woods road to the right and crosses a stream. From here the footpath ascends moderately steeply through a series of switchbacks, which lead out of the hardwood forest and up into the distinctive spruce-fir forest typical of higher elevations in southern Vermont. Throughout this area there are pleasant views to the east of Glastenbury Mtn. and Hell Hollow. The trail then climbs to a spur trail (1.9 mi.), which leads 0.2 mi. to a spring. From the spur, the Bald Mountain Trail reaches a junction with the West Ridge Trail on the right, which leads 0.1 mi. to the summit.

•••••••••••••••

MANCHESTER AREA

LYE BROOK TRAIL

Distance: 9.5 mi. (15.3 km)
Elevation Change: 2,000 ft. ascent
Hiking Time: 6¼ hr. (reverse 5¼ hr.)

ABOUT THE TRAIL: Passing through the heart of the Lye Brook Wilderness, this blue-blazed U.S. Forest Service trail is part of the Long Trail System (USGS Manchester, Sunderland). The trail starts in the town of Manchester and ends at the Long Trail near Stratton Pond. Along the way, it connects with the Branch Pond Trail near Bourn Pond. These trails (along with the Lye Brook Trail) are described in the GMC's *Long Trail Guide*.

At 9.5 mi., the trail in its entirety is lengthy for a day hike, but shelters and tent sites are located at Bourn and Stratton Ponds. A series of high waterfalls are found just 2.0 mi. from the trailhead.

Although a permit for the wilderness area is not required for most hikers, organized groups may need a permit (see group hiking, page 13). Trails in wilderness areas are primitively maintained: blazes may be few and far between; blowdowns may not be removed; and stream crossings could be difficult due to the lack of bridges.

TO THE TRAIL: From Vt. 11 and 30, 0.25 mi. east of exit 4 off U.S. 7, and about 2.5 mi. east of Manchester Center, turn south onto the East Manchester Road (0.0 mi.). Follow this road through a sweeping turn to the west, then turn left onto Glen Road (1.2 mi.) just before reaching the U.S. 7 overpass. After crossing Bourn Brook, continue straight onto the USFS Lye Brook Falls Service Road, where Glen Road makes a sharp turn to the left (1.3 mi.). The gravel service road, which parallels U.S. 7, ends at the trailhead (1.7 mi.) and a small parking area. The service road is not plowed in winter.

The Lye Brook Trail passes straight through the intersection and reaches the southern end of Bourn Pond (7.0 mi.). (The hike to this point will take about 4¾ hr. and the elevation gain is 1,950 ft.) The trail then assumes an easterly direction along a former section of the Long Trail. After crossing the Winhall River, which marks the eastern boundary of the Lye Brook Wilderness, the trail eventually reaches a junction on the left with the North Shore Trail (9.1 mi.) on the western side of Stratton Pond. Bearing right, the Lye Brook Trail crosses the pond's outlet on puncheon, passes two lean-tos, and reaches its eastern terminus at the Long Trail in Willis Ross Clearing (9.5 mi.).

Junction: From this point, the Long Trail proceeds 7.0 mi. south over the summit of Stratton Mtn. (3,936 ft.) to the Arlington–West Wardsboro Road. The Stratton Pond Trail departs the Long Trail 0.1 mi. south of the Lye Brook Trail/Long Trail junction and leads 3.7 mi. to the Arlington–West Wardsboro Road over a lowland route.

To the north, the Long Trail leads 4.7 mi. to the north end of the Branch Pond Trail and 5.6 mi. to Prospect Rock. Camping is available at Stratton Pond Shelter and the North Shore Tenting area. An overnight use fee is charged in season.

PROSPECT ROCK

Distance: 1.5 mi. (2.4 km)
Elevation Change: 980 ft. ascent
Hiking Time: 1½ hr. (reverse 1 hr.)

ABOUT THE TRAIL: From this vantage point high above Downer Glen (USGS Manchester), there are fine views of Mt. Equinox, Dorset Mtn., and the Manchester area. The unblazed and unsigned Old Rootville Road has been a popular hiking route for many years. The namesake settlement, a long-forgotten hamlet in the town of Winhall, was the creation of Henry Root. Around the Civil War, a small settlement of eight or ten buildings, including two sawmills, shipped logs and lumber west to the railroad in Manchester. No trace of the settlement remains today.

TO THE TRAIL: From Vt. 11 and 30, 0.25 mi. east of exit 4 off U.S. 7, and about 2.5 mi. east of Manchester Center, turn south onto the East Manchester Road (0.0 mi.). Turn left almost immediately onto Rootville Road, and continue 0.5 mi. to a small turnout where parking is available for five cars. Care should be taken not to obstruct the driveway nearby or block the unmaintained section of the road.

DESCRIPTION: From the end of the public road (0.0 mi.), the abandoned and badly washed out Rootville Road ascends steadily, following a flumelike stream for some distance and crossing several small streams. Eventually following easier grades, the trail continues to a junction with the white-blazed Long Trail (1.5 mi.). Continue along the road a very short distance to a spur on the right, which leads 50 yds. to Prospect Rock.

•••••••••••••••

MOUNT EQUINOX

With an elevation of 3,825 ft., Mt. Equinox (USGS Manchester, West Rupert) is the highest peak in the Taconic Mountains and also the highest peak in Vermont not in the Green Mountain Range. Common theory holds that the origin of the mountain's name is a corruption of Native American words meaning either "place of fog" or "place where the very top is."

Access to the summit is available by foot along the Burr and Burton Trail, also known as the Blue Trail, as well as by car along the paved Equinox Sky Line Drive (toll charged). From the parking area at the summit, trails from the Sky Line Inn (which is now closed) lead to several points of interest. Additionally, the Equinox Preservation

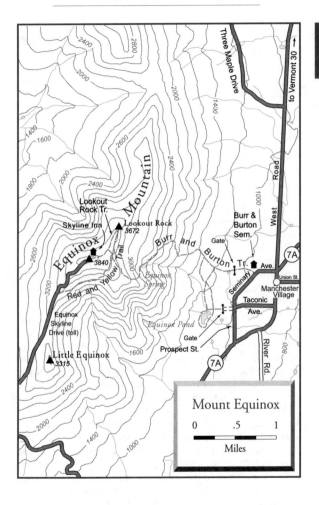

Trust (EPT), established in 1993 to protect and maintain the lands of Mt. Equinox, maintains several multiuse trails in the vicinity of Equinox Pond. For a brochure and trail map, contact the EPT at P.O. Box 46, Manchester Village, Vermont 05254; (802) 362-4700; ept@sover.net, or stop by the Equinox Resort.

BURR AND BURTON TRAIL

Distance: 2.7 mi. (4.3 km)
Elevation Change: 2,730 ft. ascent
Hiking Time: 3 hr. (reverse 1½ hr.)

ABOUT THE TRAIL: Also called the Blue Trail because of its blazing, this trail was first established and later maintained for many years by students from the Burr and Burton Seminary, now a semipublic high school renamed the Burr and Burton Academy, in the village of Manchester. The trail is maintained by the Friends of Equinox Preservation Trust, a dedicated group of volunteers who maintain all the trails on the Mt. Equinox Preserve.

TO THE TRAIL: The Burr and Burton Trail begins at the northwest corner of Burr and Burton Academy's upper parking lot—please do not park at this lot; ample parking is available nearby at the Equinox Hotel and Resort on Vt. 7A in Manchester. Hikers should leave their cars at the upper (west) end of the large parking lot at the hotel and then walk to the trailhead.

From the west end of the parking lot, follow an unpaved sandy trail (the old route of West Union Street) to nearby Seminary Avenue. Cross Seminary Avenue onto West Union Street. Almost immediately on the right is the Burr and Burton Academy parking lot. Proceed to the northwest corner of the lot to the spur trail. Take the spur past soccer fields and the academy's ropes course. At the fork in the trail bear left uphill to the red gate.

DESCRIPTION: From the red gate (0.0 mi.), the signed Burr and Burton Trail follows a woods road westerly and soon reaches successive junctions on the left with the Flatlanders Pass Trail and the Snicket Trail, both of which trend southerly on parallel routing for about 0.5 mi. to the Pond Loop Trail and the main gate access from Pond Road and Prospect Street. The Burr and Burton Trail continues uphill past a grassy woods road on the left to reach a fork (0.2 mi.). Here the Red Gate Trail takes the left fork and descends southerly for about 0.75 mi. to the Pond Loop and the main gate.

The Burr and Burton Trail takes the right fork and ascends on the woods road to a clearing and an unmarked trail crossing (0.4 mi.).

> **Junction:** Here the Trillium Trail departs on the left and descends southerly for about 0.6 mi. to Equinox Pond. The eastern leg of the Southern Vermont Art Center Loop leaves on the right and trends northerly for about 2.5 mi. to reach the lower slopes of the Southern Vermont Art Center and connections with its local trails.

The Burr and Burton Trail continues straight through the junction, and after some steady climbing, the trail crosses the much steeper western leg of the Southern Vermont Art Center Loop at a woods road junction (0.5 mi.).

Still following the woods road, the trail begins a steep and winding climb to the northwest. Eventually swinging to the southwest (1.0 mi.), the trail continues its steady ascent to the end of the road and a junction (1.4 mi.), where a marked but somewhat brushy spur trail descends 250 ft. to the gushing torrent of Equinox (Upper) Spring, which can be easily heard from the junction.

The Burr and Burton Trail, now a rough and narrow footpath, takes the right fork and continues its steady southwesterly climb past several limited but increasingly revealing views of the Manchester area and the Green Mountains. Eventually reaching the south shoulder of the mountain, the trail swings to the right (2.0 mi.) and ascends westerly on easier grades through spruce woods to a crossing of the Red-and-Yellow Trail (2.4 mi.), so named for its red-on-yellow blazing.

Junction: To the right, the Red-and-Yellow Trail makes a gradual northerly descent below the ridgeline. After passing limited views to the east, it makes an easy ascent to the ridge and continues a short distance to Lookout Rock (0.4 mi.). To the left, the Red-and-Yellow Trail descends gradually for some distance, and then begins a difficult passage over the aptly named Devil's Wagon Road. It then continues on rough, up-and-down routing past several views to the south to reach its terminus on Sky Line Drive in the saddle north of Little Equinox Mtn. (1.0 mi.).

From the junction, the Burr and Burton Trail continues in the woods and soon crosses the terminus of a narrow gravel road at a television repeater station. The trail skirts the left side of the fenced-in facility and continues for 100 ft. to its end on the Lookout Rock Trail (2.5 mi.).

Junction: To the left, the Lookout Rock Trail leads uphill to the Sky Line Inn, the upper end of the Toll Road, and the summit of Mt. Equinox (0.1 mi.) with some of the finest views in southern Vermont. To the right, the Lookout Rock Trail leads to Lookout Rock (0.3 mi.).

LOOKOUT ROCK TRAIL

Distance: 0.4 mi. (0.6 km)
Elevation Change: 188 ft. descent
Hiking Time: 10 min. (reverse 20 min.)

From the Sky Line Inn (0.0 mi.), this ridgeline trail descends to the north along the ridge past the upper end of the Burr and Burton Trail (0.1 mi.) and a granite memorial to Mr. Barbo, a faithful dog of Dr. Joseph C. Davidson, a man who wrote a history of the mountain. The trail then reaches Lookout Rock (0.4 mi.) and a junction with the Red-and-Yellow Trail. From Lookout Rock, there are excellent views to the north and east overlooking the Manchester area, Mt. Ascutney, Mt. Monadnock, and the White Mountains.

•••••••••••••••••

DORSET AREA

West of the Valley of Vermont, at the headwaters of the Batten Kill and Otter Creek, rises an impressive series of summits and ridges, long a site of quarrying activity. A variety of old roads, revived hiking trails, and snowmobile trails provide access to abandoned quarries and rocky outcrops, as well as to the summits of Dorset's higher peaks. Portions of a ridge trail connecting Owl's Head, Mt. Aeolus, Dorset Peak, and other significant summits surrounding Dorset Hollow have been reopened and are described in this section.

DORSET PEAK

Although this mountain (USGS Dorset) is one of New England's 100 highest peaks, the south (3,730 ft.) and north (3,770 ft.) summits are wooded and provide only limited views. A local flood and resultant landslides ravaged the Dorset Hollow area in late 1976, but the forest has reclaimed most of the damaged areas, leaving only traces of the event. Two trails provide access to the peak.

DORSET HOLLOW APPROACH

Distance: 3.4 mi. (5.5 km)
Elevation Change: 2,320 ft. ascent
Hiking Time: 3 hr. (reverse 1¾ hr.)

TO THE TRAIL: In the village of Dorset, just west of the Barrows House on Vt. 30 (0.0 mi.), follow the paved Dorset

Hollow Road (also Lower Hollow Road) north, turn right at the first junction onto Elm Street (0.7 mi.) and continue past a fork on the left (0.9 mi.). Continue beyond the end of the pavement (1.7 mi.) and past a fork on the left (3.6 mi.) to the end of the public road in Dorset Hollow (4.2 mi.), where limited roadside parking is available. The trail proceeds up the woods road on the left, which quickly becomes quite rough. Special care should be taken not to block any driveways in the area.

DESCRIPTION: From the end of the public road (0.0 mi.), the unsigned, unblazed trail ascends easily on an obvious woods road through areas of logging activity and reaches a hunting cabin (1.1 mi.). The trail continues following the logging road, bearing right of the cabin and ascending steeply uphill. Presently the trail crosses Jane Brook (1.5 mi.) before reaching the saddle (2.0 mi.) between Jackson Peak on the left and Dorset Peak on the right. To the left, the woods road continues to a public road at Danby Four Corners, providing access from the north. Ascent via this trail begins on page 56.

In the saddle, the trail bears right along an obvious snowmobile trail marked by an orange caution sign. The trail soon comes to another junction marked by a small cairn, where a second snowmobile trail leaves to the right (2.4 mi.); the trail turns right and ascends steeply along this trail, which is sporadically blazed with silver squares. At a second cairn (2.7 mi.), the trail turns to the right, leaving the snowmobile trail, and ascends through the ferns on an unblazed foot trail to a clearing on the south summit of Dorset Peak (2.8 mi.). An alternative access to the summit is reached by continuing straight past the cairn a short distance, where another snowmobile trail departs to the right and makes a short ascent to the summit. The clearing contains the remains of a steel tower erected in the 1930s. To the north there are good views of the Taconics.

Ignoring a smaller trail leaving the clearing to the east, the trail exits the summit clearing to the north along the

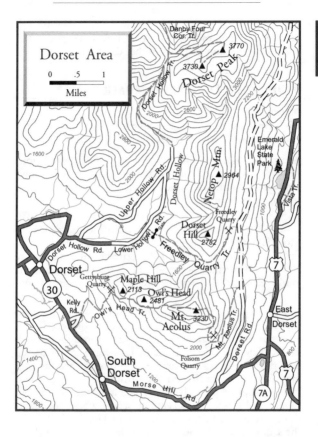

spur trail and descends to rejoin the snowmobile trail, now blazed with orange diamonds. Continuing north past a newer trail to the right, the trail reaches a sign at the crossing of another snowmobile trail (3.2 mi.). Continuing straight through this junction, the trail becomes smaller and climbs to the wooded north summit of Dorset Peak at the remains of an old cabin (3.4 mi.). A short spur to the south provides limited views in that direction.

DANBY FOUR CORNERS APPROACH

Distance: 3.7 mi. (6.0 km)
Elevation Change: 2,354 ft. ascent
Hiking Time: 2½ hr. (reverse 1½ hr.)

ABOUT THE TRAIL: This trail uses an unmarked but obvious woods road to ascend to the saddle between Dorset and Jackson Peaks and describes an alternative final ascent to the north summit of Dorset Peak.

TO THE TRAIL: From U.S. 7 in Danby, follow Brook Road west 3.9 mi. to a sharp left turn onto the gravel Dorset Mountain Road (known as Danby Mountain Road from the west). Continue south 1.3 mi. before turning sharply left onto Edmunds Road. Limited roadside parking is available. Avoid blocking the driveway of the nearby house or parking on the lawn.

DESCRIPTION: The trail begins on the south side of the road (0.0 mi.), follows a recently abandoned logging road, and, after passing through a gate, continues through an overgrown field that was a log landing. After veering to the left, the trail leaves the field and enters the woods (0.8 mi.). The trail remains on the obvious woods road and climbs steeply in places before reaching the saddle between Dorset and Jackson Peaks (2.2 mi.). The woods road continues straight ahead, descending into Dorset Hollow. In the saddle, a well-defined snowmobile trail leads east (left). An ascent to the south and north summits of Dorset Peak may be made following the path previously described in the ascent from Dorset Hollow.

An alternative ascent to the north summit may also be made using this trail. Turning left in the saddle and ascending gently, the trail crosses a small stream (2.4 mi.) then continues past a snowmobile trail leaving on the right and leading to the south summit. Continuing east and passing a poorly defined trail on the right (2.7 mi.), the trail offers limited views of the Tinmouth Valley and Danby Four Corners through the trees. The trail arrives at a junction indicated by a red marker on a tree (3.5 mi.), where a short spur to the left leads to a lookout with views east to the Green Mountains. Turning sharply right at the marker, a rocky trail ascends to the north summit of Dorset Peak at the remains of an old cabin (3.7 mi.).

MOUNT AEOLUS

Distance: 2.8 mi. (4.5 km)
Elevation Change: 1,850 ft. ascent
Hiking Time: 2½ hr. (reverse 1¾ hr.)

ABOUT THE TRAIL: Described here is an approach from the east over a limited section of the Dorset Ridge Trail, ascending Mt. Aeolus and connecting to the Owl's Head Trail (described on page 60) at Gilbert Lookout. For guidebook purposes, the quarry roads leading to the trail are considered part of the trail.

TO THE TRAIL: From South Dorset on Vt. 30, follow the paved Morse Hill Road east 2.5 mi. to Quarry Road on the left. To reach this same point from the east, follow U.S. 7 south from the East Dorset General Store 0.7 mi. to an intersection on the right with the same Morse Hill Road and proceed 1.2 mi. west to this junction. From Morse Hill Road, follow the unpaved Quarry Road (also Dorset Hill Road) 1.9 mi. north to a woods road on the left, across from a white house. Two large road signs at this junction indicate that the side road is open to the public. Roadside parking is available in the vicinity.

DESCRIPTION: From the trailhead (0.0 mi.), the Mount Aeolus Trail follows the quarry road, soon reaching a fork

(0.1 mi.) at a gate across a gravel road on the left. While the woods road continues to the right (leading about 1.0 mi. to the abandoned Freedley Quarry), the Mount Aeolus Trail turns sharply to the left, passes through the gate, and follows an old quarry road in a southerly direction. At a second fork (1.0 mi.), the trail bears left onto a narrow woods road, leaving the gravel road, which turns sharply right to a microwave transmitter. To the right of the trail, a short spur leads to the abandoned Folsom Quarry (2,060 ft.) (1.3 mi.). Opened in 1854, the quarry is now a great roofless man-made vault with vertical work faces extending about 100 ft. in height. A short distance beyond is a level area atop quarry dumps with good views of the Manchester area and Bromley Mtn.

The trail turns to the right and ascends steadily, circling above the quarry before meeting another road junction (1.8 mi.) where metal arrows point to the right. Bearing to the right, the trail continues along a series of switchbacks to a point east of the entrance to the Dorset Bat Cave (2.0 mi.), which is easily overlooked. Because of the importance of this cave as a hibernaculum for many bat species, including the endangered Indiana bat, there is an iron gate at the cave entrance to minimize disturbance of these timid creatures. This area is owned by the Nature Conservancy, which asks that the cave entrance remain undisturbed during the September-to-May hibernation period.

A short distance above the cave, the trail passes to the left of a lookout providing views to the east and south from leveled quarry rubble. The trail then turns left off the road (2.1 mi.) and ascends along a narrower footbed to a short rocky path, which climbs to the summit of Mt. Aeolus, formerly Green Peak (3,230 ft.) (2.8 mi.). A short distance south of the summit is a rocky lookout with views to the south of the Dorset-Manchester area, Stratton Mtn., Haystack Mtn., Mt. Equinox, and Mt. Greylock.

DORSET RIDGE TRAIL

Distance: 2.0 mi. (3.2 km)
Elevation Change: 980 ft. ascent
Hiking Time: 1½ hr. (reverse 1¾ hr.)

ABOUT THE TRAIL: Early last century George Holly Gilbert scouted and blazed the Dorset Ridge Trail, which formed a lengthy loop over Owl's Head, Mt. Aeolus, Dorset Peak, and other significant summits surrounding Dorset Hollow (USGS Manchester, Dorset). Portions of this trail remain obvious or have been reopened and are described here. This section of the Dorset Ridge Trail connects Mt. Aeolus with Owl's Head and Gilbert Lookout (page 60).

TO THE TRAIL: Follow the trail up Mt. Aeolus (page 57).

DESCRIPTION: Beyond the summit of Mt. Aeolus (0.0 mi.), the trail is variously marked with tape, metal trail markers, and faded paint blazes. Leaving the summit, the trail continues in a westerly direction along the narrow rocky summit ridge through stunted evergreens. Passing several views to the north and south, the trail leaves the ridge on a rocky path (0.6 mi.) and descends to the south along a fern-filled route, eventually veering west and descending to an old woods road (1.6 mi.) heading in a north-south direction in the notch between Owl's Head and Mt. Aeolus.

Turning sharply to the left (south) onto the woods road, the trail ascends over the height of land at the top of the notch, then leaves the woods road to the right (west) at a marked junction soon after starting a descent. The trail then ascends, climbing through dense spruce forest and following the south side of Owl's Head, but remaining well below the summit. The trail makes a short rocky descent to Gilbert Lookout (2,300 ft.) (2.0 mi.), where a stone plaque bearing that name is cemented to the cliff face. From this point, there are good views of Dorset Hollow, the Mettawee Valley, and the Adirondacks.

OWL'S HEAD TRAIL

Distance: 2.2 mi. (3.5 km)
Elevation Change: 1,260 ft. ascent
Hiking Time: 1¾ hr. (reverse 1 hr.)

ABOUT THE TRAIL: Described here is an approach to Gilbert Lookout from the west, over a portion of the aforementioned former Dorset Ridge Trail. In combination with the approach to Gilbert Lookout from the east over the summit of Mt. Aeolus (Green Peak) via the Dorset Bat Cave and Folsom Quarry (described previously in the text), these trails offer a lengthy day hike.

TO THE TRAIL: The trail begins on Kelly Road on the north side of Vt. 30, 1.3 mi. south of the Dorset Inn in Dorset and 1.4 mi. north from South Dorset village, or 4.7 mi. north of Manchester Center. A pull-off along Kelly Road provides roadside parking for several cars.

DESCRIPTION: From the parking area (0.0 mi.), the unsigned and unblazed trail follows a private dirt road to the east, toward a sign for Black Rock Farm. Past a white pine plantation, the road forks (0.3 mi.), and the trail bears to the right following a gravel road and continuing past two new houses until turning sharply right onto an old logging road across from the second house (0.6 mi.). The trail then follows this logging road on easy grades to an old hunting cabin (1.0 mi.) where it turns sharply to the left immediately before the camp. Here the trail may be overgrown, but begins to be marked by yellow and orange flagging. After crossing a pair of old woods roads (1.3 mi.), the trail ascends steadily to the open face of the abandoned Gettysburg marble quarry (1,720 ft.) (1.4 mi.), opened in 1866. The quarry dump, reached by a rough path on the left, offers views of the Dorset Valley.

From the quarry, the trail bears right and within 150 ft. turns left, then ascends steeply for another 150 ft. before turning abruptly to the right onto a gently ascending woods road along a ledge. Here the trail may be poorly maintained but is marked with yellow and orange flagging and tin disks. There are limited views from along the ridge, south to the upper Batten Kill Valley and west to Mother Myrick Mtn.

Eventually, the trail reaches a flat-topped ridge (1.9 mi.), which provides a good view of Owl's Head, then crosses into the saddle between Maple Hill and Owl's Head (2.1 mi.), before turning sharply left at a 12-ft.-high boulder on the right. A steep zigzag climb up the cliff, marked with reddish orange blazes, tin disks, and yellow and orange flagging, ends at Gilbert Lookout (2,300 ft.) (2.2 mi.), named for the father of the Dorset area trails, George Holly Gilbert. Here there are good views of Dorset Hollow, the Mettawee Valley, and the Adirondacks.

FREEDLEY QUARRY

Distance: 2.1 mi. (3.4 km)
Elevation Change: 900 ft. ascent
Hiking Time: 1½ hr. (reverse 1 hr.)

ABOUT THE TRAIL: This unmarked trail ascends moderately along a series of old roads to reach the long-abandoned Freedley Quarry (2,020 ft.), originally opened in 1808.
TO THE TRAIL: From the village of Dorset on Vt. 30 (0.0 mi.), follow the paved Dorset Hollow Road north, turn right at the first junction onto Elm Street (0.7 mi.), and bear right at a second junction where the Upper Hollow Road leaves to the left (0.9 mi.). Continue on the right fork (Lower Hollow Road) to a large barn on the left (2.3 mi.); the trailhead is immediately across the road at the start of a farm lane.
DESCRIPTION: From the trailhead (0.0 mi.), the unsigned and unblazed trail passes through a gate and proceeds along a farm road for 600 ft. before bearing left and passing through a tree line into a meadow. Turning left, the

trail follows the meadow around its margin to an obvious road (0.4 mi.), which it then follows, turning right and continuing into the woods. Ascending gradually, the trail reaches a height of land in the notch between Mt. Aeolus and Dorset Hill.

In the notch, the trail bears left onto a woods road (1.4 mi.), then right at a second intersection (1.5 mi.), and descends to intersect the quarry road itself (1.9 mi.). Bearing left into the Freedley Quarry, the trail continues to a large water-filled opening in the side of the mountain, which can remain frozen after cold winters until July. A marble dump just east of the quarry offers good views of the Valley of Vermont with the Green Mountains beyond. On a clear day, the view from this point extends all the way to Mt. Monadnock in southern New Hampshire.

MOTHER MYRICK MOUNTAIN

Distance: 3.8 mi. (6.1 km)
Elevation Change: 2,020 ft. ascent
Hiking Time: 3 hr. (reverse 2 hr.)

ABOUT THE TRAIL: This unmarked trail follows logging roads and snowmobile trails to a wooded summit, where there are limited views from a nearby lookout.
TO THE TRAIL: From Vt. 30 in South Dorset, follow the Dorset West Road west for 2.1 mi. to a junction on the left with the Nichols Hill Road then proceed 1.3 mi. to the end of this road. Parking for several vehicles is available in a small lot provided by a landowner.
DESCRIPTION: From the parking area (0.0 mi.), the unblazed and unsigned trail proceeds through a gate along a woods road, soon reaching junctions with roads on the right and left. Ignoring these roads, the trail continues straight, passes a log landing, and skirts the front of a hunting camp (0.3 mi.) before beginning a steep ascent. Ignoring logging trails off the main woods road, the trail

reaches the crest of a ridge in an area of activ
(1.0 mi.) and bears left along a road. In a short distance,
the road curves to the right, but the trail bears left onto an
older logging road. Ascending on gentle grades to the
southwest and south, the trail then turns abruptly to the
right (1.8 mi.), climbs more steeply, and reaches the
Taconic ridge and a second hunting cabin. At a snowmobile trail beyond the cabin, the trail turns to the left and
descends for a short distance before coming upon a major
three-way intersection. Here, the trail bears left and begins
a moderately steep climb to an intermediate summit
(2.7 mi.) and a ridge.

Continuing along the crest of the ridge and ignoring a
series of trails to the right, the trail reaches an intersection
at a sign incorrectly identifying the summit as located to
the northwest. Bearing left and ascending moderately, the
trail reaches the summit of Mother Myrick Mtn. (3,010
ft.) (3.8 mi.). A small, rocky lookout is 50 ft. northeast of
the trail, and it provides views across the Mettawee Valley
to Dorset Mtn. and Mt. Aeolus. A short distance beyond
the lookout are the remnants of a wing from a small plane
that crashed near the summit in the 1970s.

EMERALD LAKE STATE PARK

Distance: 1.0 mi. (1.6 km)
Elevation Change: 200 ft. ascent
Hiking Time: ½ hr. either direction

ABOUT THE TRAIL: The 430-acre Emerald State Park encircles Emerald Lake, the headwaters of Otter Creek, which
flows north through the Valley of Vermont on a 100-mi.
journey to Ferrisburg and Lake Champlain. The park offers swimming, fishing, motorless boating, and camping.
In addition to the Vista Trail, several shorter trails are
shown on a trail map of the park, available without charge
at the contact station.

To the Trail: Emerald Lake State Park is on the west side of U.S. 7 in North Dorset, on the flank of Dorset Mtn.

Description: The blue-blazed Vista Trail starts at a sign on the park access road, 200 ft. east of the contact station. From the trailhead, the trail travels easterly to cross the railroad tracks under the U.S. 7 highway bridge, then turns to the south and climbs through the woods to ledges above the highway (0.6 mi.). Here there is a good view of Emerald Lake and Netop Mtn. The trail continues along the ledge, descending gradually to recross U.S. 7 to reenter the park at the south end of Emerald Lake. Continuing near the shore through a marshy area, the Vista Trail continues around the west side of the lake and ends at the park beach (1.0 mi.), a short distance from the contact station.

•••••••••••••••••

MERCK FOREST AND FARMLAND CENTER

Located in the town of Rupert (USGS Pawlet, West Rupert), the Merck Forest and Farmland Center (Merck Forest) consists of more than 3,100 acres of fields and forests in the Taconic Mountains. George Merck founded Merck Forest in 1950 as a nonprofit conservation organization devoted to environmental education and recreation and is funded by memberships and contributions. The center's lands are open for public use during daylight hours throughout the year, and several backcountry cabins and shelters are available for rent. Although there are no fees for day use of the area, donations, left in the contribution boxes at each entrance, are appreciated.

The trails described below are a small part of an intricate network of more than 28 mi. of forest roads and trails

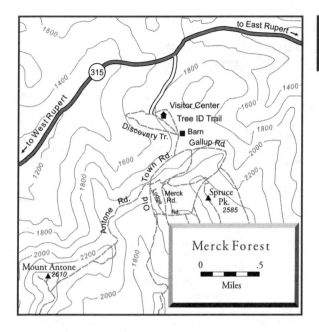

providing access to all parts of the forest. Closed at all times to motorized vehicles, most are ideally suited for walking and cross-country skiing. For more information, contact Merck Forest and Farmland Center, P.O. Box 86, Rupert, Vermont 05768; (802) 394-7836; merck@vermontel.net; www.merckforest.org.

TO THE TRAIL: From the junction of Vt. 30 and Vt. 315 in East Rupert, follow Vt. 315 west 3.0 mi. to a height of land. Turn left (south) on an unnamed gravel road with a sign for Merck Forest. A map of the trail system is available at the Joy Green Visitor Center or at the entrance sign nearby.

MOUNT ANTONE

Distance: 2.5 mi. (4.0 km)
Elevation Change: 820 ft. ascent
Hiking Time: 1¾ hr. (reverse 1¼ hr.)

DESCRIPTION: The ascent to the summit of Mt. Antone follows a series of roads. From the visitor center (0.0 mi.), the route follows Old Town Road, past sweeping views to the south, to the barn and the upper end of the Discovery Trail (0.3 mi.). After descending for some distance, the road ascends through the woods to a junction with Lodge and Antone Roads (0.8 mi.).

From the junction, Antone Road takes the right fork and follows easy grades along the ridge, passes through Clark's Clearing (1.3 mi.), and continues to a shelter at a junction (1.4 mi.), where the Clark's Clearing Trail departs to the left and a ski trail (which offers alternate routing) leaves to the right. The Antone Road continues straight ahead and soon begins a steady, winding climb to the left of the ridge. After gaining the ridge, the trail continues on easier grades, is rejoined on the right by the ski trail (1.9 mi.), and then begins a steady ascent past the Wade Lot Road and Lookout Road (2.1 mi.) to a junction with the Masters Mountain Trail and the Beebe Pond Trail (2.3 mi.). Here the Mount Antone Trail turns sharply to the right and ascends steeply to a junction with a spur trail, which leads left 0.1 mi. to a lookout. A short distance beyond, the main trail reaches the summit (2,610 ft.) (2.5 mi.) with views of Dorset Peak, the southern Adirondacks, the northern Catskills, and the White Creek Valley.

SPRUCE PEAK

Distance: 1.7 mi. (2.7 km)
Elevation Change: 750 ft. ascent
Hiking Time: 50 min. (reverse 1¼ hr.)

DESCRIPTION: From the visitor center (0.0 mi.), the route follows Old Town Road, past sweeping views to the south, to the barn and the upper end of the Discovery Trail (0.3 mi.). After descending for some distance, the road ascends through the woods to a junction with Lodge and Antone Roads (0.8 mi.). Following Lodge Road, the trail enters the woods and soon begins a winding ascent to a four-way junction (1.2 mi.).

Junction: To the right, a spur leads 300 ft. to a clearing, where there is a good view of Mt. Antone. To the left, a trail descends 0.3 mi. to Gallup Road, from which point it is 0.4 mi. to the barn.

Straight ahead through the junction, the trail slabs through the woods following Lodge Road to the left for a short distance before turning sharply to the right (1.7 mi.) and beginning a steep and winding climb to the summit (2,585 ft.). From the open rock, there is a fine view of Mt. Antone and the Merck Forest.

NATURE TRAILS

At the Merck Forest and Farm Center, there are also two self-guided nature trails, the Discovery Trail and the Tree Identification Trail, which begin at the upper parking lot and make good walks for young families. Each trail is about 1.0 mi. long, and both trails lead to the center's working 60-acre farm. Open to the public, this area includes an organic garden and barnyard animals. Discovery Trail guides can be found at the visitor center.

• • • • • • • • • • • • • • •

WHITE ROCKS NATIONAL RECREATION AREA

The Ice Beds Trail, Keewaydin Trail, and the Long Trail access the beautiful and interesting White Rocks National Recreation Area (USGS Wallingford). Directions to the common trailhead at the U.S. Forest Service's White Rocks Picnic Area are described in the Ice Beds Trail entry.

ICE BEDS TRAIL

Distance: 0.8 mi. (1.3 km)
Elevation Change: 160 ft. ascent
Hiking Time: ½ hr. (reverse ¾ hr.)

ABOUT THE TRAIL: This trail leads to spectacular views of White Rocks Cliff as well as a spot at the base of a rock slide where ice persists throughout the year. The cliff is made of Cheshire quartzite exposed by glacial action in the last Ice Age, about 12,000 years ago.

TO THE TRAIL: From U.S. 7 in Wallingford, follow Vt. 140 east. Turn south onto Sugar Hill Road (2.3 mi.), then turn right onto White Rocks Picnic Road (USFS Road 52) (2.4 mi.), and continue to the picnic area and parking (3.0 mi.). Overnight parking at the picnic area is not permitted. White Rocks Picnic Road is not plowed in winter.

DESCRIPTION: From the west side of the parking area (0.0 mi.), the blue-blazed trail quickly crosses a small stream and soon reaches the base of a rocky hogback. The trail then follows a series of switchbacks to a saddle (0.2 mi.). To the left, a spur leads a few feet to the Parapet, where there is an impressive view of White Rocks Cliff.

From the saddle, the trail ascends past several views of the cliffs to the summit at the top of the knoll (0.3 mi.). Here there is a good view to the west of the Otter Creek Valley and the Taconics. Continuing over the knoll, the trail descends to a woods road (0.6 mi.). Turning left and

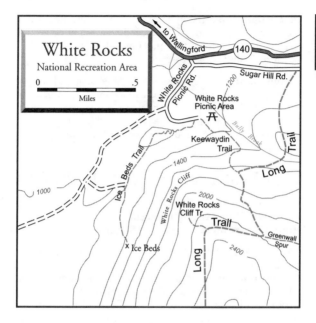

following the road, the trail descends to cross a brook (0.7 mi.), then quickly crosses a second, smaller brook and follows it upstream to its source in the Ice Beds at the base of an old rock slide (0.8 mi.).

KEEWAYDIN TRAIL

Distance: 0.4 mi. (0.6 km)
Elevation Change: 700 ft. ascent
Hiking Time: ½ hr. (reverse ¼ hr.)

ABOUT THE TRAIL: This trail links the White Rocks Picnic Area with the Long Trail, which leads to the summit of White Rocks Mtn. and White Rocks Cliff.

DESCRIPTION: From the upper end of the White Rocks Picnic Area (0.0 mi.), this blue-blazed trail follows a woods road to steadily ascend to the Long Trail (0.4 mi.) just south of Bully Brook's cascades.

> **Junction:** From the Keewaydin Trail, the Long Trail turns left, heading north, and crosses Bully Brook (0.1 mi.). Traveling beside a dramatic gulch, the trail reaches Sugar Hill Road (0.7 mi.). To the left, it is about 0.4 mi. to the White Rocks Picnic Road, and then another 0.6 mi. back to the White Rocks Picnic Area.

LONG TRAIL SOUTH TO WHITE ROCKS CLIFF

Distance: 1.1 mi. (1.7 km)
Elevation Change: 600 ft. ascent
Hiking Time: 55 min. (reverse 45 min.)

TO THE TRAIL: Follow the Keewaydin Trail 0.4 mi. to the Long Trail.
DESCRIPTION: Turning right, south, off the Keewaydin Trail (0.0 mi.), the Long Trail climbs steeply high above Bully Brook and its numerous cascades. The trail then ascends out of the mixed hardwood forest to cross a small stream. Turning sharply to the right and swinging around a spruce- and hemlock-covered promontory, the trail continues its steady climb to reach Greenwall Spur (0.6 mi.). This spur leads 0.2 mi. to Greenwall Shelter. From the junction, the Long Trail turns sharply and ascends gently to a junction on the right with the White Rocks Cliff Trail at a large stone cairn (0.9 mi.).

This trail descends from the Long Trail to an outlook with dramatic views on the very brink of White Rocks Cliff (1.1 mi.). These cliffs are a peregrine falcon nesting site, and may be closed to the public from mid-March through early August if the falcons are nesting nearby. Contact the

USFS Manchester Ranger District at (802) 362-2307 to confirm the status of the trail during nesting season.

1

•••••••••••••••••

BIRD MOUNTAIN

Located between Castleton and West Rutland, Bird Mtn. (USGS West Rutland), also known as Birdseye Mtn., is a quartz conglomerate named for Col. Amos Bird, one of the first settlers of Castleton. In 1767, while surveying the township, Colonel Bird became separated from his party and disoriented. To regain his bearings, he climbed to the summit of a nearby hill and spent the night. He awoke to a bird's-eye view of the surrounding area, and hence the mountain was named.

CAUTION: Due to a lack of signage, faded blazes, and an intricate trail network, take careful note of the trail descriptions and locations to avoid becoming lost. Use of map and compass is essential. The trails are marginally maintained and may be poorly defined or overgrown in places. Please keep the Green Mountain Club informed about changes to these trails.

The Birdseye hiking trails were established in 1979 as a service project by Camps Betsey Cox, Killoleet, Keewaydin, and Sangamon. Their names have been applied to four of the dozen lookouts and points of interest located on or near the four summits of Bird Mtn.

The trails on the summit ridge are interconnected and provide trips of varying length. Except for short sections of the North Peak and Castle Peak Trails, grades are not overly steep, and the footway generally is firm and dry.

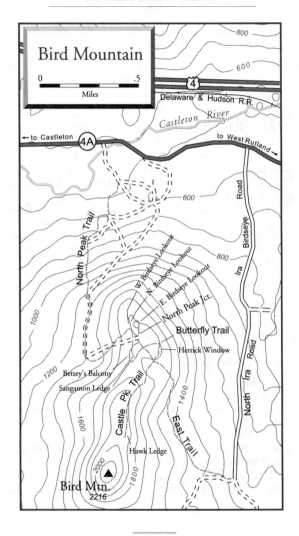

Bird Mountain

0   .5
Miles

800

600

4

Delaware & Hudson R.R.

Castleton River

← to Castleton   4A   to West Rutland →

600

Birdseye Road

800

North Peak Trail

W. Birdseye Lookout

N. Birdseye Lookout

E. Birdseye Lookout

North Peak Jct.

Butterfly Trail

Herrick Window

1000

Ira Road

North Ira Road

Betsey's Balcony

Sangamon Ledge

1200

Castle Pk. Trail

1400

East Trail

1600

Hawk Ledge

2000

Bird Mtn.
2216

1800

NORTH PEAK TRAIL

Distance: 3.4 mi. (5.5 km) round trip
Elevation Change: 1,250 ft. ascent
Hiking Time: 2¼ hr. round trip

ABOUT THE TRAIL: In addition to providing access to three impressive lookouts on the northernmost summit of the ridge, this trail serves as the approach to the Butterfly Trail and the Castle Peak Trail.

TO THE TRAIL: Trailhead parking is available at a gravel turnout and chain-link fence on the south side of Vt. 4A, 3.7 mi. west of its junction with Vt. 3 in Center Rutland, or 3.8 mi. east of the village of Castleton. The Birdseye Ski Area operated on the site from the early 1960s. Although it boasted such innovations as snowmaking and nighttime skiing, it nonetheless faced foreclosure by 1969.

DESCRIPTION: From the parking area (0.0 mi.), the trail passes to the east of the fence and follows an old ski lodge road over the Castleton River. The trail enters a field, passes a chairlift on the left, and intersects a road, where it bears right and passes a ski lift foundation. Entering a pine woods and ascending to the south, the trail crosses underneath a power line (0.2 mi.) and then takes a sharp right turn to follow another road parallel to the tree line. The trail then takes a sudden left turn, enters mixed hardwoods, and assumes a southerly direction.

After crossing a normally dry brook bed (0.3 mi.), the trail ascends on easy grades and eventually reaches a well-defined woods road (0.5 mi.), which it follows around a shoulder of the mountain. Soon after the road turns to the left and levels out, the trail bears right (0.7 mi.) and rises through open forest to cross a woods road (0.9 mi.).

Climbing easily, the trail soon crosses another woods road (1.0 mi.), at which point it enters and follows a multi-use trail, which ascends steadily at moderately steep grades. Meeting and crossing yet another well-used road, the trail begins a short but steep climb to a switchback at Killoleet Rock (1.3 mi.). Here the trail turns sharply to the left and begins a slabbing climb to the north, crossing a multiuse trail (1.4 mi.) and continuing on easier grades to Keewaydin Ledge (1.5 mi.), where there is a limited view to the west. The trail bears to the right and ascends gradually into a sag to North Peak Junction (1.6 mi.), at which point the Butterfly and Castle Peak Trails leave to the south.

The North Peak Trail continues east from the junction and quickly reaches the head of a small loop trail, which circles the summit of North Peak. Bearing to the right, the trail continues a short distance to a spur that leads right about 50 ft. to East Birdseye Lookout, overlooking the pastoral Castleton River Valley and the communities of West Rutland, Proctor, and Rutland, as well as the summits of Pico and Killington. The main trail then quickly passes over the highest point on North Peak and reaches a spur, which leads a few feet to North Birdseye Lookout, where there is an abandoned hang-glider launch platform and a view of Grandpa Knob and the Adirondacks.

The main trail then continues a few more feet to the West Birdseye Lookouts (1.7 mi.). From this point, the trail quickly returns to the head of the summit loop. Turning to the right, it is a short distance to North Peak Junction (1.8 mi.). Here the hiker may either follow other trails south along the ridge or return to the trailhead via the North Peak Trail.

BUTTERFLY TRAIL

Distance: 1.0 mi. (1.6 km)
Elevation Change: 100 ft. ascent
Hiking Time: ½ hr. either direction

ABOUT THE TRAIL: Taking its name from its staggered figure-eight routing, this trail consists of a double loop linking two views on the west side of the ridge with two lookouts on the east side. Either loop or both may be used as longer and more interesting alternate routing to Castle Peak.

DESCRIPTION: From North Peak Junction (0.0 mi.), the Butterfly Trail and the coinciding Castle Peak Trail follow a woods road south on easy grades around the west slope of Second Peak to a junction (0.1 mi.) where the Castle Peak Trail takes the left fork. The Butterfly Trail bears to the right, descends westerly into a shallow sag, and then descends very gradually to the south to reach Betsey's Balcony (0.2 mi.), where there is an excellent view to the west. After swinging to the left and making a brief climb, the trail continues south with little change in elevation to reach a junction (0.3 mi.). To the right via a spur it is about 50 ft. to another vista at Sangamon Ledge.

From the junction, the Butterfly Trail turns sharply left, following an old woods road uphill a short distance before diverging to the left and following a pleasant hogback to the end of the Butterfly Trail's west loop and a crossing of the Castle Peak Trail (0.4 mi.). To the left via the Castle Peak Trail, it is slightly more than 0.1 mi. back to North Peak Junction. To the right it is 0.7 mi. to the summit of Castle Peak.

From the trail crossing, the eastern loop of the Butterfly Trail climbs easily onto the south slope of Second Peak and then continues to a spur on the right (0.5 mi.), which leads a few feet to Herrick Window, a massive rock outcrop providing an imposing view of Herrick Mtn. and Ben's Slide, located on its north face.

From Herrick Window, the trail turns sharply to the south, makes a brief steep descent, and then descends more gradually, bearing to the southwest and descending to a woods road. To the left, this road descends 0.7 mi. to a public road, as described in the East Trail description (page 77). A few feet beyond the road, the Butterfly Trail meets a final junction with the Castle Peak Trail (0.7 mi.), which leaves to the left toward Hawk Ledge. To the right, the Castle Peak Trail follows an easy uphill grade back to the junction of the western and eastern loops of the Butterfly Trail (0.9 mi.), from which point it is 0.1 mi. to North Peak Junction.

CASTLE PEAK TRAIL

Distance: 0.8 mi. (1.3 km)
Elevation Change: 350 ft. ascent
Hiking Time: ¾ hr. either direction

TO THE TRAIL: Follow the North Peak Trail 1.6 mi. to North Peak Junction.
DESCRIPTION: Leaving North Peak Junction (0.0 mi.) with the coinciding Butterfly Trail, the Castle Peak Trail follows a woods road south on easy grades around the west shoulder of Second Peak. Reaching a junction (0.1 mi.), the trail leaves the Butterfly Trail and takes the west fork, continuing gradually uphill. Passing through the junction of the western and eastern loops of the Butterfly Trail (0.2 mi.), the Castle Peak Trail descends easily to the south and southeast along the road to a final junction with the east loop of the Butterfly Trail (0.3 mi.), which continues straight ahead.

Turning sharply right off the road at the junction, the Castle Peak Trail trends southerly and ascends gradually along the east flank of the ridge before swinging to the right (0.4 mi.) and climbing somewhat more steeply. Soon beginning a much steeper climb with several twists and turns, the trail continues into an overgrown clearing where it turns sharply to the right (0.6 mi.). At this point there are obscured views through the trees of the Rutland area and Killington Peak. Continuing in the open for some distance, the trail then returns to the woods, passes just east of the north summit of Castle Peak, and enters a very shallow sag (0.7 mi.). From the sag, the trail ascends easily to the south summit of Castle Peak (0.8 mi.), where there is a tunnel view to the west of Lake Bomoseen and limited views through the trees to the east and northeast.

From the summit of Castle Peak, the trail descends about 200 ft. to the east and south lookouts at Hawk Ledge, named for the numerous hawks to be seen soaring above Bird Brook Valley. Herrick Mtn. and the rugged dome of Bird Mtn. dominate the view to the south. Because Bird Mtn. is the nesting area for several species of hawks, it is strongly recommended that no attempt be made to cross over that summit.

EAST TRAIL

Distance: 0.7 mi. (1.1 km)
Elevation Change: 500 ft. ascent
Hiking Time: 20 min. (reverse 35 min.)

TO THE TRAIL: From its intersection with Vt. 133 in West Rutland, proceed west on Vt. 4A for 3.3 mi. and turn left (south) onto the gravel Ira Birdseye Road. Climbing to a fork (0.9 mi.), continue straight past the more-traveled route on the left, which descends to a private residence. The narrow public road passes a pull-off (1.3 mi.) and a brook before coming upon a second pull-off at a gate (1.4 mi.). Roadside parking is available for four to five cars. Caution should be taken to avoid blocking the gate or road. The trailhead is 200 ft. farther along the Ira Birdseye Road, where a woods road departs to the right.
DESCRIPTION: From the public road (0.0 mi.), the unsigned and unblazed trail follows a woods road, which curves right into a clearing, then begins a steep climb. Bearing left at a fork (0.3 mi.) and crossing a brook, the grade moderates as the trail slabs the eastern slope of the mountain. Staying on the most obvious road, the trail enters a notch and arrives at a junction (0.7 mi.) on the western loop of the Butterfly Trail.

elevation to the wooded north summit (2,090 ft.) (1.2 mi.). The trail soon turns sharply to the left, descends a short distance, then bears to the left of a scenic bog on easy grades. Reaching a lookout (1.5 mi.) where there are views over the Cold River Valley to Mt. Equinox and Dorset Peak, the trail then passes through a rocky ravine before reaching a junction in an open area on the south summit (2,080 ft.) (1.8 mi.).

Junction: To the left the West Loop (description follows) follows an occasionally obscure footpath 0.9 mi. around the western side of the mountain, rejoining the East Loop about 0.1 mi. north of the south summit.

To the right at the junction atop the south summit, the East Loop descends gently over ledges to reach the junction with the West Loop. A short distance to the left lies Rutland Lookout (1.9 mi.), where there is a good view of Rutland and the Otter Creek Valley to the north, as well as the Adirondacks and northern Taconics. Bearing right at the junction, the East Loop then leaves the ledges and descends, steeply at first, before reaching an old woods road (2.1 mi.). The trail descends along the road, soon reaching another woods road (2.4 mi.), which it follows to the right. After only 200 ft. the trail leaves this road to the right at an easily missed junction and ascends to a more recent logging road. Following this road through tall spruces, the trail reaches the junction at the head of the East Loop (2.9 mi.). Continuing straight, the trail then reaches Notch Road (3.3 mi.).

WEST LOOP

Distance: 0.9 mi. (1.4 km)
Elevation Change: 380 ft. ascent
Hiking Time: ½ hr. (reverse 40 min.)

ABOUT THE TRAIL: This trail extends the East Loop hike and includes a vista with impressive views to the east and west.

DESCRIPTION: Leaving the south summit at the southern junction of the East and West Loop, (0.0 mi.), the West Loop continues over brushy ledges, soon reaching a vista to the south (0.1 mi.). The trail descends past two more-limited views before reaching Red Rocks Lookout (0.3 mi.), where there are extensive vistas of Mendon and Little Killington to the east and of the Taconics, Mt. Equinox, Dorset Peak, and finally the Adirondacks to the west.

From the lookout, the trail descends steeply, passing under a cliff on the left, before reaching the low point of the West Loop (0.4 mi.). The trail passes atop a small cliff before ascending a switchback and reaching Rutland Lookout and rejoining the East Loop (0.9 mi.).

• • • • • • • • • • • • • • • •

SHREWSBURY PEAK

Located in the northeast corner of the town of Shrewsbury (USGS Killington Peak), Shrewsbury Peak offers good views to the east, south, and west. Two trails climb this mountain, the Shrewsbury Peak Trail and the Black Swamp Trail.

SHREWSBURY PEAK TRAIL

Distance: 2.0 mi. (3.2 km)
Elevation Change: 1,500 ft. ascent
Hiking Time: 1¾ hr. (reverse 1 hr.)

ABOUT THE TRAIL: This blue-blazed trail continues 1.8 beyond the summit to reach the Long Trail east of Little Killington. From there, the LT continues north to Cooper Lodge and a junction with a spur trail to Killington Peak.
TO THE TRAIL: The trail begins at a parking lot on the gravel CCC Road 3.0 mi. east of North Shrewsbury and 3.5 mi. west of Vt. 100. The CCC Road (also called Shrewsbury

Road) leaves Vt. 100 10.7 mi. north of the junction of Vt. 100 and 103 and 3.1 mi. south of the junction of Vt. 100 and U.S. 4. The CCC Road is not maintained in winter.

DESCRIPTION: From the parking lot (0.0 mi.), the trail swings to the left and passes just right of a well (unsafe water), where it swings to the right and ascends steadily past Russell Hill Shelter (0.2 mi.). Passing a short distance east of the summit of Russell Hill, the trail then descends across a woods road into a rocky gully (0.5 mi.). It then ascends through a "rock garden" to cross another old road (0.7 mi.). After briefly following another old woods road (0.8 mi.), it crosses some small brooks and enters conifers (1.4 mi.), climbing gradually, ascending to cross an interior property line of Coolidge State Forest (1.5 mi.).

The trail then begins a steep, winding climb through dense balsam fir to the south summit of Shrewsbury Peak (1.8 mi.). From the several rocky outlooks on the wooded summit (3,720 ft.), there are views to the southeast of Mts. Ascutney, Kearsarge, and Monadnock and to the south of Mt. Okemo (also known as Ludlow Mtn.), Bromley Mtn., and Stratton Mtn.

From the south summit, the trail descends 100 ft. to a 100-ft. spur leading to a northwest lookout, then into a shallow sag, where the blue-blazed Black Swamp Trail (description follows) departs on the right (1.9 mi.). A short distance beyond the sag, the Shrewsbury Peak Trail passes just to the left of the slightly lower wooded north summit of Shrewsbury Peak (2.0 mi.).

Note: The Shrewsbury Peak Trail continues from here for some distance into a swale (3.2 mi.), climbs to the west, crosses a brook (3.7 mi.), and reaches the Long Trail (3.8 mi.). This hike takes 3 hr. (reverse 2 hr.) and the elevation gain is 1,950 ft. North on the Long Trail, it is 1.6 mi. to a spur that leads 0.2 mi. to the summit of Killington Peak. The complete hike to Killington Peak is 5.6 mi. (9.0 km) and will take 4 hr. (reverse 3 hr.). The elevation gain is 2,700 ft.

BLACK SWAMP TRAIL

Distance: 2.1 mi. (3.5 km)
Elevation Change: 1,300 ft. ascent
Hiking Time: 1¾ hr. (reverse 1 hr.)

ABOUT THE TRAIL: This is an easier route from the CCC Road to Shrewsbury Peak and the Long Trail beyond. Because this is a spring feeding area for black bears, the Black Swamp Road is gated except for the winter months.

TO THE TRAIL: The trail begins at the intersection of Black Swamp and CCC Roads, 4.3 mi. east of North Shrewsbury, 1.3 mi. east of the Shrewsbury Peak Trail, and 2.2 mi. west of Vt. 100.

DESCRIPTION: From the CCC Road (0.0 mi.), the trail ascends the gravel Black Swamp Road to its end (0.9 mi.). The blazed trail begins here and climbs steadily on more primitive woods roads to a blue-blazed Farm and Wilderness Camps Trail on the right, which descends to Woodward Reservoir on Vt. 100. Continuing north 260 ft., the Black Swamp Trail passes a short spur leading to Shrewsbury Peak Shelter, a log lean-to with space for eight, built by the Civilian Conservation Corps. At the shelter, there is a limited view east. A rock-lined spring is located 50 ft. to the south of the shelter. From here, the trail ascends to its junction with the Shrewsbury Peak Trail (2.1 mi.), 0.1 mi. north of Shrewsbury Peak and 1.9 mi. south of the Long Trail.

• • • • • • • • • • • • • • • •

OKEMO STATE FOREST

Distance: 2.9 mi. (4.7 km)
Elevation Change: 1,900 ft. ascent
Hiking Time: 2½ hr. (reverse 1½ hr.)

ABOUT THE TRAIL: The blue-blazed Healdville Trail ascends the northwest side of Ludlow Mtn. (USGS Ludlow, Mt.

Holly), more commonly known as Okemo Mtn., to reach a former fire tower atop its summit, from which there are panoramic views of southern Vermont, southwestern New Hampshire, and northern Massachusetts. Constructed by the Vermont Youth Conservation Corps during the summers of 1991 to 1993, the Healdville Trail replaces an older, now obsolete trail described in previous editions of this guidebook.

The trail and summit lie within the town of Mt. Holly, on the western side of the 4,513-acre Okemo State Forest. The state forest tract extends into the adjacent town of Ludlow and lends its name to Okemo Ski Area found on the eastern slopes of the mountain.

TO THE TRAIL: From the junction of Vt. 140 and Vt. 103, go east 6.5 mi. to reach a junction with Station Road on the right. Follow Station Road to the south for 0.7 mi. to a grade crossing with the Green Mountain Railroad at the hamlet of Healdville. A signed parking lot is located just past the tracks on the left, at the former site of the Healdville Station. To reach Station Road from the east, follow Vt. 100/103 north from the village of Ludlow for about 1.75 mi. to a junction where the routes split, then bear west along Vt. 103 for another 2.75 mi.

DESCRIPTION: The trail leaves the parking lot (0.0 mi.) in an easterly direction over a small wooden bridge, then crosses a small stream on timbers before climbing briefly along an eroded footpath. The trail soon turns more to the south and begins a new ascent to the left of the stream below. Turning to the southeast (0.3 mi.) and beginning a steeper climb, the trail enters an older forest and passes small cascades and pools. A small stream enters from the left (0.5 mi.) and shortly thereafter the trail turns to the east (0.6 mi.), leaving the stream behind. The trail then ascends moderately over a series of switchbacks, passing two double-blazed gentle turns (1.1 mi.), followed by a string of stepping stones.

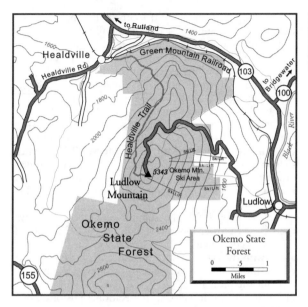

Reaching a shoulder of the mountain and turning to the south, the trail begins a half-mile traverse along the western flank of the mountain with relatively little change in elevation. Climbing again, the trail reaches a marker, 1.9 mi. from the trailhead and 1.0 mi. below the summit. Here, an overgrown and unblazed trail leads uphill to the access road, which originates at the base of the eastern slope of the mountain, continues past the Okemo Ski Area, and ends at a small parking area near the summit.

The Healdville Trail continues straight ahead and soon reaches a rock cascade before making a brief climb along a gentle contour and crossing several cuts formed by wet-season streams. Upon entering the coniferous transition zone, the trail reaches a vista (2.3 mi.) then follows a relocation, uphill from the old footbed. Passing the upper end of the relocation (2.4 mi.), the trail turns to the east and climbs more steeply, at first reaching a slightly obscured vista then coming to a beautiful open view to the west. This point offers a clear line of sight to Wallingford Pond in the Green Mountain National Forest, the largest undeveloped body of water in Vermont.

The trail continues a moderate ascent toward the summit and soon passes a chimney, the remnant of a Civilian Conservation Corps (CCC) camp. The trail soon reaches the summit of Ludlow Mtn. (3,343 ft.) (2.9 mi.), where there are fine panoramic views from the observation deck of the former fire tower. Below, only one ski resort building can be seen a short distance away in the forest, and no ski trails are visible.

From about 1920, the summit of Ludlow Mtn. was used as a fire tower lookout station. From 1932 to 1934, the CCC constructed a new steel tower on the summit, along with the access road, which ascends the eastern side of the mountain. The current tower served as an active lookout site until about 1970, was repaired and repainted in 1991, and was installed in the National Historic Lookout Register in 1998.

• • • • • • • • • • • • • • • •

DEERFIELD RIVER WATERSHED

The Deerfield River watershed encompasses a large area of southwestern Vermont and northwestern Massachusetts. The river has been dammed in many places for power generation, creating several reservoirs along the way. Near East Greenfield, Massachusetts, the Deerfield River empties into the Connecticut River. Well upstream lies Sherman Reservoir, straddling the Vermont-Massachusetts border (USGS Rowe, Readsboro), Harriman Reservoir, and then the much smaller Searsburg Reservoir. Just north of Searsburg Reservoir, the river branches; upstream along the East Branch is Somerset Reservoir, a large man-made impoundment. Beyond Somerset, along an unnamed stream, is Grout Pond. The New England Power Company (NEPCO) and the U.S. Forest Service maintain a variety of footpaths and multiuse trails along the reservoirs.

HARRIMAN TRAIL

Distance: 7.2 mi. (11.6 km)
Elevation Change: 200 ft. ascent
Hiking Time: 3¾ hr. either direction

ABOUT THE TRAIL: Also known as the Westside Trail, this route is maintained by the New England Power Company (NEPCO). The trail follows a mostly unblazed but obvious path along the west side of Harriman Reservoir, between a power company picnic area near the north end of the reservoir west of Wilmington and a small parking area at the base of Harriman Dam in Whitingham (USGS Readsboro). Blue plastic markers of the Catamount Trail are found along parts of the route where the two trails coincide. Walking and cycling are allowed on the trail. While the trail is described from the north to the south, directions to both trailheads are given.

The trail provides frequent views across the reservoir to the surrounding mountains and passes stone walls, foundations, and other reminders of past settlement. Like all other recreational facilities on NEPCO lands, this trail is open only during daylight hours; overnight parking, camping, and open fires are not permitted.

Except for short bypasses of the original stream crossings, the trail follows the roadbed of the former Hoosic Tunnel and Wilmington Railroad. This section of track, with its roller coaster grades and a switchback crossing of Harriman Dam, was constructed in 1923 to replace original routing flooded by the newly created reservoir. It remained in service until the line was abandoned in 1937. The story of the railroad is told in Bernard R. Carman's *Hoot, Toot and Whistle* (Brattleboro, Vt.: Stephen Green Press, 1963).

TO THE TRAIL (NORTHERN ACCESS): The northern end of the trail is at the power company's Mountain Mills West picnic area. From Vt. 9, about 0.3 mi. east of the Searsburg-Wilmington town line, or 2.9 mi. west of the traffic lights in Wilmington, turn south onto Woods Road and cross the Deerfield River on a steel bridge. Turn left at a junction just beyond the bridge and follow the narrow gravel road for 1.0 mi. to the picnic area, where there is an impressive view of Haystack Mtn. The trail begins at a gate barring the road to vehicular traffic.

TO THE TRAIL (SOUTHERN ACCESS): The southern trailhead is located at the Harriman Dam. From Vt. 100, about a mile west of the Whitingham post office, or about 4.0 mi. east of the center of Readsboro, turn north onto the paved Harriman Road (also Dam Road) and continue 1.9 mi. to its end at a parking area at the bottom of a hairpin turn. The trail begins at an inconspicuous opening in the chain-link fence. This access is located about 60 ft. to the left of the main gate, opposite a birch tree. The trail follows a paved road, which crosses the lower face of the dam and then ascends to its top. Here the trail bears to the left onto a dirt road, which follows the path of the railroad bed and continues along the shore toward a prominent rock cut.

DESCRIPTION (SOUTHBOUND): From the gate at the picnic area (0.0 mi.), the trail and a coinciding truck road ascend steadily to the south. After passing camps on the right and left (0.8 mi.), the trail continues with minor elevation changes, crosses a gate (1.1 mi.), and begins a brief swing to the west (1.6 mi.). The trail then resumes a southerly course before crossing high above Boyd Brook (1.9 mi.). Passing through two prominent rock cuts, then several less obvious ones, the trail enters a much longer, deeper, and

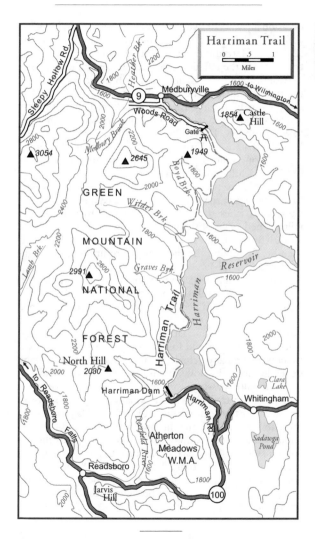

occasionally wet cut, where the railroad ties are still in place (2.7 mi.). Beyond this cut, the trail reaches a junction (2.8 mi.). Here the truck road forks to the right, and the trail bears to the left along the undisturbed railroad bed.

Continuing through another cut in the rocks (2.9 mi.), the trail soon leaves the railroad bed to the right and follows yellow blazes into the woods (3.0 mi.). Here the trail arrives at a junction with the Catamount Trail, which it follows to the left. Descending to cross Wilder Brook on a footbridge (3.1 mi.), the trail then ascends to the left to cross a stone wall (3.2 mi.) before continuing through an old farm clearing and into a reforested area.

Returning to the railroad bed (3.4 mi.), the trail crosses the former stage road to Heartwellville (3.5 mi.) and gradually approaches the reservoir. The trail then leaves the railroad bed again (4.0 mi.), descending to the left to cross Graves Brook a few feet from the reservoir (4.1 mi.). It then briefly follows the shore before returning to the railroad bed (4.3 mi.).

After rounding a pleasant point (5.2 mi.) and paralleling a long stone wall on the left, the trail swings to the right off the railroad bed (5.3 mi.), briefly ascends in open woods, and then passes through an overgrown clearing near the massive foundations of former farm buildings. The trail then joins and follows a dirt road (5.4 mi.) used by power company vehicles to its end at Harriman Dam, generally along the now-obscure route of the old roadbed.

Eventually passing through a prominent rock cut (6.4 mi.), the trail descends gradually along the shore of the reservoir to the north end of Harriman Dam (6.9 mi.). Here the trail jogs to the right for a few feet, and then descends on a paved roadway, which soon swings to the left and crosses the lower face of the dam to a closed gate in a chain-link fence. The trail follows the fence to the right for about 60 ft. to a white birch tree, at which point an inconspicuous narrow opening provides access to the parking lot (7.2 mi.).

WILMINGTON-SOMERSET TRAILS

Traveling alongside large reservoirs and rivers, these trails often follow old railroad beds. The trails were established and are maintained by the New England Power Company (NEPCO). In addition to the reservoir trails, the trails up Haystack Mtn. and Mt. Snow are described.

EAST BRANCH TRAIL

Distance: 5.0 mi. (8.1 km)
Elevation Change: 550 ft. ascent
Hiking Time: 2¾ hr. (reverse 2½ hr.)

ABOUT THE TRAIL: This trail is marked for its entire length with faded diagonal double yellow blazes. Since nearly all the trail is on power company property, overnight camping and open fires are prohibited. The trail generally parallels the Catamount Trail, which is blazed with blue diamonds.

TO THE TRAIL: The East Branch Trail and Flood Dam Trail (page 94) (USGS Mt. Snow) share a common trailhead on Somerset Road (USFS Road 71), which leads to Somerset Reservoir. This road leaves Vt. 9 (0.0 mi.) about 1.5 mi. east of its junction with Vt. 8 and 5.6 mi. west of the traffic lights in Wilmington. After reaching the end of the pavement (0.3 mi.), the road passes the dam at Searsburg Reservoir (1.0 mi.) before reaching a small lot where limited parking is available at the trailhead (2.1 mi.).

DESCRIPTION: Descending from Somerset Road (0.0 mi.), the trail crosses the West Branch of the Deerfield River on a suspension bridge and proceeds gradually uphill. The trail soon turns sharply uphill to the right at a junction with the Flood Dam Trail (0.1 mi.), which departs to the left.

The East Branch Trail continues across a low ridge and crosses the East Branch of the Deerfield River on a suspension bridge (0.4 mi.). The trail then reaches an old railroad bed and joins the Catamount Trail as it comes in from the right. Along this railroad bed are several scenic overlooks of the river as well as views of Mt. Snow to the northeast. The trail crosses several streams (1.2 to 1.6 mi.), some at fords and others on hewn timbers that span the stream channel.

After crossing the last brook, the trail bears to the right, leaves the railroad bed (1.6 mi.), and crosses another brook on a hewn timber. The trail returns to the railroad bed (2.0 mi.), crosses two more streams, and bears to the right off the main roadbed (2.3 mi.). Following a spur railroad bed running up a stream, the trail quickly bears right, away from the river.

After crossing the brook (2.7 mi.), the trail crosses a red-blazed boundary and enters the Green Mountain National Forest (2.9 mi.), where the route was formerly marked with blue blazes. The trail follows the brook channel and crosses it (3.0 mi.), then bears right at the first fork in the brook (3.1 mi.) and left at the second fork (3.2 mi.). (The trail is difficult to follow in this area, so care should be taken to look for blazes.) The trail begins to level off and crosses the brook for the last time (3.3 mi.). Descending across a red-blazed boundary line, the trail crosses back onto NEPCO land (4.1 mi.). Here there are views of Mt. Snow and several beaver ponds. The trail continues to descend gradually alongside a small stream into a large clearing (4.5 mi.), where the East Branch Spur Trail leads left to the East Branch of the Deerfield River.

The main East Branch Trail turns sharply to the right at this junction and follows the upper edge of a small meadow. After returning to the woods (4.6 mi.), the trail once again reaches the East Branch (4.7 mi.), following its east bank for several hundred feet, then again turning away to the right. Climbing a moderate grade, the trail levels off and passes to the right of an old mill foundation (4.9 mi.) then ascends to the right and reaches the Somerset Reservoir access road (5.0 mi.), just below the east end of the dam.

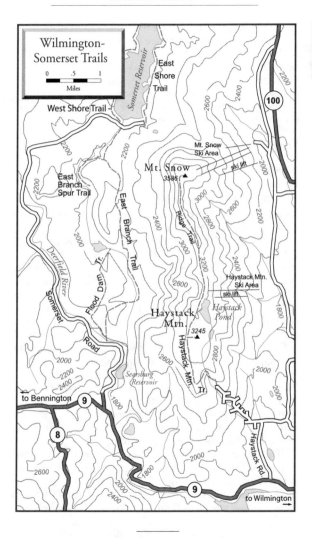

Wilmington-
Somerset Trails

0   .5   1
Miles

Somerset Reservoir

East
Shore
Trail

West Shore Trail

Mt. Snow
Ski Area

Mt. Snow
3586

ski lift

East
Branch
Spur Trail

East Branch Trail

Ridge Trail

Deerfield River

Flood Dam Tr.

Haystack Mtn.
Ski Area

ski lift

Somerset

Haystack
Pond

Haystack
Mtn.

3245

Road

Searsburg
Reservoir

Haystack Mtn. Tr.

to Bennington

9

8

to Wilmington

Haystack Rd.

To the left, the access road descends a short distance to the dam's outlet and continues south, past the parking lot to the southern end of the West Shore Trail (page 96). The access road leads 9.7 mi. back to Vt. 9.

To the right on the access road, it is a few hundred feet uphill to the top of the dam. It is about 0.3 mi. to parking and boat launching areas and 0.5 mi. to a picnic grove and the southern end of the East Shore Trail (page 95).

FLOOD DAM TRAIL

Distance: 2.3 mi. (3.7 km)
Elevation Change: 280 ft. ascent
Hiking Time: 1¼ hr. (reverse 1¼ hr.)

ABOUT THE TRAIL: Marked with single yellow blazes, the trail is sporadically maintained and may be overgrown in places.
TO THE TRAIL: This trail diverges from the East Branch Trail 0.1 mi. from the trailhead on Somerset Road (page 91).
DESCRIPTION: A short distance north of the Deerfield River suspension bridge, the Flood Dam Trail branches left where the East Branch Trail makes an abrupt right turn (0.0 mi.). The Flood Dam Trail passes through overgrown clearings and woods along an old roadbed (0.1 mi.) and continues parallel to the Deerfield River on level ground before arriving at a fork (0.4 mi.). To the left, a dead-end spur continues along the river for a short distance. The Flood Dam Trail follows the right branch of the fork away from the river. The trail continues to the base of a hill (0.5 mi.), turning more northerly as it begins a gradual climb up a rocky section of trail. Climbing through mature hardwood forests, the trail reaches its highest point at the unmarked Windham-Bennington county line (1.2 mi.).

The Flood Dam Trail continues generally to the northeast across this flat-topped mountain, begins a very gradual descent, and then levels out (1.7 mi.). Turning sharply to the right, the trail descends again to the bottom of a hill, crosses a small stream (1.8 mi.), and continues northeasterly around a spruce and hardwood forest to another stream (1.9 mi.). The trail meets an old railroad bed (2.0 mi.) and turns sharply to the left, where there are views of a large area of beaver activity. The trail follows the railroad bed and ends at a clearing on the shore of the pond (2.2 mi.). The foundations of the old flood dam, which dates back to at least the turn of the past century, can be seen from this point. The dam and railroad beds found in this area are remnants of logging activity in the nineteenth century.

EAST SHORE TRAIL

Distance: 5.7 mi. (9.2 km)
Elevation Change: minor
Hiking Time: 3 hr. (reverse 3 hr.)

ABOUT THE TRAIL: This trail follows high ground near the east shore of scenic Somerset Reservoir (USGS Mt. Snow, Stratton Mtn.), dropping down to skirt many coves. The trail offers views across the water to Mt. Snow, Stratton Mtn., and other area landmarks. The double-yellow-blazed route follows, in part, the Catamount Trail (a cross-country ski trail) and a former woods road. At the northeast arm of Somerset Reservoir, the Catamount Trail leaves the East Shore Trail to continue 0.5 mi. to Grout Pond, where several trails lead 1.2 mi. to the Grout Pond parking area. From the point where the Catamount Trail departs, the East Shore Trail continues 4.0 to 5.0 mi. to its end on the north shore of the reservoir and the West Trail Loop, part of the Grout Pond network; however, this portion of the East Shore Trail is overgrown and difficult to follow.

TO THE TRAIL: The East Shore Trail begins at the end of the Somerset Reservoir access road, 10.0 mi. from the junction of Somerset Road and Vt. 9, and about 0.3 mi. north of the dam. From Vt. 9, turn north onto Somerset Road (USFS Road 71) and continue past the trailhead for the East Branch Trail (2.1 mi.) (page 91). Bear right at a fork (6.3 mi.) off Somerset Road onto the Somerset Reservoir access road, and continue to a small trailhead parking area just beyond a larger parking lot on the right, near the end of the road (10.0 mi.).

DESCRIPTION: From the end of the road (0.0 mi.), the trail crosses a small stream on a bridge and follows an old road to a cove. After swinging around the east end of the cove (0.2 mi.), the trail enters the woods, passes between several large rocks (0.7 mi.), and crosses a small stream. It then skirts a small cove on puncheon (1.1 mi.) before ascending a small knoll (1.6 mi.), descending to another cove, and climbing another knoll (1.8 mi.). Dropping to yet another cove, the trail follows the shore to the right, partly on puncheon, before leaving the cove (2.0 mi.) to cross a brook on a wooden bridge (2.2 mi.).

Turning northerly, the trail ascends and crosses an old woods road (2.5 mi.), and then slabs a slope to reach the high ground atop a ridge. From the high point on the slope and a winter view of the Mt. Snow–Haystack Mtn. ridge, the trail descends to the shoreline and joins with the Catamount Trail (3.2 mi.) before crossing a large brook.

The trail continues on higher ground, enters a clearing on the shore (3.5 mi.), and continues north to a point on the shore closest to Streeter Island (4.2 mi.). The trail swings to the right around a cove before crossing a small brook (5.0 mi.) and then a rocky stream (5.3 mi.) where a bridge has washed out. The trail crosses the stream and then reaches a sign (5.7 mi.) indicating it is 6.0 mi. back to the dam at the outlet of Somerset Reservoir.

WEST SHORE TRAIL

Distance: 5.6 mi. (9.0 km)
Elevation Change: 130 ft. ascent
Hiking Time: 3 hr. (reverse 2¾ hr.)

ABOUT THE TRAIL: This trail follows the high ground on the west side of Somerset Reservoir to an indefinite terminus on the reservoir's shoreline. The trail is overgrown and unblazed along much of the route and peters out after 5.5 mi. Care must be taken to stay on the trail. Map and compass and the knowledge of how to use them are recommended. For an alternate route that is easier to follow, walk along the grassy service road, which continues north on gentle grades for a couple of miles—out of sight of Somerset Reservoir—and makes a pleasant path through the woods.

To the Trail: Follow directions to the East Shore Trail (page 95). The trail begins at the junction of the access road and a chained service road at the base of the west end of the dam. Parking is available at the trailhead and other nearby locations. (A NEPCO sign for the West Side Trail may be seen nearby.) The route is marked with double yellow blazes.

Description: From the access road (0.0 mi.), the trail follows the service road up the face of the dam for about 150 yds. before turning left onto a woods road. Soon after leaving the service road (0.2 mi.), the trail descends toward the reservoir, reaching the water's edge at a rock ledge (0.4 mi.). The trail continues around two small coves (0.7 mi. and 0.8 mi.) and crosses a large brook, entering another cove (1.3 mi.) before rising to higher ground.

After returning to the shore and crossing another stream (1.7 mi.), the trail again leaves the reservoir at a rocky cove (1.9 mi.) and slabs the slope for some distance on occasionally rough ground before continuing with minor elevation changes to a former town road (2.5 mi.). The trail follows the old road and its paralleling stone walls uphill to the left through an overgrown farm site (2.8 mi.) and then descends gradually, bearing to the right at an old woods road junction (3.2 mi.) and soon reaching a trail junction (3.3 mi.). To the left, a red-blazed snowmobile trail follows old roads.

The West Shore Trail descends on the right fork and soon returns to the reservoir (3.4 mi.). Continuing along or near the shore, the trail crosses a large brook at the en-

trance to a cove (4.2 mi.) and swings to the right away
from a woods road, which also uses the brook crossing.
Once again turning into the woods (4.4 mi.), the occasionally obscurely routed trail goes a short distance inland,
crosses a low spur ridge (4.9 mi.), and gradually descends
to the shore (5.2 mi.). The trail follows the rocky beach for
a short distance, returns to the shoreline, and then continues on higher ground and becomes ill-defined in the
woods (5.6 mi.). Note: From here, the trail is unmaintained and very difficult to follow to its ending on the west
bank of the East Branch of the Deerfield River. On the east
bank of the East Branch is the East Shore Trail; do not
cross the river; it is deep and the currents are strong.

GROUT POND RECREATION AREA

A major logging site until it was purchased by the Boy
Scouts of America in 1950, Grout Pond was acquired by
the U.S. Forest Service in 1979. The 1,600-acre area is
managed for a variety of recreational use. Nine campsites
and three lean-tos are available on a first-come, first-served
basis. Some of the sites are accessible by car, others only by
foot or boat. The area also offers swimming and boating
(electric motors only, with a portage required for access).
A U.S. Forest Service caretaker may be in residence during
the summer and fall. Additional information and a trail
map are available from the U.S. Forest Service's Manchester office and at the trailhead.

More than 12.0 mi. of multipurpose trails encircle the
70-acre pond along mostly flat terrain. The trails are
marked with blue diamond-shaped blazes and are open
year-round. In the winter, snowmobiles are restricted to
USFS Road 262 and a portion of the trail system designated by orange diamond blazes.

To the Trail: To reach the Grout Pond Recreation Area
from the east, follow the Stratton Road (also known as the
Arlington Road) west from Vt. 100 in West Wardsboro for

6.3 mi. to Grout Pond Road (USFS Road 262). From the west, follow Kelley Stand Road east from U.S. 7 in Arlington for about 12.0 mi. to reach the same spot. Turn south onto Grout Pond Road and continue 1.3 mi. to a parking lot near the pond.

DESCRIPTION: From the parking lot, the Pond Trail Loop heads southeast to make a 2.5 mi. counterclockwise circuit around the pond. From a junction near the south end of the pond, about 0.75 mi. from the parking lot, it is 0.5 mi. along the Catamount Trail to a junction with the East Shore Trail. This trail, described on page 95, originates from the dam at the outlet of Somerset Reservoir about 6.0 mi. to the south.

HAYSTACK MOUNTAIN

Distance: 1.8 mi. (2.9 km)
Elevation Change: 1,025 ft. ascent
Hiking Time: 1½ hr. (reverse 1 hr.)

ABOUT THE TRAIL: From the partially wooded, conical summit (3,445 ft., USGS Mt. Snow), there are views of Haystack Pond and Mt. Snow (formerly Mt. Pisgah) to the north and Harriman Reservoir and Lake Sadawga to the south (USGS Readsboro). More distant views include Mt. Ascutney to the northeast, Mt. Monadnock in New Hampshire to the southeast, Mt. Greylock to the south, and Glastenbury Mtn. to the north. For most of its length, this is a combination hiking and cross-country ski trail, marked with occasional blue diamonds.

TO THE TRAIL: From Vt. 9, 1.0 mi. west of the traffic light in Wilmington, or 5.8 mi. east of Vt. 8, turn north into the Chimney Hill Development on Haystack Road (0.0 mi.). Bear right at a turn where Town Farm Road leaves to the left (0.3 mi.), continue north on Haystack Road, past junctions on the right and left, until reaching a four-way intersection (1.2 mi.).

At this point, turn left onto Chimney Hill Road, then turn right at the next junction (1.4 mi.) onto Binney Brook Road. Bear left at a fork and begin a steep and winding climb past several roads to the right and left. At the junction where Binney Brook Road ends on Upper Dam Road (2.3 mi.), turn right and proceed uphill to another intersection (2.4 mi.). Bear left, still on Upper Dam Road, to reach the trailhead, which is on the right (2.5 mi.) and marked with a U.S. Forest Service sign. Limited roadside parking is available in the vicinity.

DESCRIPTION: From Upper Dam Road (0.0 mi.), the trail ascends northwesterly on a jeep road. The trail turns left off the road at a crossing of Binney Brook (0.6 mi.), and then trends southwesterly for some distance before climbing steadily in a northward direction to a junction with the Ridge Trail on the west slope of the mountain (1.5 mi.). Here the trail turns to the right and follows the blue-blazed route to the summit (1.8 mi.). Note: As indicated by postings in the area, this is a watershed protection zone for the town of Wilmington. Camping is not allowed along the trail or on the summit.

RIDGE TRAIL

Distance: 3.5 mi. (5.6 km)
Elevation Change: 385 ft. ascent
Hiking Time: 1¾ hr. (reverse 2 hr.)

ABOUT THE TRAIL: This combination cross-country skiing and hiking trail connects Haystack Mtn. with Mt. Snow. Although it is minimally marked, it is an obvious path and is as wide as a road.

DESCRIPTION: From a junction below the summit of Haystack Mtn. (0.0 mi.), the Ridge Trail continues straight ahead to the north. The trail follows easy up and down routing just west of the height of land to reach the Haystack Mountain Ski Area near the upper lift station (1.0 mi.). The trail then continues in a northerly direction, on or near the ridgeline, to the summit facilities of the Mount Snow Ski Area (3.5 mi.). Although the trail does not cross the summit of Mt. Snow, it does connect here with a network of trails maintained in season by the Mount Snow Adventure Center at Crisports, a shop in the Grand Summit Resort Hotel. Hikers may obtain trail maps for self-guided interpretive hikes, take a guided hike, or rent hiking boots. There is a trail access fee of $5.25 (in 2001) to hike from this center. The center is open May 29 through October 11, from 8:00 A.M. to 5:00 P.M. For more information, call the center at (802) 464-4040.

LITTLE POND

Distance: 2.6 mi. (4.2 km)
Elevation Change: 330 ft. ascent
Hiking Time: 1¾ hr. (reverse 1¼ hr.)

TO THE TRAIL: This secluded pond (USGS Woodford) is reached by an unblazed and unsigned woods road that leaves a U.S. Forest Service parking lot on the north side of Vt. 9 at a height of land about 1.6 mi. east of the Prospect Mountain Ski Area and about 1.6 mi. west of Woodford State Park.
DESCRIPTION: From the highway (0.0 mi.), the woods road ascends through the woods to a power line crossing (0.5 mi.), where there are views to the east and west. After dipping into a hollow, the road continues through overgrown fields to a fire ring at the site of an old camp (0.8 mi.). Nearby, there are limited views east to Haystack Mtn. and the Hoosic Range. The road then ascends gradually through the woods around a shoulder of Hager Hill and ignores a snowmobile trail departing to the right. The road then reaches a fork (2.4 mi.), where a more recent logging road veers left. To the right an older road descends to the west shore of the pond (2,602 ft.) (2.6 mi.).

• • • • • • • • • • • • • • • •

RAMBLES

Lake Shaftsbury State Park

About the Trail: This 84-acre park surrounds small and picturesque Lake Shaftsbury. The park has group camping facilities and a day-use area, with a fee charged in-season.

To the Trail: State Park Road leaves Vt. 7A just north of the village of Shaftsbury, about 10.5 mi. north of Bennington, and leads 0.5 mi. to the park contact station.

Description: A brochure is available at the contact station describing the 0.75-mi. Healing Springs Nature Trail, which nearly circles the lake. The trail begins at the western end of the dam, which forms the lake's outlet, and follows the north shore for a distance before crossing a boardwalk onto Hemlock Island. The trail follows the ridge of this glacial esker to another bridge, where it crosses to a peninsula on the south shore of the lake. The trail continues through an oak forest to a boardwalk over Warm Brook before ending at the group picnic shelter near a parking lot southeast of the lake.

Lake St. Catherine State Park

About the Trail: Lake St. Catherine State Park occupies 117 acres on the east shore of Lake St. Catherine. Formerly the site of a slate quarry, the remains of old slate mills and their rubble piles are still visible. Camping facilities and a day-use area, including a beach, are available. A fee is charged in-season.

To the Trail: The park entrance is 3.0 mi. south of Poultney on the west side of Vt. 30.

Description: A brochure is available at the park contact station describing the 1.0-mi. Big Trees Nature Trail loop, which ascends gently to a low ridge in old pastureland. The trail passes a series of labeled trees, many rare for their exceptional size, before ending at the site of an old farmstead. From this point, a hiking trail continues west to the lake, where a spur leads to the swimming area. The hiking loop then turns to the east and passes the park campground before returning to the contact station.

DELAWARE AND HUDSON RAIL TRAIL

ABOUT THE TRAIL: Comprised of two discontinuous but nearly equal lengths of abandoned roadbed, the Delaware and Hudson Rail Trail follows the Vermont portion of a rail route that once connected the slate-producing regions near Rutland with Albany, New York. As it passes through the pastoral Vermont landscape of western Rutland and Bennington Counties, it encounters seventeen bridges and overpasses, including two railroad bridges nearly 100 ft. long in Poultney and West Pawlet. This 19.8-mi. multiuse trail is owned by the Vermont Transportation Agency and maintained by the Department of Forests, Parks, and Recreation. An excellent flyer describing the access, history, and permitted uses of the trail is available from the Pittsford office of the Vermont Department of Forests, Parks, and Recreation (see page 347).

TO THE TRAIL: The northern segment of the trail runs from Castleton to Poultney. Parking is available at Castleton State College on Vt. 4A, and the trail can be accessed immediately to the west on South Street. The trail follows a southerly course and eventually reaches a southern access for the northern segment in Poultney just east of the junction of Vt. 30, Vt. 31, and Vt. 140.

The northern end of the southern segment of the trail is several miles to the south in the village of West Pawlet on Vt. 153. The trail continues to the south, at first following the Indian River before arriving at the village of Rupert. Here the trail bears to the west and reaches a terminus in West Rupert on Vt. 153, where very limited parking is available.

The trail leaves Vermont to enter New York in three places. Since the New York sections of the trail have not been developed for recreational use, and in some cases ownership of the rail bed has reverted to adjacent private landowners, passage over these portions of the old roadbed is not assured.

HAPGOOD POND RECREATION AREA

The USFS Hapgood Pond Recreation Area with a picnic area, campground, and swimming is reached from the village of Peru, located a short distance to the north of Vt. 11, east of the Bromley Mountain Ski Area. In the village, bear left on the blacktop Hapgood Pond Road. Continue for 1.7 mi. to the entrance of the recreation area. The Land and Man Forest Trail, 0.8 mi. long, circles the pond.

BIG BRANCH TRAIL

ABOUT THE TRAIL: This U.S Forest Service trail descends to the Big Branch River from the Big Branch Picnic Area in the Green Mountain National Forest. Many dramatic views of the river are afforded from an adjoining trail.

TO THE TRAIL: Go east from U.S. 7 in the village of Danby on the paved Mount Tabor Road/USFS Road 10 (seasonal) through the village of Mt. Tabor to the signed Big Branch parking area (2.6 mi.) on the south side of the road.

DESCRIPTION: The picnic area provides a good vantage point high above the Big Branch River with a broad southwestern view of the Otter Creek Valley and Dorset's peaks. At a break near the center of a split-rail fence, the Big Branch Trail begins a steep descent via switchbacks to the boulder-filled river (0.2 mi.). At the river's edge, narrow trails proceed in both directions, giving impressive views of the rushing water and gargantuan boulders in the riverbed.

WOODFORD STATE PARK

ABOUT THE TRAIL: Woodford State Park occupies 398 acres on a mountain plateau surrounding Adams Reservoir. At an elevation of 2,400 ft., it is the highest Vermont state park and is covered in a high-altitude, spruce-fir-birch forest. A number of campsites are available, and a day-use fee is charged in-season.

TO THE TRAIL: The park entrance is on the south side of Vt. 9, about 11.0 mi. east of Bennington and 3.2 mi. west of Vt. 8. Out-of-season, parking is available at a U.S. Forest Service parking lot on Vt. 9, north and east of the park entrance.

DESCRIPTION: A blue-blazed hiking trail located mostly within the park encircles the 23-acre reservoir, closely following its western shore. Following a clockwise loop, the trail may be found at any of three points along an access road that leaves the contact station to the left and continues to the park campgrounds. The first trailhead is on the left, as the access road ascends a hill. Starting on a wide snowmobile trail, the foot trail veers to the right at a power line crossing. The second access is a left into the woods at a playground, and the third access is on the left 100 yds. farther, just before the access road descends a hill.

The hiking trail heads south, closely following the eastern park boundary, then bears west through a small section of the George Aiken Wilderness where there are limited views to beaver ponds. The trail then recrosses state park land to enter the Green Mountain National Forest, reaching a junction at the south end of Adams Reservoir. Distance from access road to reservoir is about 1.0 mi. (1.6 km).

Junction: To the right, a trail returns to the state park, reaching the campground at site 64, where the access road leads back to the contact station.

To the left, the trail follows the west side of the reservoir, reentering state park land, and eventually reaching a junction where the Atwood Trail leaves to the right and provides a short alternate route along the shoreline. The trails reconverge several hundred feet ahead and soon reach a parking lot at the park day-use area (1.7 mi.). The contact station lies a short distance beyond.

Region 2
Southeast Vermont

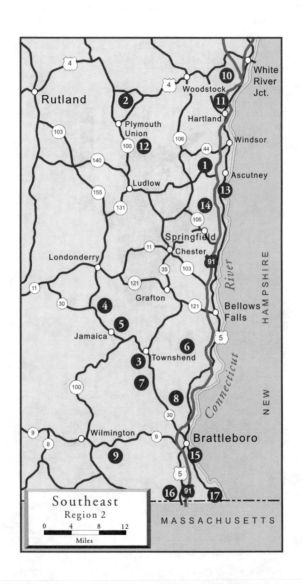

REGION 2
Southeast Vermont

lthough this part of Vermont lacks the larger
south-north mountain ridges of much of the
rest of the state, there are plenty of places to explore by foot. Trails wend their way along rivers, climb to
the few peaks, and wander through natural areas with rare
plant species. Many trails are multiuse and good for walking, cross-country skiing, hiking, and often cycling.

To the west, the main range of the Green Mountains has
petered to foothills; to the east, the broad Connecticut
River separates the state from neighboring New Hampshire. Mixed between is a jumble of hills and rivers draining
to the great Connecticut. Throughout the region, rivers
flow southeast in a tree-branch pattern, creating an unor-
ganized-looking topography. Mt. Ascutney, a monadnock
looming from the Connecticut River Valley, is the largest
and most prominent mountain in the region.

MOUNT ASCUTNEY

A monadnock, Mt. Ascutney (3,150 ft.) is the dominant physical feature of southeastern Vermont and is
rich in history. The mountain's quartz syenite rock has

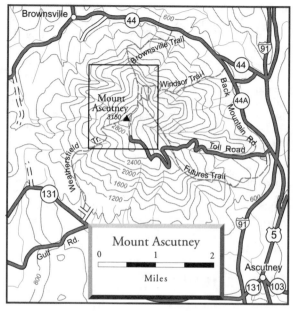

Mount Ascutney

| 0 | 1 | 2 |

Miles

withstood the erosion and glaciation that has worn away the softer rocks of the surrounding Piedmont peneplane. Located in the towns of Windsor and West Windsor (USGS Mt. Ascutney), the mountain derives its name from the Algonquin words *Cas-Cad-Nac* or *Mahps-Cad-Na*, meaning "mountain of the rocky summit," or *Ascutegnik*, meaning "meeting of the waters."

The mountain's first hiking trail was built in the 1850s. Today, four trails approach from the base of the mountain and connect near the summit. The Brownsville, Windsor, and Weathersfield Trails derive their names from the towns or villages that roughly mark their town of origin. The Futures Trail ascends through Ascutney State Park, which occupies about 2,000 acres on the eastern slope of the mountain. All trail descriptions include mileages to the summit. The Civilian Conservation Corps (CCC) developed the park between 1935 and 1939, constructing the original stone buildings as well as a 3.8-mi. paved auto road, which ascends some 2,250 ft. to within 0.75 mi. of the summit. There are camping facilities near the base of the mountain and picnic facilities along the mountain road and near the summit. Day-use and camping fees are charged in-season. The park entrance is on the west side of Vt. 44A, which runs between U.S. 5, north of Ascutney and Vt. 44, east of Brownsville.

The trail system is maintained largely by the Ascutney Trails Association, established in 1967. The group has restored and improved these historic trails and publishes a fascinating guidebook, the *Mount Ascutney Guide*. Describing the trails in detail, the guide also gives historical information and natural history of the area. The guide is available from the association (see page 345) or from the Green Mountain Club.

WINDSOR TRAIL

Distance: 2.7 mi. (4.3 km)
Elevation Change: 2,520 ft. ascent
Hiking Time: 2½ hr. (reverse 1¼ hr.)

TO THE TRAIL: Marked with white blazes, this trail begins at a small parking lot on the southwest side of Vt. 44A, also known as Back Mountain Road. From U.S. 5 in Windsor, head west on Vt. 44 for roughly 2.5 mi. to reach the intersection with Vt. 44A. Turn sharply to the left onto Vt. 44A, and continue south 0.2 mi. to reach the trailhead and parking lot on the right, marked by a small, white Ascutney Trails Association (ATA) sign on the opposite side of the road. The lot is 1.5 mi. north of the entrance to Ascutney State Park, also located on Vt. 44A.
DESCRIPTION: From Vt. 44A (0.0 mi.), the white-blazed

trail follows the southern boundary of an open field. Beyond the upper end of the field, the trail passes through birches and pines and soon enters the woods. The trail then begins an increasingly steep climb on a wide woods road to reach a spur on the left (0.8 mi.), which leads a short distance to Gerry's Falls on Mountain Brook.

Continuing past the side trail, the Windsor Trail soon crosses the right branch of the brook (0.9 mi.), then follows the left branch upstream a short distance before swinging to the right and slabbing westerly to recross the right branch (1.1 mi.). The trail then continues over and around a low shoulder of the mountain to reach a trail junction at Halfway Spring (1.6 mi.), the former site of a logger's cabin.

Junction: From the junction, two ascent routes diverge, rejoining in 0.2 mi. To the right, the 1857 Route climbs to a spring and log shelter, built in 1968 by the ATA, then rejoins the Windsor Trail a short distance beyond.

From Halfway Spring, the Windsor Trail follows the 1903 Route left at the fork, then turns sharply to the left and ascends steeply to the south to reach a junction with the Blood Rock Trail (1.7 mi.).

Junction: To the left, this blue-blazed trail climbs steeply for about 0.25 mi. to reach Blood Rock, where there is a good view to the north. Caution should be exercised around the face of the ledge, which has been blocked by a railing. The trail then swings to the west to rejoin the Windsor Trail about 0.5 mi. above the junction.

Bearing right at the junction, the Windsor Trail is soon rejoined by the 1857 Route (1.8 mi.). It then begins a steady climb past the upper end of the Blood Rock Trail (2.0 mi.), and reaches a junction with the Futures Trail a short distance beyond (2.2 mi.). The Windsor Trail then reaches another junction (2.4 mi.) where a spur on the left leads to Castle Rock and a view of the Connecticut River Valley.

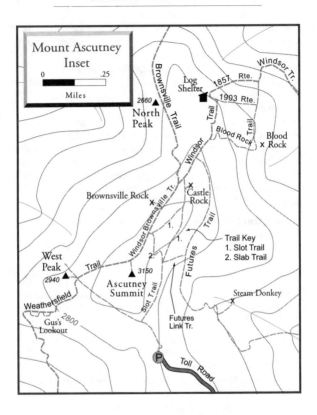

The Windsor Trail then reaches yet another junction, where it is joined on the right by the Brownsville Trail. From this point, the trails coincide in a final ascent to reach the open area at the Stone Hut site (3,110 ft.) (2.5 mi.). To the right, a short spur leads to Brownsville Rock, where there are extensive views of much of the Green Mountain Range. As the trail continues atop the ridge toward the true summit, it passes a junction with the Slot Trail on the left, which descends 0.7 mi. to the Mountain Road parking lot. The Windsor/Brownsville Trail continues through the woods to a public observation tower, then reaches a junction with the Weathersfield Trail at the bottom of a short spur, which ascends to Ascutney summit (3,150 ft.) (2.7 mi.).

Two communications towers dominate the mountain's highest summit, making views from this area mediocre. Hikers will be more satisfied with the vistas from Brownsville Rock, Castle Rock, and the nearby observation tower.

2

A cabin and tower were originally constructed on the summit of Mt. Ascutney in 1920 for forest fire surveillance. The CCC built a new steel tower in 1938 to 1940, and the site remained operational until 1952, when airplane patrols were established in the area. The concrete footings from this 1940 tower, which was removed in 1988, can be found about 300 ft. south of the present tower, which was constructed in 1989 by the state of Vermont. Using steel elements of the old tower, a 24.5-ft. tall observation tower was rebuilt (without a cabin), which affords panoramic views from treetop level to the White Mountains, Green Mountains, Berkshires, and Taconics.

BROWNSVILLE TRAIL

Distance: 3.2 mi. (5.2 km)
Elevation Change: 2,400 ft. ascent
Hiking Time: 3½ hr. (reverse 1¾ hr.)

TO THE TRAIL: This trail begins just past a wood-framed house on the south side of Vt. 44, 4.3 mi. west of its junction with U.S. 5 in Windsor and 1.1 mi. east of the Mt. Ascutney Ski Area. From the south, the trailhead is located 2.8 mi. north of Ascutney State Park and 1.2 mi. north of the beginning of the Windsor Trail, making a loop hike over these two trails possible. Parking for the Brownsville Trail is available off the highway in a gravel lot with a trail-head bulletin board.

DESCRIPTION: From the parking lot (0.0 mi.), this white-blazed trail crosses a short grassy stretch in a former pasture before entering the woods in a southerly direction. The trail bears to the left to cross a wooden bridge over a seasonally dry wash before ascending briefly on wooden stair treads. At the top of the stairs, the trail bears right and zigzags steeply uphill to an old road. Turning right to follow the road, the trail continues on easier grades, soon reaching the former Norcross granite quarry (1.1 mi.), one of four that operated at various times in the area.

Beyond the grout (granite waste) pile, the old road ends and the trail turns sharply left, climbing steeply to a spur leading a short distance to Quarry Top Lookout, which offers views to the north (1.2 mi.). Climbing steadily through the woods, the trail eventually approaches a ski trail (1.6 mi.). Here the trail swings sharply left and climbs on switchbacks to Knee Lookout (2.0 mi.), where there is a view to the east. The trail then continues on easier grades to the summit of North Peak (2.4 mi.) and a nearby vista where there are views to the west. Continuing on easy grades for some distance, the trail then resumes a steep climb via switchbacks to a junction with the Windsor Trail (2.9 mi.).

Bearing right at the junction, the Brownsville Trail and Windsor Trail coincide in their ascent to the Stone Hut site (3.0 mi.) atop the summit ridge. Here, a short spur trail to the right leads to Brownsville Rock, where there are extensive views west to the Green Mountain Range and the hamlet of Brownsville. Atop the ridge, the trail continues south on easy grades, passes the observation tower, and reaches a junction with the Weathersfield Trail at the bottom of a short spur leading to Ascutney summit (3.2 mi.). Additional information on the summit area may be found in the description of the Windsor Trail, previously described.

FUTURES TRAIL

Distance: 4.8 mi. (7.7 km)
Elevation Change: 2,600 ft. ascent
Hiking Time: 3¾ hr. (reverse 2½ hr.)

ABOUT THE TRAIL: Marked with blue blazes, this trail leads from Ascutney State Park to the Windsor Trail, about 0.5 mi. below the summit of Mt. Ascutney. Although it takes longer to ascend via this route, it offers several interesting views that compensate for the additional effort.

TO THE TRAIL: Follow directions to Ascutney State Park on page 112. From the contact station near the park entrance, follow the signs for the Futures Trail, which point to the first road on the left, then follow the campground road to the trailhead at campsite 22.

DESCRIPTION: From the campsite (0.0 mi.), the trail winds south past the ruin of a stone fireplace dating to the 1930s. The trail continues climbing south and west through a series of switchbacks before reaching Bare Rock Vista (1.0 mi.), which offers views of the summit to the northwest and south to the Connecticut River Valley below.

Bearing right, the trail descends to traverse a mature hardwood forest before reaching a small stream (1.5 mi.) and then another small stream on the left (2.0 mi.). Ascending, the trail crosses under power lines before reaching a parking lot along the Mountain Road (2.1 mi.) where a picnic shelter is located opposite. Without crossing the road, the trail bears to the west and returns to the woods, crossing two additional power lines (2.4 mi.) and then the Mountain Road (2.8 mi.).

The trail ascends gently to a pair of streams (3.2 mi.). Just beyond the second stream, the trail reaches a junction (3.4 mi.) where a spur trail leads 0.1 mi. to the right to a "steam donkey." This steam engine was used in the early 1900s to pull logs up the mountain for use in building the road and fire tower. The Futures Trail bears left at the junction, soon reaching another junction (3.6 mi.), where the Futures Link Trail bears left.

Junction: Here the Futures Link Trail leads 0.1 mi. to a four-way intersection with the Slot and Slab Trails, which provide two shortcuts to the summit. The four-way intersection lies at about the midpoint of the Slot Trail (0.7 mi. long), which links the parking area atop the Mountain Road to a point on the Windsor/Brownsville Trail near the summit of the mountain. Continuing straight ahead at the intersection, the Slab Trail provides an additional shortcut to the summit, bypassing the upper half of the Slot Trail and reaching the Windsor/Brownsville Trail (0.2 mi.) in a saddle a short distance north of the observation tower and Ascutney summit.

The Futures Trail bears right at the junction and ascends steeply, finally reaching its terminus at a junction with the Windsor Trail (4.2 mi.). To the left, the Windsor Trail soon reaches a junction with the Brownsville Trail, and these two trails coincide to make a final ascent to the Stone Hut site and Brownsville Rock a short distance below the observation tower and Ascutney summit (4.8 mi.). Additional information on the summit area may be found in the description of the Windsor Trail on page 115.

SLOT TRAIL

Distance: 0.7 mi. (1.1 km)
Elevation Change: 350 ft. ascent
Hiking Time: ¾ hr. (reverse ½ hr.)

ABOUT THE TRAIL: The Slot Trail begins at the top of the Mountain Road and climbs on moderate grades to reach the Windsor/Brownsville Trail in a saddle a short distance north of the Ascutney summit. It gets its name from a portion of the trail that passes through a high-walled slot.
DESCRIPTION: From the parking area (0.0 mi.), the trail ascends gradually to a four-way intersection (0.3 mi.).

Junction: To the right, the Futures Link Trail descends 0.1 mi. to reach the Futures Trail at a point 3.6 mi. above the trailhead in Ascutney State Park. To the left, the Slab Trail ascends 0.2 mi., rejoining the Slot Trail just below the ridge.

Continuing straight ahead, the Slot Trail soon reaches another junction (0.5 mi.), with the southern end of the Castle Rock Trail.

Junction: The Castle Rock Trail provides a short link (0.1 mi.) connecting the Slot Trail in the south with the Windsor Trail in the north. Castle Rock lies at the midpoint of the trail and provides an excellent view east to the Connecticut River Valley.

Turning left at the junction, the Slot Trail makes a winding ascent, is rejoined by the Slab Trail, and reaches the white-blazed Windsor/Brownsville Trail in a saddle 0.1 mi. north of the Ascutney summit (0.7 mi.).

WEATHERSFIELD TRAIL

Distance: 2.9 mi. (4.7 km)
Elevation Change: 2,062 ft. ascent
Hiking Time: 2½ hr. (reverse 1½ hr.)

ABOUT THE TRAIL: This blue-blazed trail ascends the southwestern side of the mountain and is on state and town (West Windsor) forestlands.

TO THE TRAIL: From Vt. 131, 3.3 mi. west of I-91 exit 8, and 3.8 mi. east of Vt. 106 at Downers, turn north onto Cascade Falls Road. Bear left at a fork and continue 0.3 mi. to a right turn leading to a parking area and the trailhead.

DESCRIPTION: From the parking area (0.0 mi.), the trail begins a gradual ascent following an old woods road, soon crossing Little Cascade Falls (0.4 mi.). Ascending steeply over a rock outcrop, the trail enters a deep rock cleft, and then ascends on easier grades, passing several overlooks

(0.6 mi.). Descending, the trail reaches Crystal Cascade Falls (1.1 mi.) where Ascutney Brook tumbles 84 ft. over a sheer cliff. The trail then makes a steep and winding climb to the top of the cascade, turns sharply to the right, and continues up the east side of the brook. After crossing Cascade Brook, the trail meets and follows an old woods road, which soon becomes strewn with boulders.

Following the road as far as Halfway Brooks (1.7 mi.), the Weathersfield Trail then turns to the left and begins a winding and moderately steep climb through the woods. (Here a bypass to the right leaves the trail to join it again at Gus's Lookout.) After passing several lookouts, the trail crosses an open rock area at the base of West Peak and continues a short distance to Gus's Lookout (2.3 mi.) where there is an excellent view of the Connecticut River Valley. The lookout is named for Augustus Aldrich, a charter director of the ATA and man of many talents who died, at the age of 86, while hiking Mt. Katahdin in 1974.

Beyond the lookout, the trail resumes its steady, winding climb past a spur to West Peak Spring (2.4 mi.), and then reaches two more spurs. One goes a few hundred feet to West Peak (2,940 ft.) (2.6 mi.), and the other leads to a hang-glider launching site. Passing the spurs, the Weathersfield Trail makes a final winding climb to reach a junction with the Windsor/Brownsville Trail at the bottom of a short spur below the communications antennas on Ascutney summit (2.9 mi.). The summit area and nearby observation tower offer extensive views of the White Mountains, Green Mountains, Berkshires, and Taconics. Other features in the summit area are in the description of the Windsor Trail, page 115.

• • • • • • • • • • • • • • • • •

COOLIDGE STATE PARK, SLACK HILL

Distance: 3.6 mi. (5.8 km)
Elevation Change: 500 ft. ascent
Hiking Time: 2¼ hr. (reverse 1¾ hr.)

ABOUT THE TRAIL: Coolidge State Forest was first established in 1925 and now encompasses 16,166 acres scattered through seven towns. For management purposes, the forest is divided into eastern and western districts by Vt. 100. Camp Calvin Coolidge was established in Coolidge State Forest in Plymouth on June 9, 1933 as the third Civilian Conservation Corps (CCC) camp in Vermont, on the present site of Coolidge State Park. Now occupying about 500 acres in the forest's eastern district, the park contains camping and day-use facilities, with a fee charged in-season. Several hiking trails are available, including a 3.6-mi. loop that passes near the summit of Slack Hill (2,174 ft., USGS Plymouth).

TO THE TRAIL: The paved access road to Coolidge State Park leaves the east side of Vt. 100A, 4.3 mi. south of Bridgewater Corners and 2.7 mi. north of Plymouth Union. From the highway, travel 0.9 mi. uphill to the park contact station.

DESCRIPTION: Marked with blue blazes, the clockwise trail loop to the summit begins at the park contact station (0.0 mi.). To the right of a firewood shed, follow the signed Slack Hill Trail, which climbs gently through open woods to a signed junction (0.5 mi.). Bearing left at the junction, the trail climbs moderately through a mixed hardwood forest before leveling off and passing to the east of the summit, which has been encumbered with blowdowns. The trail then descends to a vista (1.5 mi.) where there is a narrow view of Mt. Ascutney to the southeast. The trail continues to descend gently, through a hardwood forest, and then passes through a stand of white pine with

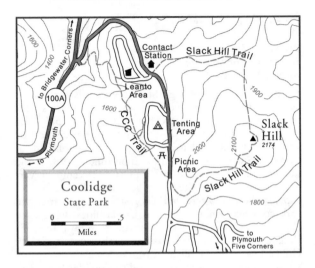

Coolidge
State Park

0 _____ .5

Miles

little change in elevation, eventually reaching the paved park access road (2.5 mi.).

Junction: The access road leads about 0.75 mi. right to the contact station.

Continuing the loop across the road, the CCC Trail starts in the park picnic area, continuing to a picnic pavilion with massive fireplaces at either end. Passing through the pavilion, the trail soon reaches a junction (3.0 mi.) where a spur to the right leads to the park tenting area. Continuing straight ahead, the trail descends into a ravine to cross a stream, then climbs to reach another junction (3.5 mi.).

Junction: To the left at the junction, a 0.5-mi. spur trail descends fairly steeply to reach a picnic shelter (currently closed) and Vt. 100A, at the beginning of the park access road, 0.9 mi. below the contact station.

Bearing right at the junction, the trail quickly reaches its terminus on a gravel roadway forming the western side of a road loop through the park's lean-to area. Bearing right along the road and continuing straight through a junction forming the head of the loop, it is a short distance to the contact station on the park access road (3.6 mi.). Alternatively, bearing left along the road to walk the longer leg of the road loop, there are occasional views west to Killington Peak and other summits in the Green Mountain Range. This route adds about 0.5 mi. to the hiking distance.

2

• • • • • • • • • • • • • • • •

WEST RIVER AREA

BALD MOUNTAIN, TOWNSHEND

Distance: 1.7 mi. (2.7 km)
Elevation Change: 1,100 ft. ascent
Hiking Time: 2 hr. (reverse 1 hr.)

ABOUT THE TRAIL: This small mountain is located in Townshend State Forest. Although the fire tower that once graced the summit of Bald Mtn. (1,680 ft., USGS Townshend) is long gone, several small clearings offer views of Townshend Reservoir, the West River Valley, Stratton Mtn., Bromley Mtn., and New Hampshire's Mt. Monadnock.

Townshend State Park occupies about 41 acres in the 856-acre Townshend State Forest. The park was established as a CCC camp during the Great Depression and currently offers camping facilities. An access fee is charged in-season. Swimming, picnicking, and access to the Ledges Overlook Trail (description follows, see maps on pages 124 and 129) are available at the Townshend Dam Recreation Area, managed by the Army Corps of Engineers.

TO THE TRAIL: To reach the trailhead in Townshend State Park, follow Vt. 30 north 2.1 mi. from the Townshend village common, or south for 2.4 mi. from the post office in West Townshend to reach Townshend Dam. At the dam,

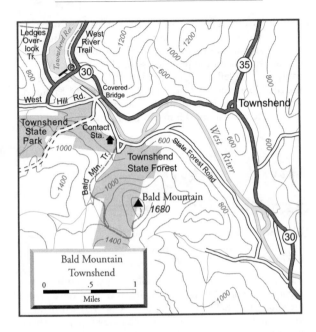

Bald Mountain
Townshend

0   .5   1
Miles

turn west and cross the spillway on a narrow bridge and continue straight to an intersection. Turn left onto the gravel West Hill Road, which leads to the Scott Covered Bridge (the longest single-span covered bridge in Vermont). Bear right at the bridge onto the state forest road and continue parallel to the West River to the park entrance on the left. Parking is available inside the park near the contact station.

DESCRIPTION: The blue-blazed trail starts at the contact station (0.0 mi.) and follows the paved campground road toward campsite 25, where it turns left and crosses a brook on a wooden bridge (0.1 mi.). The trail then bears left to follow an old woods road to the south, parallel to the brook, ascending on moderate grades. Eventually reaching a sign, the trail recrosses the brook on stones (0.5 mi.) and starts up a moderately steep grade. The trail soon leaves the woods road to the left, following a smaller skid road. Reaching a switchback to the left, the trail leaves the skid road and continues on to cross two woods roads before passing through a hemlock forest. The trail reaches an old cellar hole (1.1 mi.) and climbs moderately to a rocky section before leveling off and bearing to the left (1.2 mi.). Turning to the northeast, the trail passes an alder swamp on the right (1.5 mi.), and then makes a steep climb to the north, mostly on bedrock, to the summit of Bald Mtn. (1.8 mi.).

This spot was one of the earliest forest fire lookouts in Vermont. The station was established in 1912, and soon an observation tower was built. Between 1932 and 1934, the CCC constructed a steel tower at the site. In 1949 to 1950 this tower was relocated to Mt. Olga in Wilmington, where it is still standing and is used as an observation tower for the general public.

In 1996, the eastern return leg of the old loop trail, which continued over the summit and down the north side of the mountain, was closed due to severe erosion. Until this section is reopened, hikers should use only the western half of the trail and not proceed beyond the summit.

LEDGES OVERLOOK TRAIL

Distance: 1.7 mi. (2.7 km)
Elevation Change: 450 ft. ascent
Hiking Time: 1½ hr. either direction

ABOUT THE TRAIL: Maintained by the U.S. Army Corps of Engineers, this trail loop begins and ends at a wooded picnic grove on the west shore of Townshend Reservoir (USGS Townshend). Refer to the map on page 129.

TO THE TRAIL: From Townshend village, follow Vt. 30 north 2.1 mi. to Townshend Dam. At the dam turn west and cross the spillway on a narrow bridge. Turn right onto an access road (0.0 mi.) and pass the beach (0.5 mi.) and picnic area (0.6 mi.) to the signed trailhead on the left. Ample parking is available on the east side of the road.

DESCRIPTION: The two ends of this yellow-blazed trail are separated by a short section of the paved access road. A register box at the southern trailhead contains brochures with a map outlining the clockwise loop.

From the register box (0.0 mi.), the trail enters the forest to follow a woods road, quickly crosses another woods road and a stone wall, and then begins a steady ascent to the west. Eventually reaching a stone wall, which it follows for a distance, the trail bears left off the road (0.2 mi.) onto a southerly course through a mixed hardwood-softwood forest. The trail soon reaches and follows another road to the left on easier grades (0.3 mi.) before turning sharply to the west and crossing another stone wall. After resuming a steady climb, the trail turns to the north (0.5 mi.) and reaches the end of the woods road (0.6 mi.). Following easier grades, the trail soon reaches a rock outcrop (0.7 mi.), and then continues to an old clearing at the top of a rock ledge (0.8 mi.). From this vantage point, there is a panorama of the West River Valley, including Townshend Reservoir and Dam and the Scott Covered Bridge. Bald Mtn. lies to the southeast, and the long ridge of Rattlesnake Mtn. lies to the east.

Continuing north from the lookout, the trail climbs a short steep grade, then meanders along the top of the ridge parallel to the marked property line. In this woodland savanna, a grassy lawn lies beneath a grove of hop-hornbeam trees. Leaving the property line (1.0 mi.), the trail gradually descends, following a well-worn footpath marked with faded yellow blazes. The trail bears right onto a woods road, which it follows along a steady descent to the east, then southeast. Bearing slightly to the left off the woods road, the trail reaches another woods road, which it follows to the right. The trail passes some old foundations on the right (1.5 mi.) before again leaving the woods road. The trail crosses another woods road, then descends on easier grades to reach a dirt road. Bearing to the left onto this road, the trail quickly turns to the right at a road junction then reaches the paved access road (1.7 mi.) across from the Burrington Picnic Pavilion, about 400 ft. north of the register box.

2

WEST RIVER TRAIL

When complete, the multiuse West River Trail will stretch 16.0 mi. from Townshend Dam, located between the villages of Townshend and West Townshend, to the west and north to South Londonderry. Walkers, cyclists, and cross-country skiers enjoy the route, which closely follows the West River and in many places utilizes the former bed of the West River Railroad. Marked with lavender and green West River Trail markers, four sections of the trail are open. The Friends of the West River Trail (page 345) maintain the trail. Conditions may change as sections of the trail are rerouted or improved. Here the trail is divided into four sections described in a northbound direction.

Conceived as a connecting link between the Connecticut River and Lake Champlain, the West River Railroad operated from 1879 to 1935 between Brattleboro and South Londonderry, first as a narrow gauge line and later as a standard gauge railroad. Much of the route from Jamaica southward remains well defined; many sections of roadbed and several bridge abutments are readily visible from Vt. 30. The story of the West River Railroad is told in Victor Morse's *36 Miles of Trouble* (Brattleboro, Vt.: Stephen Greene Press, 1959).

TOWNSHEND DAM TO WEST TOWNSHEND

Distance: 3.0 mi. (4.8 km)
Elevation Change: minor
Hiking Time: 1½ hr. either direction

ABOUT THE TRAIL: Utilizing the old railroad bed and an abandoned section of Vt. 30, this section of the West River Trail (USGS Townshend) traverses the river bottomland along the east side of Townshend Reservoir and the West River. Located entirely on U.S. Army Corps of Engineers property, much of the first half of the trail may be underwater in the spring, or when the Townshend Dam inundates the area for flood control purposes. Contact the corps office at the dam at (802) 365-7703 for trail information.

Townshend Dam was constructed between November 1958 and June 1961 and stretches 1,700 ft. in width and 133 ft. in height. With a drainage area of 278 square miles, the 1,010-acre lake has a maximum impoundment of 11 billion gallons.

TO THE TRAIL: At this time, this portion of the West River Trail is only accessible from the south. The trail starts at a large paved parking area on the southwest side of Vt. 30 at the Townshend Dam, 2.1 mi. west of the common in Townshend village, or 2.4 mi. south of the post office in West Townshend.

DESCRIPTION: From a sign at the western end of the parking area (0.0 mi.), the trail descends steeply through a young forest to a cleared area behind the concrete spillway of the dam and then turns to the right onto an old roadway. The trail then descends more gradually to the edge of the reservoir and into open, brushy land amid many broken tree limbs caused by ice damage from stored water.

With Rattlesnake Mtn. lying straight ahead, and the West River Railroad bed visible in the trees to the right, the trail continues to the north to reach and follow the blacktop roadway of a former section of Vt. 30 (0.2 mi.), abandoned when Townshend Dam was constructed.

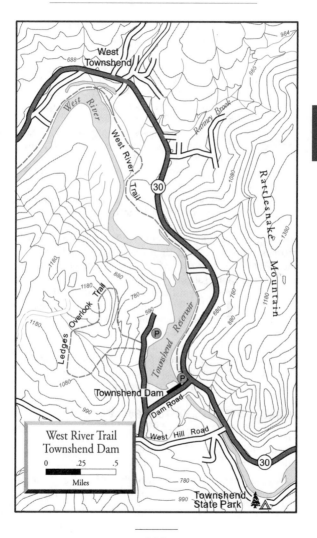

West
Townshend

West River

West River Trail

30

Rainey Brook

Rattlesnake Mountain

Townshend Reservoir

Ledges Overlook Trail

P

P

Townshend Dam

Dam Road

West Hill Road

30

Townshend
State Park

West River Trail
Townshend Dam

0   .25   .5

Miles

2

The trail crosses a log boom and yellow gate (0.7 mi.) before arriving at a junction with a road on the right. Bearing left at the junction, the trail soon reaches the top of the reservoir, where the waterway narrows and the West River veers to the far side of the valley. The trail follows a winding course past a series of small rock outcrops before eventually meeting the river again, where both turn to the right (1.7 mi.). The West River Trail soon turns left off the old Vt. 30 roadbed (1.9 mi.), passes through a yellow gate, and crosses Ranney Brook on a wooden bridge. (Continuing along the roadbed for an additional 0.4 mi. leads to the present Vt. 30, 0.3 mi. south of the post office in West Townshend.)

The trail, now a footpath, wends its way through a brushy area before crossing a large open field where the route is marked by West River Trail markers mounted on posts. At the far side of the field (2.2 mi.), the trail enters another brushy area and then follows the barely discernable West River Railroad bed past a row of large white pine trees on the right. Just beyond the trees lies the location of the former West Townshend railroad station. The trail leaves the roadbed briefly to cross a small stream, then rejoins it before coming to a washout (2.6 mi.). The marshy stream here must be crossed on a beaver dam.

The trail enters a wooded area and leaves the almost imperceptible railroad bed to parallel a channel of the West River. The trail ends at posted private land (3.0 mi.) with the main channel of the West River on the left.

JAMAICA STATE PARK TO COBB BROOK

Distance: 1.9 mi. (3.1 km)
Elevation Change: 350 ft. ascent
Hiking Time: 1½ hr. (reverse 1 hr.)

ABOUT THE TRAIL: This segment of the West River Trail follows the roadbed of the former West River Railroad east and north for about 2.0 mi. along the West River (USGS

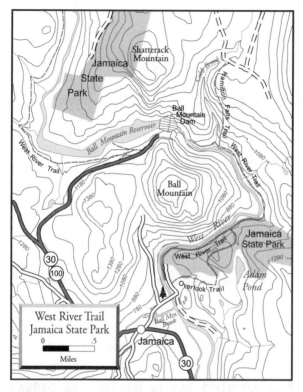

West River Trail
Jamaica State Park
0   .5
Miles

Jamaica, Londonderry). The West River Trail also connects with the Overlook Trail and the Hamilton Falls Trail
in Jamaica State Park, described on pages 136 to 137.

TO THE TRAIL: Jamaica State Park is located about 0.5 mi.
off Vt. 30, 4.5 mi. west of West Townshend village, and
about 9.0 mi. south and east of South Londonderry. From
Jamaica village, turn north off Vt. 30 at a sign for the state
park, pass the elementary school, and cross a bridge over

the West River to reach the park entrance on the left. The park offers a variety of camping and day-use facilities, with a fee charged in-season.

DESCRIPTION: From a gate at the northern end of the state park day-use parking area (0.0 mi.), the West River Trail follows the old railroad grade upstream and passes a series of wire cables stretched to the opposite bank of the West River (0.5 mi. to 0.8 mi.), which are used for setting slalom courses for kayak races. The trail then reaches a junction (1.0 mi.) where the north end of the Overlook Trail (page 136) departs to the right to ascend Little Ball Mtn. before returning to the state park campground.

The roadbed crosses several small streams, passes old foundations in thick undergrowth on the left (1.6 mi.), and then skirts the posted boundary of private property for some distance before reaching a junction with an old road on the right (1.9 mi.). Here a sign marks the beginning of the Hamilton Falls Trail (described on page 137).

Although this segment of the West River Trail ends at this junction, the old railroad bed continues straight ahead to cross Cobb Brook on rocks beside the ruins of old bridge abutments (0.1 mi.). The roadbed degenerates into a foot trail as it reaches the base of the Ball Mountain Dam (0.3 mi.). While a small spur trail leads to the top of the dam, plans call for the West River Trail to cross the face of the dam on a new route and continue to the Ball Mountain Dam access road.

BALL MOUNTAIN DAM TO WINHALL CAMPGROUND

Distance: 4.1 mi. (6.6 km)
Elevation Change: minor
Hiking Time: 2 hr. either direction

ABOUT THE TRAIL: This section of the West River Trail (USGS Jamaica, Londonderry) starts on the access road to the Ball Mountain Dam and follows a woodland path along the slopes above Ball Mountain Reservoir before dropping to the river's edge. The trail then follows a road along the former bed of the West River Railroad on the south and west shores of the West River to reach the Army Corps of Engineers' Winhall Campground.

To the Trail: The Ball Mountain Dam access road leaves the north side of Vt. 30/100 1.5 mi. west of the general store in the village of Jamaica, or 3.4 mi. east of the junction of Vt. 100 and Vt. 30 in Rawsonville. The trailhead is located on the west side of the access road 1.5 mi. north of Vt. 30/100, beyond a yellow gate and adjacent to a sign describing the Ball Mountain Dam. Parking is available in a lot near a building on the right 0.1 mi. south of the trailhead, or just beyond the trailhead on the left. The Ball Mountain Dam access road is closed from 3:00 P.M. to 7:00 A.M.

Description: From the yellow gate (0.0 mi.), follow the narrow paved road a short distance to a sign for the West River Trail. Departing the road to the left, the trail descends gradually through a young forest to meet a junction with an old road. The trail turns to the left and immediately meets a gravel road on the outside of a hairpin turn (0.1 mi.). Following the left leg of the road uphill for a very short distance, the West River Trail then bears right onto the broad grassy roadbed. Remaining on level grades, the trail narrows to a footpath to traverse a steep hillside, then crosses a rocky, washed-out area before entering an aspen-birch forest. The trail continues through rocky swales before descending to cross several small brooks on a bank overlooking Ball Mountain Reservoir.

The trail, now marked with occasional orange blazes, enters a hemlock forest (0.9 mi.) and makes a short but steady climb before dropping to cross a larger brook on a broad rock slab. Turning to the right onto an old woods road (1.2 mi.), the trail soon enters the open lands where the West River enters the head of the Ball Mountain Reservoir. The rocky slopes of Shatterack Mtn. can be seen to the east across the water, while Glebe Mtn. is visible looking upstream across the valley.

The trail crosses a brook to the right of a waterfall (1.4 mi.) and continues as a footpath through a hardwood forest. After climbing a short, steep pitch, the trail takes a winding route through hemlocks atop a large rock outcrop, passes an Army Corps of Engineers benchmark on the left, then turns onto a woods road at a point above the West River (1.9 mi.).

Soon leaving the road to the right (2.2 mi.), the West River Trail crosses a brook in a dense hemlock stand. Emerging into a white pine forest, the trail descends to a clearing and reaches a junction at the end of a dirt road (2.4 mi.). To the right, a path leads a short distance to the West River. The stone abutments of Pratt's Bridge, where the West River Railroad crossed the river, are visible to the left. Though the railroad was abandoned about 1937, the bridge remained until destroyed by ice in the 1970s.

The West River Trail turns to the left at the junction and follows the dirt road, which coincides with the roadbed of the West River Railroad. The road passes through a mixture of open lands and trees, with a number of views to the West River on the right, finally arriving at the southern end of the Winhall Campground (4.1 mi.).

WINHALL CAMPGROUND TO SOUTH LONDONDERRY

Distance: 1.8 mi. (2.9 km)
Elevation Change: minor
Hiking Time: 2 hr. either direction

TO THE TRAIL: The Army Corps of Engineers Winhall Campground, located in the town of Londonderry, is reached by turning east onto the paved Winhall Station Road from Vt. 100, 2.4 mi. north of the junction of Vt. 30 and Vt. 100 in Rawsonville or 1.5 mi. south of the bridge in South Londonderry.

From a sign for the campground at the junction of Vt. 100 and Winhall Station Road (0.0 mi.), bear left almost immediately, then right at the next junction (0.2 mi.) to reach the campground gatehouse (0.9 mi.). The West River Trail enters the campground from the south. Past the gatehouse, descend to a fork, turn right to cross a bridge over the Winhall River (1.0 mi.), and continue through the open camping areas along the West and Winhall Rivers. Parking is available at the end of the campgrounds where the road enters the woods (1.8 mi.), but vehicular traffic is permitted the next 1.7 mi. along the road to the site of Pratt's Bridge.

North of the Winhall Campground, the West River Trail is a dirt road extending toward the village of South Londonderry. The road is gated and utilizes the roadbed of the West River Railroad. The start of this section of the West River Trail is separated from the northern end of the previous section (from Ball Mountain Dam) by a 1.5-mi. road walk through the Winhall Campground. The trail is reached from the gatehouse by walking past the bridge over the Winhall River and proceeding straight onto a gravel road that parallels the north side of the river. Parking is available near the amphitheater on a mowed area 0.7 mi. beyond the bridge. The trailhead is located a short distance farther down the dirt road at a yellow gate on the edge of the woods.

Description: From the yellow gate (0.0 mi.), with the West River visible to the right, the roadbed eventually passes over the abutments of a stone culvert that permitted cattle to pass beneath the railroad (1.3 mi.). The West River Trail reaches its current northern terminus at a second yellow gate (1.8 mi.). While the roadbed does continue 0.9 mi. to reach South Londonderry, it is on private land. No parking is available along this section of the route.

JAMAICA STATE PARK

Occupying 756 acres along a bend of the West River in the town of Jamaica, Jamaica State Park was recognized in 1996 as the best state park in Vermont. Semi-annual water releases from Ball Mountain Dam, located upstream from the park, draw large numbers of whitewater paddling enthusiasts to the area in April and October. The preceding description of the West River Trail contains information about access to the park and the trails described below.

OVERLOOK TRAIL

Distance: 2.0 mi. (3.2 km)
Elevation Change: 475 ft. ascent
Hiking Time: 1½ hr. either direction

ABOUT THE TRAIL: This trail and 1.0 mi. of the West River Trail makes a nice loop hike. One end of the trail departs the West River Trail, and the other end departs from a fence near the Hackberry Lean-to.
TO THE TRAIL: Follow directions to Jamaica State Park on page 131. From the entrance to the park, walk 1.0 mi. north along the West River Trail.
DESCRIPTION: The blue-blazed Overlook Trail departs to the right at a signed junction, across the river from a sheer rock wall. The trail's sometimes obscure steep initial climb over tree roots and rocks is in stark contrast to the easy, flat roadbed of the West River Trail. The Overlook Trail passes to the right of a large meadow (0.4 mi.) before skirting the left side of the remains of a pond. This area may be wet depending on the season and rainfall. The trail soon reaches a sign pointing to the right, where a large boulder is visible at the summit ahead.

Turning to the right, the trail follows a series of switchbacks, beginning at a white birch with a triple trunk. The trail continues to climb until reaching a rock outcrop at the summit of Little Ball Mtn. (1,164 ft.), where care should be taken near the steep ledges. The trail reaches a vista offering a marvelous view of the West River Valley, as well as the Green Mountains to the west. The trail follows blue blazes painted on both trees and rocks to a second vantage point (1.0 mi.), which offers a view of the town of Jamaica. From this point the trail continues along the summit ridge and passes the boulder that was visible from below. Here, the underside of the large rock is worn away, creating a small cave.

The trail loop continues down the west side of the mountain to return to the park. Turning to the right, the trail descends, steeply in places, eventually reaching a sign pointing to the right (1.4 mi.). The trail soon reaches and follows an old logging road, which gently descends to an opening in the park fence near the campground. Entering the camping area at the Hackberry lean-to, the day-use parking lot is reached to the right along the access road.

HAMILTON FALLS

Distance: 1.1 mi. (1.8 km)
Elevation Change: 500 ft. ascent
Hiking Time: 1 hr. (reverse ½ hr.)

ABOUT THE TRAIL: This unmarked but obvious route departs the West River Trail 1.9 mi. north of its trailhead in Jamaica State Park (page 131) and ascends to one of the highest and most spectacular waterfalls in Vermont.

DESCRIPTION: Leaving the former West River Railroad bed to the right (0.0 mi.), the trail to Hamilton Falls turns to the right and ascends steadily on an old road high above Cobb Brook, passing local views of the stream and its environs from increasing heights. The trail reaches the top of a ridge and an unmarked junction on the left (0.8 mi.), where a spur slabs downhill for about 325 ft. to the base of

Hamilton Falls. From this vantage point, there is an attractive view of the falls from the bottom; it is unsafe to attempt to climb the falls from this location.

The top of the falls is reached by following the main trail as it continues on the old road to a junction with a narrow public road (1.0 mi.). Here the trail follows the road downhill to the left and soon turns to the left again onto a footpath that leads about 250 ft. to the top of Hamilton Falls (1.1 mi.). As noted by the prominent signs, these spectacular falls should be enjoyed with great caution; at least ten people have died here in recent years.

• • • • • • • • • • • • • • • • •

WINDMILL HILL–PUTNEY MOUNTAIN

Located in eastern Windham County, the Windmill Hill–Putney Mountain ridge (USGS Newfane, Townshend) runs north and south, extending 16.0 mi. between Cambridgeport and Dummerston. The ridge is known as Windmill Hill or Windmill Mtn. in the north, where it follows the town line between Athens and Westminster. To the south, along the town line between Putney and Brookline, it is referred to as Putney Mtn. The ridge rises steeply on the west side, then slopes gently to the east. At its highest point, in the Putney Mtn. section, it drops nearly 1,000 ft. into the town of Brookline.

The Windmill Hill–Pinnacle Association and the Putney Mountain Association have been instrumental in developing trails and protecting land along the ridge. Eventually, the two organizations hope to create a trail and protect wildlife habitat from Prospect Hill in Dummerston to Saxtons River.

These two organizations are nonprofits and need membership support to protect land and maintain the trails. Please help them out! Both organizations publish maps and brochures for their trails. The Windmill Hill–Pinnacle Association can be reached at 1915 Patch Road, Putney, Vermont 05346. The Putney Mountain Association is at P.O. Box 953, Putney, Vermont 05346; (802) 387-6635.

Hiking trails ascend to high points on either end of the ridge, at the summit of Putney Mtn. in the south and to the Pinnacle in the north.

2

PUTNEY MOUNTAIN

Distance: 0.6 mi. (0.9 km)
Elevation Change: 140 ft. ascent
Hiking Time: ⅓ hr. either direction

ABOUT THE TRAIL: This trail, popular among area residents, follows the top of the Putney Mtn. ridge before ascending a short distance to the summit of Putney Mtn. From the summit there are good views to the west over the hills of the West River Valley to the Green Mountains, including Stratton Mtn., and east to New Hampshire's Mt. Monadnock. The summit is an excellent place to view hawks during the fall migration. The trail is in the Putney Town Forest or on lands protected by the Putney Mountain Association.

TO THE TRAIL: From U.S. 5 at the general store in the center of Putney Village (0.0 mi.), follow Westminster West Road (the portion of the road in the village is also known locally as Kimball Hill Road) northwest to a junction on the left with West Hill Road (1.1 mi.). Follow West Hill Road, keeping right at a fork (2.5 mi.) and bearing left at a sharp curve where Aiken Road leaves to the right (3.0 mi.). Turn right onto the unpaved Putney Mountain Road (3.4 mi.), immediately bear right at a fork, and continue past a fork on the right to the parking lot for the trail (5.6 mi.), located on the right at the crest of the mountain ridge where the road curves sharply to the right.

DESCRIPTION: The unblazed trail begins at the far end of the parking lot (0.0 mi.) next to a sign reading "Welcome to Putney Mountain." Here the West Side Trail leaves to the left.

> **Junction:** The West Side Trail is a slightly longer alternate route to the summit. It drops off the ridge and slabs the steep western side passing through tall hemlocks before climbing steeply to the summit.

The main trail immediately passes over a large outcrop of bedrock polished smooth by the continental glacier and meets a rutted road (0.1 mi.). The trail continues north through a mixed forest containing an occasional red pine, a tree not commonly found in Vermont.

The trail splits and rejoins itself several times along its course. It passes a large ash tree, known as the Elephant Tree due to its peculiarly shaped limb (0.5 mi.), and then forks. Bearing right, the trail climbs past a stone wall to a second fork. Both trails soon lead to the clearing on the summit of Putney Mtn. (1,660 ft.) (0.6 mi.). To the west, Stratton Mtn. is dominant, while Mt. Snow and Haystack Mtn. are also visible. To the east, the view encompasses much of southwestern New Hampshire, from Mt. Monadnock to Mt. Sunapee.

THE PINNACLE

The Pinnacle is a high point on Windmill Hill located 2.0 mi. west of the village of Westminster West. Long held in private ownership, the Pinnacle was a popular destination for area residents. Recent purchase of lands along the ridge by the Windmill Hill–Pinnacle Association (WHPA) has secured public access to the area. Two trails provide access to the ridge. The Jamie Latham Trail accesses the Pinnacle from the north, while the Holden Trail climbs the ridge from the east.

JAMIE LATHAM TRAIL

Distance: 2.1 mi. (3.4 km)
Elevation Change: 226 ft. ascent
Hiking Time: 1¼ hr. (reverse 1 hr.)

ABOUT THE TRAIL: This trail is named for Jamie Latham, a young man from Westminster West who spent many hours visiting the Pinnacle. The trail is a memorial to Latham, who died in 1991. The route ascends the Pinnacle from the north and is marked occasionally, mostly at turns, with white wooden diamonds containing a green arrow.

TO THE TRAIL: From U.S. 5 at the general store in the center of Putney Village, follow the Westminster West Road north and west for 6.9 mi. to the village of Westminster West. Reaching a junction at the end of an S curve in front of a church, turn left onto West Road. From the north, the same junction may be reached by leaving Vt. 121 in the village of Saxtons River west of Bellows Falls and following the Westminster West Road south for 5.8 mi.

From the church (0.0 mi.), follow the gravel West Road to a junction and bear right onto Old Athens Road (0.6 mi.). At a white wooden gate with a road leading straight ahead to a private estate (1.5 mi.), the Old Athens Road turns sharply to the left. (From here, the road turns into a class 4 road with the condition of the road varying from season to season. It is generally passable by all but very low-clearance vehicles if caution is used.) At an intersection at the bottom of a short downgrade (1.9 mi.), the Old Athens Road bears left. From here the road deteriorates and may not be passable as it crosses a small swamp. A large parking lot and kiosk are on the left (2.7 mi.).

DESCRIPTION: From the kiosk (0.0 mi.), the trail leads to the far southeast corner of the clearing to two picnic tables (0.1 mi.). Following an old logging road through a recently harvested mixed forest, the trail descends to a swale and climbs to where an old road comes in from the left

(0.4 mi.). After descending to cross a second swale and climbing briefly in a section where several overgrown roads branch off, the Jamie Latham Trail turns to the right (0.7 mi.) onto an old logging road now filling in with briars.

Climbing moderately, the trail follows the logging road to its end at a small clearing with a picnic table (0.9 mi.). Continuing as a footpath, the trail almost immediately reaches and briefly follows a stone wall to the right before turning to the left and crossing the wall at a property corner. As the trail climbs moderately, it passes several hemlock groves before crossing another stone wall (1.3 mi.) near the top of the grade, and then continues into a lovely, open hardwood forest.

The trail soon turns to the left onto a wider trail (1.5 mi.) with occasional faded green-and-blue-painted blazes. As the forest becomes a mixture of hardwoods and softwoods, the trail reaches an intersection (1.8 mi.) with an older trail to the summit. Bearing right, the trail follows a wide, well-established path.

The footbed turns to bedrock as the trail climbs toward the summit and an overgrown clearing. After passing a junction with the Holden Trail on the left, the Jamie Latham Trail continues straight to a clearing at the top of the Pinnacle (1,690 ft.) (2.1 mi.). A cabin, located here, is available for overnight camping. To reserve the cabin, contact the WHPA (see page 139). Views from the summit extend from Hedgehog Gulf at the base of the Pinnacle west to the Green Mountains.

HOLDEN TRAIL

Distance: 1.5 mi. (2.4 km)
Elevation Change: 458 ft. ascent
Hiking Time: ¾ hr. (reverse ¾ hr.)

ABOUT THE TRAIL: This trail climbs the Pinnacle from the east on an old woods road.
TO THE TRAIL: From the church in Westminster West (see

directions to the Jamie Latham Trail on page 141) (0.0 mi.), follow the gravel West Road passing the Old Athens Road on the right (0.6 mi.). Continue left on West Road to Windmill Hill Road North (1.0 mi.). Follow this road uphill until it turns to a class 4 road (1.8 mi.), and then continue to a parking lot and the trailhead (2.1 mi.).

DESCRIPTION: This white-blazed trail begins at a kiosk and an elaborate and artistically decorated gate (0.0 mi.). From the gate, the trail follows an old woods road climbing steadily to reach a trail sign (0.5 mi.). From here, the trail turns right onto another woods road. Following the woods road, the trail makes a gentle and variable climb, and then descends slightly (0.9 mi.) to a moist area where short relocations and puncheon segments depart briefly from the road. A series of gentle switchbacks (1.2 mi.) bring the trail to the intersection (1.4 mi.) with the Jamie Latham Trail at the top of the ridge. Continuing left at this junction it is a short flat distance to the summit clearing (1.5 mi.).

• • • • • • • • • • • • • • • •

NEWFANE TOWN FOREST

WHITE FERN TRAIL

Distance: 2.3 mi. (3.7 km)
Elevation Change: 370 ft. ascent
Hiking Time: 1¼ hr. either direction

ABOUT THE TRAIL: The White Fern Trail is a pleasant path that follows a stream through the Newfane Town Forest and passes a 1987 timber harvest area frequently criss-crossed by skidder trails. The logged area exemplifies a forest's ability to recover from disturbance. The trail was cleared and blazed in 1999 by local volunteers. One main 2.0-mi. loop trail with a 0.7-mi. alternate route is accessed by a trail leading from a designated parking area. A map may be available at the trailhead or at the town office.

TO THE TRAIL: From the village of Newfane (0.0 mi.), head south on Vt. 30. Pass the Newfane Elementary School on the left immediately before turning right onto Grimes Hill Road (2.5 mi.). Continue on this road to the stop sign in Williamsville (4.2 mi.) and turn left onto Depot Road. Cross a single-lane bridge and then climb for a short distance to a small cemetery on the right. Just after the cemetery is the entrance (4.8 mi.) to the Newfane town garage with a small trailhead parking area just within the entrance on the right.

DESCRIPTION: From the parking lot, proceed 150 ft. down the gated town garage access road. The trail entrance is marked by a sign and an arrow on the right side of the road, just before reaching a complex of buildings and sandpiles. From the trailhead (0.0 mi.), the white-blazed trail leads through white pines interspersed with large, old apple trees. Soon entering a mix of successional woods, the trail crosses a few small streams and several old skidder ruts as the trail climbs easily to Chaos Junction (0.5 mi.).

A sign at the junction indicates that trails bear left to Mushroom Road and right to the waterfalls. Bearing left, the trail follows a gentle, mostly straight, even grade along an old woods road to the lower junction (0.6 mi.), where the Golden Gateway Trail, a yellow-blazed parallel route, bears left (see description following).

Mushroom Road climbs gradually to the upper junction (0.9 mi.) with the Golden Gateway Trail. The main white-blazed trail turns right off the log road into the woods shortly before reaching the highest point of the loop. Large vines give this area of the woods its name, Tarzan's Forest. The trail begins to descend gradually and then moderately (1.0 mi.) before reaching the edge of Town Brook (1.1 mi.). Along this bedrock stream, there are several miniature waterfalls, flumes, and pools. The trail climbs and descends along the slopes of the drainage cut before climbing out of the vale a final time (1.7 mi.) onto even ground before returning to Chaos Junction (1.8 mi.).

GOLDEN GATEWAY TRAIL

Distance: 1.3 mi. (2.1 km)
Elevation Change: 150 ft. ascent
Hiking Time: 40 min. either direction

DESCRIPTION: The Golden Gateway Trail bears left off Mushroom Road (0.0 mi.) and enters the woods along a flat stretch before crossing a small stream (0.7 mi.). The trail gradually climbs before veering right onto an old log road (0.9 mi.). The trail climbs easily along a fairly straight course to the high point on the loop (1.0 mi.), where it bears right off the old road and begins a steady, easy descent through the woods. The trail reaches the extension of Mushroom Road (1.2 mi.), turns right onto it, and descends to the upper junction (1.3 mi.) with the white-blazed trail, which emerges from the woods on the left.

• • • • • • • • • • • • • • • •

BLACK MOUNTAIN

Distance: 3.2 mi. (5.2 km) loop
Elevation Change: 975 ft. ascent
Hiking Time: 2 hr. either direction

ABOUT THE TRAIL: Located in the town of Dummerston, the Nature Conservancy's 374-acre Black Mountain Preserve supports extensive pitch pine and scrub oak communities, and harbors several rare plant species. The plant communities are more like those of Massachusetts than Vermont due to the acidic nature of this granite mountain. The mountain rises quickly from the West River and has a rough horseshoe-shape, with the opening facing to the south (USGS Newfane). The old roads and trails in the preserve, not all of which are described here, are open to the public during daylight hours for foot travel only; fires and overnight camping are not allowed. Although a blazed Nature Conservancy trail leads to the summit (1,280 ft.) from the west, many of the other routes on the mountain are unmarked, including a shorter route on private property from Black Mountain Road.

TO THE TRAIL: From Vt. 30 north of West Dummerston, cross the West River (0.0 mi.) on the Dummerston covered bridge and turn right onto Quarry Road. Follow this road south as it becomes Rice Farm Road and continue to an unmarked gravel road on the left (2.2 mi.) leading to the trailhead. Parking for three vehicles is available on the river side of Rice Farm Road.

DESCRIPTION: Leaving the public road (0.0 mi.), the initially unmarked Black Mountain Trail follows the old road uphill about 100 yds. to a cabled gate and a Nature Conservancy sign. The trail follows the road to the top of the hill, where the first white blazes and a trail sign are found. Bearing right, the trail begins a gradual ascent, reaching an older woods road on the right (0.3 mi.), which is the unmarked end of the return route. The blazed Black Mountain Trail continues straight ahead to cross a wetlands on wooden planking and eventually ascends to a TNC register box (0.4 mi.).

After skirting the upper edge of an overgrown clearing, the trail enters the woods (0.5 mi.) and begins climbing along a series of switchbacks where care should be taken to follow the blazes. The trail reaches a ridge (1.1 mi.) below the true summit, where it bears left for a distance before veering to the right and meandering through an extensive cluster of mountain laurel. The trail reaches its highest point a short distance below the summit, then begins an easy descent and emerges onto a large rock outcropping and vista (1.4 mi.), from which there are views to the south of the West River Valley, Connecticut River Valley, the Vermont Yankee nuclear station, and New Hampshire's Mt. Monadnock.

The trail continues along the rock outcropping, following the blazes, and leaves the summit area to the north. At a woods road junction (1.6 mi.), the trail turns to the right onto the road and eventually leaves TNC property at a sign, where the blazing ends (1.8 mi.). The now unblazed trail reaches an unmarked road junction in a sag (1.9 mi.).

Junction: This unmarked road leads uphill about 0.5 mi. through old quarries to reach a T-junction. To the right, along a wide gravel path, it is about 0.4 mi. to a summit and views. Straight ahead, the trail leads to Black Mtn. Road. These side trails are on private property, so please respect the land and buildings.

2

Turning sharply to the right from the junction, the trail descends to the south near a brook. After crossing a small tributary (2.3 mi.) the trail swings to the right of a beaver dam (2.5 mi.) and continues on easier grades to a woods road junction, where it takes the more conspicuous right fork (2.7 mi.). The trail continues with minor changes in elevation to the end of the trail loop (2.9 mi.) on the Black Mountain Trail. To the left, it is 0.3 mi. to the Rice Farm Road trailhead. Note: due to the lack of blazing on this descent route, careful observation is required to follow the sometimes indistinct path.

• • • • • • • • • • • • • • • •

MOUNT OLGA

Distance: 2.0 mi. (3.1 km)
Elevation Change: 520 ft. ascent
Hiking Time: 1¼ hr. either direction

ABOUT THE TRAIL: From the old, but maintained, fire tower on the summit of Mt. Olga (2,415 ft., USGS Wilmington), there are good views of southern Vermont, southwestern New Hampshire, and northern Massachusetts.

To the Trail: The two trails to the summit, which form a loop, begin in Molly Stark State Park. The park entrance is on the south side of Vt. 9, about 3.5 mi. east of Wilmington Village or 15.0 mi. west of Brattleboro. The park offers a variety of camping accommodations; a day-use fee is charged in-season.

Description: Leaving the park road opposite the contact station (0.0 mi.), the blue-blazed main trail quickly crosses Beaver Brook on a wooden bridge and climbs gradually to the east through the woods. The trail soon reaches a junction of two stone walls (0.1 mi.), where it turns left to follow one of the walls for about 100 ft. before bearing to the right. The trail then ascends a moderate grade before beginning an easier climb through evergreens. The trail reaches another stone wall (0.4 mi.) before beginning a steep and winding climb and then reaching a junction with the summit trail (0.7 mi.).

> **Junction:** The 0.1-mi. summit trail bears to the left and climbs to the crest of Mt. Olga at a fire tower. An old road that serviced the abandoned Hogback Mountain Ski Area leads several hundred feet east to the ski trails, from which there are good views to the northeast.

Mt. Olga became a fire lookout site in 1930 when a wooden tower with an octagonal cab was constructed on the summit. From 1949 to 1950, the wooden tower was removed, and the present steel tower was moved to Mt. Olga from Bald Mtn. in Townshend. The tower was last used as a fire lookout in 1974. The tower was listed in the National Historic Lookout Register in 1996.

From the previously mentioned junction just below the summit (0.7 mi.), the blue-blazed Mt. Olga Trail follows a campground sign and descends through the woods on easy grades, eventually passing between two large rocks and crossing a small stream on a crude wooden bridge. The trail then bears left onto an old road (1.1 mi.), which it follows for a short distance before bearing left again off the road and crossing a small stream on stepping stones. The trail soon reaches a stone wall on the right, which it follows to its end, passing a junction (1.5 mi.) on the right with the Ghost Trail.

Junction: The blue-blazed Ghost Trail provides an alternate route to the contact station. Follow the trail south off the Mount Olga Trail to skirt the camping area on easy grades. The trail crosses over a small brook on a wooden bridge, passes two unused fireplaces, and crosses another brook before ending on a service road a short distance from the contact station.

The Mount Olga Trail continues straight ahead then crosses a small stream on a bridge, before reaching the loop road in the camping area (1.6 mi.). To the right, it is 0.2 mi. to the park headquarters and the contact station.

● ● ● ● ● ● ● ● ● ● ● ● ● ● ● ● ●

RAMBLES

QUECHEE GORGE

ABOUT THE TRAIL: Located in the town of Hartford, Quechee Gorge (USGS Quechee) is a part of the Quechee Recreation Area, owned by the Army Corps of Engineers as part of the North Hartland Dam flood control basin. The 611-acre area is leased and operated by the Vermont Department of Forests, Parks, and Recreation, which maintains camping facilities at Quechee State Park.

TO THE TRAIL: From I-89 exit 1, proceed west on U.S. 4 about 3.0 mi. Just before the road crosses over Quechee Gorge, turn right onto Dewey's Mill Road and continue 0.1 mi. to the overlook picnic and parking day-use area on the left, where parking is available for five vehicles.

DESCRIPTION: From the picnic area, blue-blazed spur trails lead to the north and south. To the north, a trail leads 0.2 mi. to a dam and hydroelectric plant, previously the site of the Dewey Woolen Mill. From the dam, the trail continues straight ahead 0.4 mi. across an isthmus to reach Country Club Road opposite a local inn.

To the south of the picnic area, a trail proceeds along the gorge wall, protected from the cliff edge by a fence. The trail soon reaches an overlook, marked by a bench on the right. Straight ahead, the trail passes under the road bridge, which is 165 ft. above the water. The bridge was built in 1911 for the Woodstock Railroad (1875–1933) to replace its original Howe Truss bridge of wood timbers and iron. With the abandonment of the railroad, the bridge and the roadbed in this area became part of U.S. 4. The story of the Woodstock Railroad, of which some of the structures and roadbed are still visible, is told in Mead's *Over the Hills to Woodstock*.

The trail continues to the south and soon arrives at an unmarked junction. Bearing right, the trail descends to the bottom of the gorge, where the rushing waters turn into a placid river at the upstream end of the North Hartland Reservoir. Further exploration is possible along the obvious footpath that continues downstream, but this eventually peters out.

Quechee State Park is located south of U.S. 4, east of the gorge. Two access trails lead from the state park camping areas to the previously described trail along the eastern edge of the gorge itself. These short spur trails are reserved for state park campers only.

ESHQUA BOG

ABOUT THE TRAIL: Located in the town of Hartland, Eshqua Bog is a 40-acre sanctuary jointly owned and managed by the Nature Conservancy and the New England Wild Flower Society. The site contains a variety of cold-climate holdover plants that largely disappeared from Vermont at the end of the last glacial period some 10,000 years ago. In late spring and early summer, a variety of wildflowers can be found at the site, including several varieties of orchids and a spectacular vernal display of hundreds of lady's-slippers in bloom. A 0.5-mi. white-blazed loop trail roughly circles the property, but the focal point of the preserve is a two-acre fen traversed by a boardwalk. A fen is a type of wetland where water comes from a local aquifer rather than rainfall or nearby streams or ponds.

TO THE TRAIL: From its junction with Vt. 12 in Woodstock Village, follow U.S. 4 east a short distance to the edge of the village, where the main road makes a sharp left. Proceed straight here onto Hartland Hill Road (0.0 mi.), which soon turns to the southeast. Turn right onto the un-signed Garvin Hill Road (1.1 mi.) and follow this gravel road to a small pull-off on the right (2.3 mi.) where limited parking is available. The entrance to the preserve is located a short distance beyond the pullout.

DESCRIPTION: Past the entrance, the trail reaches a registration box and junction. While the boardwalk departs to the left and cuts across the center of the wetland, the loop trail goes to the right, skirting the edge of the bog in a mature hardwood forest. The trail climbs steeply up a bank at the northern end of the bog before meeting the western end of the boardwalk. The loop trail continues straight ahead on level ground around the south end of the bog and returns to Garvin Hill Road about 40 yds. south of the entrance.

The boardwalk crosses the center of the fen, and offers an excellent opportunity to examine closely the wealth and variety of the wetland plant life. While cattails abound, more exotic species such as turtleheads, insectivorous pitcher plants, northern green orchids, and tall white bog orchids are identified by small signs. Due to the fragile nature of the ecosystem, extreme care should be taken to remain on the boardwalk in the fen area!

CAMP PLYMOUTH STATE PARK

ABOUT THE TRAIL: Located along the east shore of Echo Lake in the town of Plymouth, the 295-acre Camp Plymouth State Park occupies the site of a former Boy Scout camp (USGS Ludlow). In 1855, gold was discovered along the banks of nearby Buffalo Brook resulting in mining operations, which continued for some 30 years; panning for gold remains a popular activity in the park to the present day. Camping is limited to a group camping area; obtain information at the park contact station. The park has a variety of day-use facilities, including a beach; a fee is charged in-season. A short hiking loop heads north from the park entrance to a vista overlooking the lake.

TO THE TRAIL: Camp Plymouth State Park is located off Vt. 100, several miles south of Coolidge State Park. From the village of Tyson on Vt. 100 at the south end of Echo Lake, about 5.0 mi. south of Vt. 100A in Plymouth Union, and about 5.5 mi. north of Vt. 103 in Ludlow Village, proceed east on Kingdom Road about 1.0 mi. to a crossroads. Turn left onto Scout Camp Road and continue about 1.0 mi.; the park entrance is on the left side of the road.

DESCRIPTION: The Echo Lake Vista Trail begins on a dirt road on the east side of Scout Camp Road, a few paces north of the park entrance (0.0 mi.). The trail follows the road for a short distance, then leaves it on the left along a footpath, which soon reaches an old cemetery. Continuing straight ahead, the trail climbs steadily, eventually reaching a vista (0.5 mi.) overlooking Echo Lake and the park. From the vista, the trail drops down the backside of the ridge and switches back, turning sharply to the south. The trail follows Buffalo Brook for a short distance before crossing the brook and joining the dirt road the trail began on. Bear right on the road to get back to the park (1.5 mi.). Please note there is no bridge at the stream crossing. Crossing on the large rocks may be tricky during high water or icy conditions.

WILGUS STATE PARK, THE PINNACLE

ABOUT THE TRAIL: Located in Wilgus State Park with camping and picnic areas, this low hill offers good views of the New Hampshire hills to the east.

TO THE TRAIL: The blue-blazed loop trail begins on U.S. 5, opposite the entrance to the park, 1.1 mi. south of the junction of U.S. 5 and Vt. 131 in Ascutney village. Parking arrangements should be made with the park manager.

DESCRIPTION: From the highway (0.0 mi.), the trail climbs a bank and swings to the left, following a pleasant woods road on easy grades. Eventually turning to the right off the old road (0.3 mi.), the trail climbs to a lookout just below the wooded summit (0.5 mi.).

From the lookout, the trail passes over the summit (640 ft.) and makes a steep and winding descent through the woods to the highway (0.9 mi.). Following the park access road, it is 0.25 mi. south to the contact station and park entrance.

SPRINGWEATHER NATURE AREA

ABOUT THE TRAIL: Located in the town of Weathersfield and encompassing nearly 70 acres of fields and forests, the Springweather Nature Area was developed by the Ascutney Mountain Audubon Society and the U.S. Army Corps of Engineers following construction of the North Springfield Flood Control Dam. Three blazed trails, totaling about 2.0 mi., wander through the site and offer a variety of moderate loop hikes.

TO THE TRAIL: From its intersection with Vt. 11 in Springfield (0.0 mi.), follow Vt. 106 north along the Black River. Turn right onto Reservoir Road (1.9 mi.) and continue past the flood control dam to the signed nature area access road on the left (3.4 mi.). Bear right at the first intersection, and proceed north a short distance to the main parking lot on the right (3.6 mi.). Two of the trailheads are located across the gravel road at a bulletin board, where a map of the site is posted. The access road continues to the north past this parking lot, ending at another parking area on the Black River, where the third trail may be accessed.

DESCRIPTION: The Blue Trail loop leaves the bulletin board to the left, crosses a small brook, and climbs quickly to an open field. The trail crosses the field to reach a hemlock grove atop a small hill, where there are views across the lake to Mt. Ascutney. Here the trail turns to the right but soon bends back to the left to reach a high bank over the lake, which it follows to the south. The trail then leaves the lake along a mowed path, eventually reaching a junction.

To the left, a short spur leads back to the head of the loop; to the right an alternate route leads to a small pond and the access road, a short distance south of the trailhead.

The Red Trail departs the bulletin board to the right and soon reaches a series of junctions and small trail loops. Bearing to the left toward the lake, this trail also reaches the high bank above the water, which it follows to the north. At the farthest point on the loop from the trailhead, the Red Trail reaches a junction on the left with the Green Trail. Bearing to the right, the Red Trail curves southward to parallel the access road and return to the head of the loop.

The Green Trail, from its junction with the Red Trail, continues along the bank overlooking the lake before turning away and also heading toward the access road. The trail quickly reaches a junction, where a spur to the right leads a short distance to the access road, north of the main parking lot. The more interesting route bears to the left and soon reaches a stream, near the site of Barretts Mill and an old bridge. The trail takes a short but steep route to cross the stream before continuing to a parking area at the north end of the access road.

FORT DUMMER STATE PARK

ABOUT THE TRAIL: Fort Dummer State Park occupies 217 acres in the Connecticut River Valley just outside Brattleboro. Bordering the foothills of the eastern edge of the Green Mountains, the chestnut oak hardwood forest found in the park is more typical of southern New England than Vermont. The park contains a relatively short hiking loop (about 1.25 mi.) leading to two vistas overlooking the Connecticut River. A variety of camping facilities are available, and a day-use fee is charged in-season.

TO THE TRAIL: Fort Dummer State Park is located a short distance south of Brattleboro. From I-91 exit 1, follow U.S. 5 north 0.25 mi. to a traffic light, and turn east onto Fairground Road (0.0 mi.). Continue past the high school and town garage to an intersection near the bottom of a winding hill (0.5 mi.). Turn right to follow South Main Street and its continuation, Old Guilford Road, to a dead end at the park (1.6 mi.).

DESCRIPTION: From the park contact station, follow the paved road to its end at an intersection where dirt roads lead to the left and right to the two campgrounds. The trailhead is located a few yards to the north of the intersection, at a sign for the Sunrise Trail. A blue-blazed trail leads a short distance to a junction marking the head of the loop. Bearing left at the junction onto a lesser used red-blazed trail, the northern leg of the loop crosses over a small footbridge and continues an easy ascent, soon reaching another junction.

> **Junction:** To the left, a yellow-blazed lookout spur leads a short distance to an opening with views atop a granite ledge. While the original site of Fort Dummer was flooded when the Vernon Dam was constructed in 1908, its former location is visible on the western bank of the river at a point near the lumber company. From this overlook, there are also views southward to the Vermont Yankee nuclear station, and beyond to Mt. Monadnock in New Hampshire and northern Massachusetts.

The main trail continues right at the junction, soon reaches another vista, and then reaches a junction where a trail leaves to the right on a more direct route to the beginning of the loop. Continuing straight ahead, the southernmost leg of the loop follows marginally longer routing to reach the same spot.

SWEET POND STATE PARK

ABOUT THE TRAIL: Once a private estate, Sweet Pond State Park (USGS Brattleboro) has a mile-long hiking trail that follows most of the undeveloped shoreline of the name-sake pond. Several log benches at the ends of short spur trails offer pleasant sites for enjoying the pond and its surroundings from different angles. The park does not contain any developed facilities, nor is there any overnight camping. There is no entrance fee.

TO THE TRAIL: From U.S. 5 in Guilford (0.0 mi.), follow the paved Guilford Center Road west 1.7 mi. and turn left onto the paved Weatherhead Hollow Road. Continue south past the end of the pavement (4.7 mi.) and the north end of Weatherhead Hollow Pond. Turn right at a fork (5.7 mi.) and ascend a narrow gravel road. Turn right again at the next intersection (6.1 mi.) and follow the gravel Sweet Pond Road uphill, past two forks to the right and a view of the outlet dam (7.4 mi.). At the Sweet Pond State Park sign (7.7 mi.), turn right, then quickly bear to the left to reach the parking area (7.8 mi.).

DESCRIPTION: From the parking area (0.0 mi.), the blue-blazed trail descends southwesterly for a short distance before swinging sharply to the left and following an easy northward route through the woods parallel to the pond. The trail soon enters a Norway Spruce plantation and passes a spur to the right (0.1 mi.) that leads a few feet to a bench on the shore. After passing another short spur (0.2 mi.), the trail crosses two tiny inlet brooks in a wet area and continues through a clearing to yet another spur (0.4 mi.). The trail then crosses the main inlet on a board-walk (0.5 mi.) a short distance below a beaver dam.

From the inlet the trail soon enters an old hemlock forest and follows up and down routing above the east shore of the pond. After passing two spurs (0.8 mi. and 0.9 mi.) leading to views from the ledges, the trail reaches its terminus at the concrete outlet dam (1.0 mi.). Just beyond the dam is Sweet Pond Road, which can be followed uphill for 0.3 mi. back to the park entrance road.

BLACK GUM SWAMP

ABOUT THE TRAIL: Black Gum Swamp, located in J. Maynard Miller Municipal Forest in Vernon (USGS Bernardston), is the unlikely home of black gum trees (*Nyssa sylvatica*), some of which are more than 400 years old. Several other species of ferns and plant life that are normally found only in the southern United States flourish in this spot as well. Apparently established some 3,000 to 5,000 years ago when the region's climate was far warmer, these trees and plants have somehow managed to adapt to the present less-favorable environment.

A compact network of four color-coded trail loops provides access to two sections of the swamp, a scenic overlook, and other areas within the municipal forest. There are no individual trail signs, but the generally well-defined trails are marked with diamond-shaped blazes. An interpretive bulletin board at the trailhead parking lot features a large map of the area and its color-coded trail system, regulations governing use of the forest, and interesting facts about its history and features. Trail maps, supplied by the Vernon Recreation Department, are in an adjacent mailbox.

> **Note:** Hikers are reminded of the requirement to remain on the trails when viewing the environmentally sensitive High Swamp and Lower Swamp.

TO THE TRAIL: From Vt. 142 in the Central Park area of Vernon, about 7.25 mi. south of U.S. 5 in Brattleboro, turn west onto Pond Road. (This junction is 1.3 mi. south of the village of Vernon and several hundred feet north of a white church and the Vernon highway garage on Vt. 142.) From the highway (0.0 mi.), follow the paved Pond Road through the railroad underpass and past a road on the right. Turn right onto the paved Huckle Hill Road (1.2 mi.) and proceed uphill past several intersections before turning right onto the paved Basin Road (2.5 mi.).

The road ends (3.2 mi.) at the trailhead parking lot and a large sign for the Black Gum Swamp and J. Maynard Miller Municipal Forest.

DESCRIPTION: The red-blazed High Swamp Trail (0.5 mi. in length) leaves the parking area to the west and ascends a narrow gravel roadway to a dead end opposite a private dwelling. Turning sharply to the right, it makes a brief and fairly steep ascent to meet the west end of the Overlook Trail, and then ascends westerly on easier grades. After circling three sides of High Swamp, the trail descends easterly through the woods and past a junction with the southern leg of the Lower Swamp Trail to complete its loop.

The green-blazed Overlook Trail (0.4 mi. in length) leaves the parking lot along a forest road that begins a few feet east of the municipal forest sign. After a moderately steep climb on the road, the trail reaches a clearing on the right (0.2 mi.), which offers two picnic tables and an excellent view across the Connecticut River Valley to Mt. Monadnock and its neighbors. Opposite the clearing, the trail turns left into the woods, climbs gradually for a short distance to its highest point, and then descends to meet the High Swamp Trail. Left along this trail is a short distance back to the parking lot.

The blue-blazed Mountain Laurel Trail (1.5 mi.) shares the forest road portion of the Overlook Trail as far as the clearing. Swinging off the road to the west, the trail climbs gradually through an area of white birches and patches of mountain laurel, passes an old woods road to the right, and then trends southwesterly to a woods road crossing at the edge of a large clearing. Here the trail is joined by the Lower Swamp Trail at a sharp turn to the left, and both trails coincide over an up-and-down route through the woods to reach their end on the western side of the High Swamp Trail.

The silver-blazed Lower Swamp Trail (1.2 mi. long) begins and ends its triangular loop on the High Swamp Trail. From the southern side of the High Swamp, the

Lower Swamp Trail leaves westerly through the woods on easy circuitous routing to avoid wet areas. After skirting the northern edge of the Lower Swamp (and the Massachusetts State Line), the trail reaches a woods road junction. It turns sharply to the right and follows a woods road northerly to a junction with the Mountain Laurel Trail at the edge of a large clearing. The Lower Swamp Trail turns sharply to the right and follows up-and-down routing through the woods with the coinciding Mountain Laurel Trail to rejoin the High Swamp Trail on the western side of its namesake.

REGION 3
West Central Vermont

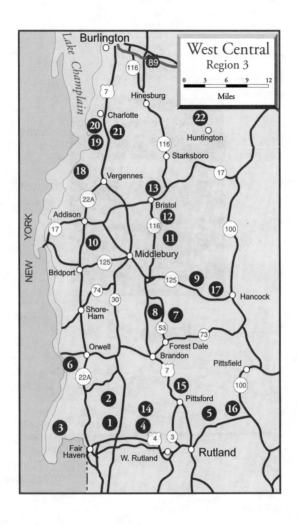

REGION 3
West Central Vermont

T he Lake Champlain Valley plays a prominent role in this region. For the most part, the Champlain Valley is gentle rolling country, but several steep escarpments and an intermittent series of hills along or near the shore stand out as landmarks. Many scenic trails travel near other lakes, including Lake Bomoseen and Lake Dunmore. Moosalamoo, a region of upland state and forest-service land, offers scenic walking and multiuse trails.

The eastern part of the west central region is dominated by the Green Mountains, which are well-defined ranges in this region. The first range rises abruptly from the Champlain Valley as a steep front that includes the Hogback Mountains and West Mtn. of the Bristol-Monkton area and extends southward through Robert Frost Mtn. and Mt. Moosalamoo and to Blue Ridge Mtn. near Sherburne Pass. The second or main range of the Green Mountains lies somewhat farther to the east. Several scenic gaps, used for east-west highways, make prominent breaks in the otherwise generally even skyline of the main range.

North of the Rutland area, the Taconic Mountains and the Valley of Vermont gradually lose their identity, and north of Brandon, the Champlain lowlands, home to enormous swamps, become the major physiographic feature of the western portion of the state.

LAKE BOMOSEEN AREA

Situated at the extreme northern end of the Taconic Mountain Range, Lake Bomoseen is the largest lake lying entirely within the boundaries of Vermont. The terrain is characterized by a series of north-south ridges heavily wooded with hemlock–white pine forest. Numerous smaller ponds are located throughout the area, but 202-acre Glen Lake, with its nearly undeveloped shoreline, offers the most spectacular scenery.

Within the 2,940-acre Bomoseen State Forest lie two state parks. Bomoseen State Park, in the southern part of the forest, offers picnicking, swimming, and boating, as well as extensive camping accommodations and access to a pair of short trails. In the north, Half Moon State Park offers more secluded campsites and restricted day-use activities. Hikers wishing to hike only the two short trails, but not camp at the park, may be turned away. This park is a good base camp for exploring the area.

The two state parks are connected by the Glen Lake Trail, which extends nearly 6.0 mi. along the shore of Glen Lake and over varied terrain between the state parks.

BOMOSEEN STATE PARK

To the Trail: Located along the western shore of Lake Bomoseen in the town of Castleton, Bomoseen State Park is easily reached from exit 3 off U.S. 4 in Fair Haven by following the paved Scotch Hill Road north for 4.5 mi. through the hamlet of West Castleton. Alternatively, from Vt. 4A in the village of Hydeville, follow the paved Creek Road north 4.0 mi., roughly following the west shore of Lake Bomoseen. Fees are charged in-season.

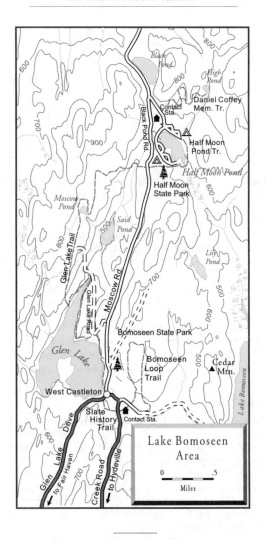

Lake Bomoseen
Area

0 .5

Miles

BOMOSEEN LOOP TRAIL

Distance: 1.5 mi. (2.4 km)
Elevation Change: minor
Hiking Time: 1 hr. either direction

DESCRIPTION: This blue-blazed trail explores a small portion of the Bomoseen Wildlife Preserve, which lies along the western lakeshore. The trail starts in a meadow behind the contact station and soon crosses Cedar Mountain Road. Proceeding through an old hayfield and past scattered rock walls, foundations, and apple trees at an old farm site, the trail crests a low hill where there is a good view of Glen Lake to the west. The trail continues through a mixed pine and hardwood forest with an open understory and returns to the state park.

SLATE HISTORY TRAIL

Distance: 0.75 mi.(1.2 km)
Elevation Change: minor
Hiking Time: ½ hr. either direction

ABOUT THE TRAIL: The story of the rise and fall of the local slate industry is told in a self-guided trail passing through a now-abandoned village of the West Castleton Slate Company. Sixty to seventy buildings once stood between Lake Bomoseen and Glen Lake where the West Castleton Mill operated between 1850 and 1929. A pamphlet describing the trail is available at the park contact station and is recommended for exploration of the site.

TO THE TRAIL: Leave the Bomoseen State Park entrance, walk a short distance south on the public Creek Road (West Shore Drive), and then turn right onto a mowed path. Although the trail is only about 0.75 mi. in length, some time may be required to explore the ruins of the works and town and examine the preserved slate houses.

GLEN LAKE TRAIL

Distance: 5.9 mi. (9.5 km)
Elevation Change: 500 ft. ascent
Hiking Time: 3½ hr. either direction

ABOUT THE TRAIL: Constructed by the Vermont Youth Conservation Corps in 1987, this blue-blazed trail connects Bomoseen State Park with Half Moon State Park. The trail follows the shoreline of Glen Lake for some distance before swinging north through an area of beaver activity and reaching its terminus at Half Moon Pond State Park.

TO THE TRAIL: The trailhead is at the Glen Lake boat access in West Castleton. From Glen Lake Road, a short distance west of the entrance to Bomoseen State Park, turn north onto the unsigned Moscow Road, and proceed a short distance to the boat access on the west. Parking is available on the east side of the road.

DESCRIPTION: From the boat access (0.0 mi.), the trail departs to the northwest and very shortly reaches the shore of Glen Lake. Following the shore through a cedar-hemlock forest, the trail soon reaches the dirt Said Road (0.5 mi.), which it follows a short distance west around a marsh. Departing the road to the left (0.6 mi.), the trail heads back toward the water and reaches a point jutting into the lake (0.9 mi.). Continuing north and again joining the Glen Lake Road (1.6 mi.), the trail bears left along the road, soon departing to the left again (1.7 mi.) and wandering between lake shore and woods. Continuing southward along the lake's western shore, the trail reaches a junction (2.4 mi.), where a short spur to the left leads to a vista overlooking Glen Lake and the hills to the east.

Past the spur, the trail leaves Glen Lake and climbs through the woods near a ridge. The trail passes by a small pond or seep (3.3 mi.) in an area of beaver activity before reaching Moscow Pond (3.6 mi.) and following its margin around to the north. The trail continues northward through beaver meadows, reaching a vista overlooking the area at a small sign (4.6 mi.). After crossing a stream on piles of slate (5.0 mi.), the trail reaches Moscow Road a short distance farther on (5.5 mi.).

Junction: After a turn south onto Moscow Road, it is about 2.5 mi. back to the Glen Lake boat launch and the start of the Glen Lake Trail.

Continuing straight ahead, the trail reaches the Half Moon Pond Trail in Half Moon State Park and the terminus of the Glen Lake Trail (5.9 mi.). Via the Half Moon Pond Trail, it is a short distance east or west to the state park campgrounds located on either shore of Half Moon Pond.

Half Moon State Park

3

Part of Bomoseen State Forest, Half Moon State Park is located in the town of Hubbardton and occupies a small sheltered basin surrounding Half Moon Pond. Half Moon State Park contains two short trails that are open only to those camping in the park.

To the Trail: From the south, follow the unpaved Moscow Road north from Bomoseen State Park for about 3.0 mi. Alternatively, from exit 4 off U.S. 4 in Castleton, follow Vt. 30 north about 7.5 mi. and turn west onto the paved Hortonville Road. Continue west for about 2.0 mi. then turn left on Black Pond Road. Follow this road south 1.5 mi. to the state park entrance.

Daniel Coffey Memorial Trail

This blue-blazed trail leaves the north side of the park access road about halfway between the contact station and the camping area. The trail ascends easily for about 0.5 mi. on a winding woods road through open forest. The final 0.25 mi. of trail scrambles over a rocky ridge and descends to secluded High Pond, a small body of open water rimmed by thick brush and sphagnum moss.

HALF MOON POND TRAIL

This trail is an easy 0.4-mi. lakeside walk around the eastern side of Half Moon Pond connecting the campgrounds on the north and south shores. Near the southwest end of the nature trail is a junction with the Glen Lake Trail, which crosses Moscow Road and proceeds southerly to Bomoseen State Park.

•••••••••••••••••

SHAW MOUNTAIN

Distance: 2.4 mi. (3.9 km) round trip
Elevation Change: 300 ft. ascent
Hiking Time: 1¾ hr. (reverse 1¼ hr.)

ABOUT THE TRAIL: Owned by the Nature Conservancy and located in the southwest corner of Benson, the Shaw Mountain Natural Area is notable for the presence of a great diversity of plant and animal life. The area is recognized for its ecological significance by the Vermont Non-Game and Natural Heritage Program and includes twenty-five rare plant species and seven distinct natural communities. A flyer available at the site identifies many plants found near the single hiking trail, which leads from the road access to a loop atop a limestone uplift forming the north summit (715 ft., USGS Benson).

TO THE TRAIL: From Vt. 22A in the town of Benson, about 7.0 mi. north of its junction with U.S. 4 in Fair Haven, turn west onto Mill Pond Road (also known as Lake Road) (0.0 mi.), following signs for the villages of Benson and Benson Landing. Continue straight through a crossroads in the village of Benson (0.7 mi.), and proceed west along Benson Landing Road to a second four-way intersection

(1.7 mi.). Turn left onto Park Hill Road, and proceed south to a junction on the right (2.1 mi.) with Money Hole Road. Bear right and proceed past a road entering on the left (2.6 mi.). The trailhead, near a wooden sign on the left (3.7 mi.), is easy to miss. Parking is available for three cars.
DESCRIPTION: From the parking lot, the lightly used trail ascends steeply to a sign and register. Following white and blue markings, the trail then descends to cross a marshy area on a footbridge before ascending moderately to reach an unmarked junction at the head of the summit trail loop. Care should be taken to note the location of this junction for the return leg of the loop, since this portion of the trail is not well defined. Turning to the right at the junction to make a counterclockwise circuit, the trail ascends gently to the west and passes through an open oak-hickory forest near the heavily forested, viewless north summit. Continuing around the south side of the ridge, the trail returns to the start of the summit loop.

• • • • • • • • • • • • • • • •

TACONIC MOUNTAINS RAMBLE

This network of trails links some highly varied terrain in a relatively small area—sheer rock cliffs, waterfalls, deep forests, rolling meadows, high peaks with wide mountain views, and the most extensive oriental garden in Vermont, if not New England. The trails are on private property surrounding the owners' home, and they invite walkers to share the land on the understanding that there will be no smoking and no fires—not ever.
TO THE TRAIL: From U.S. 4 west of Rutland, take exit 5 (0.0 mi.) onto an unnamed paved road signed north to the Hubbardton Battlefield. Just before reaching the battlefield, turn left onto the unpaved St. John Road (6.0 mi.). Turn left (6.3 mi.) onto a private drive, the first possible

left turn from St. John Road. Continue to a parking area on the left (6.8 mi.), just beyond the second cattle guard and a short distance uphill from the house.

Trails are blazed in red except for two in yellow. Triple blazes indicate the beginning or end of a trail; double blazes mean a sharp change in direction.

JAPANESE GARDEN, MOUNT ZION MINOR, AND MOOT POINT

Distance: 1.2 mi. (1.9 km) round trip
Elevation Change: 115 ft. ascent
Hiking Time: ¾ hr. either direction

DESCRIPTION: From the parking area (0.0 mi.), the trail goes downhill and passes near the right-hand end of the house (where trail maps are usually available at no charge). From the field below the house, there are views southwest to the cliffs of Mt. Zion Minor, south to Bird Mtn. and the Herrick Mtns., and east to the central range of the Taconic Mountains. The trail continues downhill to an arched bridge and the Japanese Garden (0.2 mi.), with pools, waterfalls, stone lanterns, an island reached by another arched bridge, and views of the cliffs above.

At the north end of the garden is a large boulder with a ladder partway up it. Take the trail around the right-hand side of this rock to the start of the red-blazed trail leading uphill. This trail weaves among massive boulders as it climbs to a junction (0.25 mi.) with the yellow-blazed Cave Trail.

Take a sharp left, ascend to a switchback, pass under a 20-ft. rock overhang, and mount a short, steep section leading to the top of the Mt. Zion Minor ridge. Farther south along this ridge is the best viewpoint from Mt. Zion Minor (0.3 mi.), overlooking the Japanese Garden 115 ft. below. There are also wide views of the Taconics from north to southeast.

At this point the trail turns sharply west, crossing the ridge and reaching the red-blazed Moot Point Trail (0.4 mi.). Go left, follow along mossy ledges, cross a small marsh on stepping stones, pass a woods road, and ascend to a ledgy ridge overlooking valleys on both sides. This leads to Moot Point (0.6 mi.), with fine views of the distant northeast to southeast, including Bird Mtn., and of the nearer southwest.

Retrace the same route back to the junction with the Cave Trail on the right, but continue past it on the red trail. This descends by two switchbacks to reach the yellow Cave Trail once again (1.0 mi.). Turn left on it, cross a bridge, ascend among hardwoods along a ravine, and intercept the red Springs Trail. Taking this to the left continues the hike on up to Mt. Zion Major (see the following description). Going right and crossing the stream leads to the parking area.

MOUNT ZION MAJOR AND BOULDER MAZE

Distance: 0.8 mi. (1.3 km) round trip
Elevation Change: 260 ft. ascent
Hiking Time: ¾ hr. either direction

DESCRIPTION: From the parking area (0.0 mi.) go downhill toward the right-hand end of the house, turning to the right just before reaching a utility shed. The red-blazed Springs Trail starts at a blazed post in the field, a short distance west of the shed. Enter the woods, cross a stream, and pass the yellow Cave Trail on the left, as previously described (0.1 mi.). Ascend toward Mt. Zion Major through mixed hardwoods and conifers, with one switchback. At the second switchback, the yellow Cliff Trail branches off to the right (0.3 mi.).

Junction: The Cliff Trail presents an alternate route to Mt. Zion Major and offers many panoramic views. It is spectacular but challenging, for it follows the base of the cliffs through several quite steep ups and downs. It could be dangerous for children and inexperienced hikers and is impossible for dogs.

The red-blazed Springs Trail continues past this switchback and another above it, attaining a fairly level plateau and soon emerging onto an open rocky ridge with sweeping views from northeast to southeast. It then dips slightly, traveling closer to the cliff edge, finally ending at the 1,220-ft. peak of Mt. Zion Major (0.5 mi.). This rock outcropping is an impressive lookout, with views of the distant Adirondacks to the northwest, over the nearby Hubbardton Battlefield, and along the Taconic Mountains to the east and southeast.

The return trip is on the Mickie Trail, also blazed red, which starts near the edge of the peak plateau opposite the ending of the Springs Trail. It descends steeply through four switchbacks, crosses a log bridge, and reaches the base of the cliffs, soon passing the north end of the yellow Cliff Trail on the right. Continuing down, it winds through a maze of boulders (0.6 mi.) and enters the forest, where grazing cows are occasionally seen. The trail crosses a stream on stepping stones and shortly enters a field just north of the cattle guard beside the parking area (0.8 mi.).

NORTH WOODS TRAIL

This rather short red trail is almost completely level. In conjunction with various much longer loops through various fields on both sides of the Monument Hill Road, it makes a relaxed and scenic ski trail in winter, and in summer a quiet, undemanding amble. The trail starts near the point where the access road emerges from the woods (0.0 mi.) and enters a large field north of the house. It meanders in a roughly M-shaped course through an open, almost parklike stand of pines interspersed with small meadows and ends at the North Lookout (0.5 mi.), which is just to the left (east) of a lone pine. This spot offers perhaps the most panoramic mountain vistas on the property.

FALLS AND CANYON TRAILS

Distance: 2.3 mi. (3.7 km) round trip
Elevation Change: 235 ft. ascent
Hiking Time: 1½ hr. either direction

> **NOTE:** Those wishing to shorten the walk to the waterfalls may wish to park on Monument Hill Road. From the main parking area, drive out the access road, turn right on the St. John Road, and right again on the Monument Hill Road. Go downhill past several houses, along a straight stretch, past one more house on the right, through a right turn, and then a left. Just beyond it is a low point in the road, with a turnoff into the field on the right.

DESCRIPTION: From the main parking area (0.0 mi.), go downhill to the southeast, past the left-hand end of the house. Descend between occasional pines to a small bridge crossing the brook, near a white birch on the opposite bank. Go uphill a short distance, then continue southeast down an open field with wide mountain views. Pass between two groups of trees growing from old foundations and reach a crossing at the low point of the Monument Hill Road (0.4 mi.) to the alternate parking area.

Walk east across the paved road and enter another large field. Go uphill to the northeast, following a sometimes-discernible farm track through an opening in the line of stones and trees (0.6 mi.). Continue in roughly the same direction to the high point of this field (360 degree view). Looking northeast, find the tallest pine on the edge of the field, roughly 250 ft. south of the northeast corner. The red-blazed Falls Trail starts just left of this tree (0.7 mi.). It crosses two small brooks, presently ascends a grassy hill crowned with white birches, and descends to the first of the waterfalls (1.0 mi.).

The trail goes upstream along the left-hand bank, past several other falls and a narrow gorge, finally crossing the stream above the highest cascade (1.1 mi.). It then heads downhill to the southwest and joins a woods road, at which point the red blazes end. Descend this road, taking the more-used left fork farther along at 1.4 mi. Some 50 ft. after a stream crossing (1.5 mi.), the Canyon Trail branches off to the left.

This unmeasured but lengthy red trail turns several times before descending to the bottom of a deep canyon. Blazing ends at this point, but hiking can continue, often on the rock floor of the stream. (This surface may be extremely slippery; also, without waterproof boots, wet feet are almost inevitable.) The hike goes on past numerous waterfalls interspersed with level stretches to a long deep canyon with two high falls dropping into it at the far end, one from each side. The hike proceeds for some distance farther, finally ending with a series of low falls from very wide rock shelves stretching across the stream. At this point, turn left and go north to an unblazed woods road leading downhill to the start of the Canyon Trail.

From here, follow the edge of a small field southwest beside a brook, cross it (1.6 mi.), and continue west across a larger field to the Monument Hill Road crossing used earlier (1.8 mi.). Departing at this point from the route previously taken, go west through another field, cross a stream, and ascend northwest to the highest point of land, entering a woods road on the narrow north edge of this field. Emerge into the area below the Japanese Garden (2.1 mi.), go through the garden, and proceed uphill to the parking area.

• • • • • • • • • • • • • • • • •

BLUE RIDGE MOUNTAIN

Distance: 2.4 mi. (3.9 km)
Elevation Change: 1,490 ft. ascent
Hiking Time: 2 hr. (reverse 1¼ hr.)

ABOUT THE TRAIL: Located in the towns of Mendon and Chittenden, Blue Ridge Mtn. has a number of peaks. The highest and southernmost summit (3,278 ft., USGS Chittenden) is reached by the blue-blazed Canty Trail, which is maintained by the Killington Section of the Green Mountain Club.

TO THE TRAIL: From U.S. 4 in the village of Mendon (0.0 mi.), proceed east to a junction with the paved Old Turnpike Road on the left, where U.S. 4 curves right (2.2 mi.). Turn north onto Old Turnpike Road, and continue to the trailhead at a gated private lane on the north side of the road (2.8 mi.). Parking for five cars is available on the shoulder of the public road; special care should be taken not to block the private lane.

DESCRIPTION: From Old Turnpike Road (0.0 mi.), the Canty Trail passes around the gate and follows the lane northwest, bearing left at two forks. Continuing left around the main building of Tall Timbers Camp, the trail leaves the lane to the left, following a footpath into a swampy area (0.2 mi.). The trail crosses a brooklet, crosses it again, then trends to the left around a knoll before crossing the brook a third time (0.4 mi.).

Climbing steeply up the north bank, the trail passes to the right of a possible glacial kettle hole before descending from the low ridge onto a woods road. Following the road on stones across a small brook (0.5 mi.), the trail passes through a recently logged area and crosses another brook (0.7 mi.). Upon approaching a larger brook, the trail turns right from the woods road, crosses the brook on a series of stones (0.8 mi.), and climbs steeply up the west bank to join another woods road. Continuing its ascent, the trail

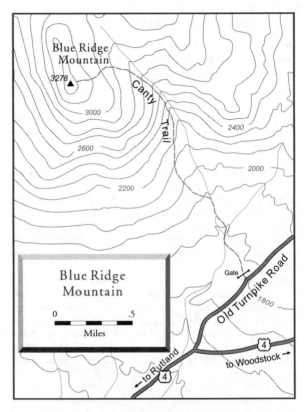

bears left at a fork where the right branch recrosses the brook (1.0 mi.) then follows the main road near the brook for a distance, ignoring several skid roads to the left.

Entering the Green Mountain National Forest (1.3 mi.), the trail begins a steep climb to a spur (1.6 mi.), which leads 100 ft. to a large cascade. Continuing on easier grades, the trail passes within 100 ft. of a flatter cascade

(1.7 mi.) before trending away from the brook to the west. Entering an evergreen forest, the woods road peters out, and the trail makes a sharp left turn (2.1 mi.) to climb through mossy woods to a junction, 50 ft. south of the summit (2.4 mi.). Following the right branch, there is a limited view from the summit ledge ranging from Spruce Mtn. in Plainfield in the northeast to nearby Mendon Peak in the south. More extensive views may be found by following the left spur 150 ft. to Rutland Lookout, a rock outcrop southwest of the main summit. Here the view extends from the Coolidge Range in the south, southwest to Mt. Equinox, Dorset Peak, the Taconics as far north as Grandpa's Knob, and west into the Adirondacks. The city of Rutland lies in the valley below.

3

• • • • • • • • • • • • • • • •

MOUNT INDEPENDENCE

Occupying a peninsula on the east shore of Lake Champlain in the town of Orwell, this low hill (306 ft.) has a commanding view of the narrow lake and nearby Fort Ticonderoga (USGS Ticonderoga). For this reason, it was fortified by the Americans to bolster the weak defenses of Fort Ticonderoga following its capture by the Green Mountain Boys in 1775.

A strong show of force at Independence and Ticonderoga plus the lateness of the season prompted the British to give up their plans for recapturing the fort in late 1776. The following spring, however, they made the American positions untenable by laboriously hauling their heavy artillery to the summit of Mt. Defiance, a craggy hill on the west shore, which the Americans had thought inaccessible. The hasty retreat from Fort Ticonderoga and Mt. Independence gave the British control of the lake again and set the stage for the battles of Hubbardton, Bennington, and Saratoga.

Most of the Mt. Independence area is owned by the Fort Ticonderoga Association and the state of Vermont and is open to the public between Memorial Day and mid-October. Four scenic foot trails lead past the marked sites of the well-preserved remains of the fortifications. This area is the site of ongoing archaeological excavations. Hikers should respect these sites in particular, and the whole area in general, and leave them undisturbed, since collecting artifacts is prohibited by law. For more information, call (802) 759-2412 or contact Vermont Division of Historic Preservation, RD 1, Box 3546, Vergennes, Vermont 05491.

To the Trail: Follow Vt. 73 west from Vt. 22A near Orwell. Take the first left off Vt. 73 onto the paved Chipman Point Road (formerly Vt. 73A), and after about 3.5 mi., turn right onto Mount Independence Road. After the pavement ends, the road parallels Lake Champlain, eventually reaches a fork, and makes a sharp left-hand turn toward a small marina. Parking is in a designated area at the top of the hill; the museum and visitors center is on the right. A brochure and map of the area is available at the center and is highly recommended for exploring local historical remains.

Description: The trailheads are reached by passing through a gate near the visitor center and ascending in a northerly direction through a meadow for about 0.3 mi. to the trail information outpost, where the four trails diverge from an informational signboard.

The Orange Trail (2.5 mi. long) crosses the highest point of the mountain and continues to a junction at the northern tip of the peninsula, where a short loop leads to the shore and back. Continuing straight ahead, the trail descends to the water along the slope of an old road, reaching the spot where a floating bridge led across the lake to Fort Ticonderoga. The trail continues around the west side of the peninsula past a rock outcrop and a junction with the Blue Trail on the right. The Orange Trail then returns to the starting point via parallel routing along the eastern side of the peninsula, at one point passing through a large area of black chert, a toolmaking stone.

The Blue Trail (2.2 mi. long) is slightly more difficult, leaving the information outpost to follow the route of a Revolutionary War supply road along the west side of the peninsula and intersecting the Orange Trail near its tip. Some of the original stonework, built by American troops, remains visible along the roadbed. A quarry site along this trail was used by the French for stone that was hauled across the ice to build Fort Carillon, later renamed Ticonderoga by the British.

The Red Trail (0.6 mi. long) departs to the west and soon reaches a lookout where there are fine views. Mt. Defiance lies directly across the lake to the west, and to the north the red roofs of Fort Ticonderoga are clearly visible.

The White Trail (0.8 mi. long), leads east from the information outpost and reaches the site of a battery position, which affords a view over East Creek toward Orwell and up the lake toward Larabees Point.

• • • • • • • • • • • • • • • •

MOOSALAMOO

The 20,000-acre Moosalamoo region includes a large network of hiking, biking, cross-country skiing, and snowmobile trails on Green Mountain National Forest (GMNF) and Branbury State Park lands. Silver Lake, the cliffs at Rattlesnake Point, and the Falls of Lana are natural highlights in this area (USGS East Middlebury), which is bounded on the north by Vt. 125, on the west by Lake Dunmore, on the south by Vt. 73, and on the east by the Long Trail. *Moosalamoo* is Abenaki for "the moose departs" or "he trails the moose."

Moosalamoo is roughly bisected by USFS Road 32 (also known as the Goshen-Ripton Road or the North Goshen

Road). The majority of the summertime day-use destinations lie to the west of this road. A free map printed by the Moosalamoo Partnership is widely available and is invaluable for year-round exploration of this broad area. Contact the Green Mountain National Forest, Branbury State Park, or the Green Mountain Club for a copy of the brochure.

Branbury State Park is on the eastern shore of Lake Dunmore and is transected by Vt. 53. The park site at the foot of Mt. Moosalamoo was formerly a farm, then a summer boy's camp before becoming the 69-acre Branbury State Park in 1945. Named for its location in Brandon and Salisbury, the park offers a variety of camping accommodations. Day-use facilities include a large sandy beach on Lake Dunmore. A park access fee is charged in-season.

On the eastern shore of Silver Lake, in the northwest corner of Leicester, is the U.S. Forest Service Silver Lake Campground. The area is accessible only by two non-motorized multiuse trails and a foot trail. Primitive camping without charge at fifteen established sites is available on a first-come, first-served basis.

The USFS Moosalamoo Campground is in the northeast corner of the town of Goshen, west of USFS Road 32. The campground lies on USFS Road 24B and is accessible to motor vehicles during the summer camping season, when a fee is charged.

BRANBURY STATE PARK NATURE TRAIL

TO THE TRAIL: Follow Vt. 53 north about 6.0 mi. from Vt. 73 at Forest Dale, or from the junction of U.S. 7 and Vt. 53 south of Middlebury, follow Vt. 53 south 3.5 mi. Branbury State Park is on the east side of Lake Dunmore.

DESCRIPTION: About 0.3 mi. long, the nature trail begins and ends on the east side of Vt. 53 just beyond a private camp, 0.2 mi. north of the park entrance. A nature trail guide is available at the park, where naturalists are on duty during the camping season.

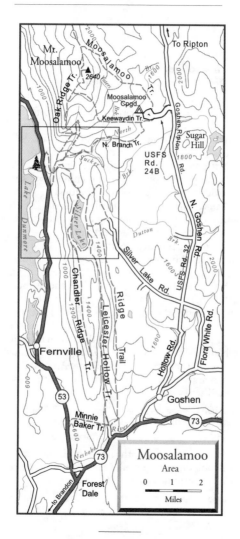

Mr. Moosalamoo

Moosalamoo Brook

To Ripton

2640

Oak Ridge Tr.

Moosalamoo Cpgd.

Keewaydin Tr.

N. Branch Tr.

North Br.

Goshen-Ripton Rd.

Sugar Hill

USFS Rd. 24B

Sucker Br.

N. Goshen Rd.

Lake Dunmore

Silver Lake

Dutton Brk.

USFS Rd. 32

Silver Lake Rd.

Ridge Trail

Chandler Ridge

Leicester Hollow Tr.

Hollow Rd.

Flora White Rd.

Fernville

53

Minnie Baker Tr.

Goshen

73

Neshobe River

73

to Brandon

Forest Dale

Moosalamoo
Area

0   1   2
Miles

3

FALLS OF LANA TRAIL

Distance: 0.7 mi. (1.1 km)
Elevation Change: 200 ft. ascent
Hiking Time: ½ hr. either direction

ABOUT THE TRAIL: This trail provides access to the Falls of Lana picnic area, an important way point for reaching other trails in the western portion of the Moosalamoo area. Hikers not staying in Branbury State Park, where the trail starts, will find ample free parking a short distance south at the head of the Silver Lake Trail, which also ascends to the picnic area. Used in combination, these two trails provide interesting loop possibilities.

TO THE TRAIL: The blue-blazed Falls of Lana Trail starts in the Branbury State Park camping area on the east side of Vt. 53, opposite the state park entrance.

DESCRIPTION: The trail departs the paved road in the rear of the campground between sites 22 and 23 (0.0 mi.) and ascends the ridge to a softwood plateau. Bearing right and ascending the rocky hillside, the trail reaches a spur on the right (0.3 mi.), which leads to a pool below the falls. After ascending steeply, the trail reaches an overlook with views of Lake Dunmore (0.4 mi.). Bearing right, the trail soon reaches a junction with a trail on the left, which descends to the Nature Trail. The Falls of Lana Trail ascends moderately to reach the Falls of Lana Picnic Area (0.5 mi.) and is poorly marked as it passes north through the picnic area to a signed trail junction.

> **Junction:** To the left, the Rattlesnake Cliff Trail provides access to Rattlesnake Point, other trails leading to Mt. Moosalamoo and the USFS Moosalamoo Campground.

Turning to the right, the Falls of Lana Trail crosses Sucker Brook on a bridge and follows a woods road downstream to its terminus at the Silver Lake Trail (0.7 mi.).

> **Junction:** From this junction, it is a 0.5 mi. descent along the Silver Lake Trail to Vt. 53, from which point it is 0.4 mi.

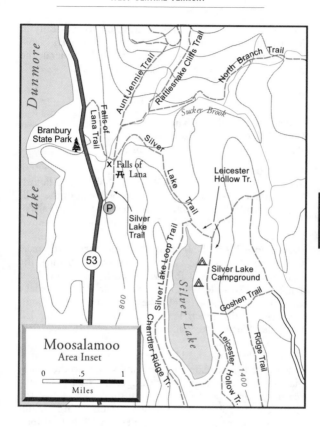

Moosalamoo
Area Inset

0   .5   1

Miles

north via the highway to the park. The Falls of Lana are located a short distance downhill and can be viewed from above via unmarked spurs off the Silver Lake Trail.

In this area Sucker Brook has carved a deep gorge in the solid rock. When U.S. Army General Wool visited the site in 1850, his fellow travelers decided that Sucker Brook

Falls was too prosaic a name. During his tour of duty in Mexico, the general had become known as General Llana, the Spanish word for wool. In tribute to the general, the party christened the site the Falls of Lana.

RATTLESNAKE CLIFFS TRAIL

Distance: 1.6 mi. (2.6 km)
Elevation Change: 870 ft. ascent
Hiking Time: 1¼ hr. (reverse ¾ hr.)

ABOUT THE TRAIL: This blue-blazed U.S. Forest Service trail links the Falls of Lana Picnic Area and Rattlesnake Point.

TO THE TRAIL: The trail begins at the north end of the Falls of Lana Picnic Area, which is easily accessed by the Falls of Lana Trail or the Silver Lake Trail about 0.5 mi. from their trailheads.

DESCRIPTION: From the trail junction where the Rattlesnake Cliffs Trail departs the Falls of Lana Trail (0.0 mi.), the Rattlesnake Cliffs Trail follows a woods road. The Aunt Jennie Trail soon leaves to the left, while the Rattlesnake Cliffs Trail continues straight ahead to a junction (0.3 mi.) with the North Branch Trail on the right. Taking the left fork, the Rattlesnake Cliffs Trail follows a woods road across a small stream.

After climbing steadily for some distance, the trail crosses the brook again (0.9 mi.) and swings to the south. Slabbing the east slope of the ridge, the trail eventually reaches a junction (1.5 mi.) where the upper end of the Aunt Jennie Trail rejoins from the left. Continuing straight ahead for a short distance, the Rattlesnake Cliffs Trail soon reaches a second junction, where the Oak Ridge Trail leaves to the right to ascend to the summit of Mt. Moosalamoo. Taking the left fork, the trail leads a short distance to Rattlesnake Cliffs (1.6 mi.), where there are spectacular views of Lake Dunmore, the Otter Creek watershed, and the Adirondacks.

AUNT JENNIE TRAIL

Distance: 1.2 mi. (1.9 km)
Elevation Change: 850 ft. ascent
Hiking Time: 1 hr. (reverse ¾ hr.)

TO THE TRAIL: This blue-blazed U.S. Forest Service trail departs the Rattlesnake Cliffs Trail to the left 0.1 mi. north of the Falls of Lana Picnic Area.

DESCRIPTION: From the Rattlesnake Cliffs Trail, the Aunt Jennie Trail ascends steadily on an old woods road through a mixed hardwood-softwood forest until it levels out briefly before swinging to the north. The trail climbs more steeply to the base of Rattlesnake Cliffs and passes through a huge boulder field. It then swings to the east and continues to climb steeply using switchbacks, eventually crossing an old woods road. The trail then begins a more moderate ascent, traversing the east slope of the cliffs before reaching its terminus on the Rattlesnake Cliffs Trail a short distance east of the lookout.

3

OAK RIDGE TRAIL

Distance: 8.0 mi. (12.9 km)
Elevation Change: 1,200 ft. ascent
Hiking Time: 4¾ hr. (reverse 5¼ hr.)

ABOUT THE TRAIL: The Oak Ridge Trail extends from the Rattlesnake Cliffs Trail (page 186) north to Vt. 125 west of Ripton. The southern portion of the trail provides an ascent to the summit of Mt. Moosalamoo from the western side of the Moosalamoo area. The lesser used northern section of the trail continues past the summit and makes a long descent to Vt. 125.

TO THE TRAIL: This blue-blazed U.S. Forest Service trail departs the Rattlesnake Cliffs Trail to the left 0.1 mi. north of the Falls of Lana Picnic Area.

DESCRIPTION (NORTHBOUND): The Oak Ridge Trail leaves the Rattlesnake Cliffs Trail to the north at a junction (0.0 mi.) located just west of the northern terminus of the Aunt Jennie Trail. From the junction, the trail climbs to the north and follows the flat, but narrow, top of a ledge, which drops precipitously to the west. Continuing on easy grades past limited views of Lake Dunmore to the west and south toward Silver Lake, the Oak Ridge Trail soon reaches a junction where the Keewaydin Trail enters from the left. The two trails coincide for a short distance, climbing to the top of a knoll (0.9 mi.) where the Keewaydin Trail departs to the right.

The Oak Ridge Trail dips into a shallow sag, then makes a steep and winding climb to the southern end of the Mt. Moosalamoo summit ridge (1.2 mi.). Here there is a fine view to the east of the main range of the Green Mountains from Middlebury Gap south to Brandon Gap. The trail continues north along the ridge, soon reaching a signed junction (1.4 mi.). To the right, a spur trail leads a short distance past the signed summit of Mt. Moosalamoo (2,640 ft.) and drops to an open ledge where there is another fine vista. From this spot, the view of the spine of the main range extends from Middlebury Gap, northward along the Vermont Presidential Range, and past the peaks of Lincoln Mtn. to Camel's Hump and Mt. Mansfield.

Descending northerly past the summit spur, the Oak Ridge Trail passes an overlook on the right (1.5 mi.), where there are wide views to the east and south. After passing another view to the east, the trail reaches a junction (1.8 mi.) on the right with the Moosalamoo Trail, which descends 2.3 mi. to the USFS Moosalamoo Campground west of the Goshen-Ripton Road (USFS Road 32). The Oak Ridge Trail ends its descent in a shallow sag, just beyond which is another view to the east (2.0 mi.). The trail then follows up-and-down routing on or near the ridgeline past views to the east and west (2.6 mi.), just below the northernmost summit (2,310 ft.) of the ridge.

After passing over the summit (2.7 mi.), the trail makes a winding descent away from the ridge and then continues in a generally easterly direction on easier grades over routing that includes portions of old woods roads. Shortly after ending its descent and resuming a northerly direction, the trail rises to cross USFS Road 92 (4.3 mi.). To the right, the road leads 0.75 mi. east to Goshen-Ripton Road (USFS Road 32), from which point it is 0.7 mi. north to Vt. 125 just east of Ripton Village and 2.5 mi. south to the USFS Moosalamoo Campground entrance.

The Oak Ridge Trail continues north, crossing Hale Brook, then USFS Road 92A (4.5 mi.). Ascending easily, the trail swings to the northwest in the vicinity of a brook crossing (5.2 mi.), crosses another small stream (5.8 mi.), and then swings around a hill (1,641 ft.) to cross a low ridge (6.0 mi.) a short distance below the summit. The trail then descends to a junction with an old road and a utility line (6.7 mi.). The trail follows the road downhill to the west, bears to the right at another junction (7.9 mi.), and continues a short distance to reach its terminus at a parking area adjacent to Vt. 125 (8.0 mi.).

MOOSALAMOO TRAIL

Distance: 2.3 mi. (3.7 km)
Elevation Change: 800 ft. ascent
Hiking Time: 1½ hr. (reverse 1 hr.)

ABOUT THE TRAIL: This trail climbs to the summit of Mt. Moosalamoo from the east. It departs the USFS Moosalamoo Campground and ascends to meet the Oak Ridge Trail a short distance north of the summit. Via this latter trail it is a short climb to the summit of Mt. Moosalamoo.
TO THE TRAIL: To reach the USFS Moosalamoo Campground from the north, turn south off Vt. 125 onto Goshen-Ripton Road (USFS Road 32) at a junction located 5.2 mi. east of U.S. 7 in East Middlebury. Continue

south on USFS Road 32 for 3.3 mi., to the signed camp-ground access road on the right. The same point is reached from the south by following USFS Road 32 north for about 6.2 mi. from Vt. 73 east of Forest Dale. Continue west along the access road for 0.7 mi. to reach the camp-ground. The trailhead is at the rear of a parking lot on the north side of the access road just before the gated camp-ground entrance. Parking is available for a dozen cars.

DESCRIPTION: The Moosalamoo Trail climbs around and over a knoll and shortly crosses the north branch of Voter Brook on a plank footbridge (0.5 mi.). From this point, the trail begins a gradual and steady ascent, eventually swinging to the northwest and following an old woods road through a mature hardwood forest. Leaving the woods road and ascending more steeply, the Moosalamoo Trail ends at a signed junction with the Oak Ridge Trail (2.3 mi.). Following this trail to the left, it is 0.25 mi. to the Mt. Moosalamoo summit (2,640 ft.), where there are views to the east and north from two overlooks.

NORTH BRANCH TRAIL

Distance: 2.2 mi. (3.5 km)
Elevation Change: 650 ft. descent
Hiking Time: 1 hr. (reverse 1½ hr.)

ABOUT THE TRAIL: The North Branch Trail connects the USFS Moosalamoo Campground with the Falls of Lana Picnic Area, and provides possibilities for loop hikes across Mt. Moosalamoo.

TO THE TRAIL: The North Branch Trail starts at the Moos-alamoo Campground directly across the road from the parking area for the Moosalamoo Trail.

DESCRIPTION: From the Moosalamoo Campground (0.0 mi.), the blue-blazed North Branch Trail follows easy grades on high ground and soon crosses USFS Road 24B.

The trail then descends steeply for a short distance to reach a junction with the Keewaydin Trail on the right. Continuing straight ahead, the North Branch Trail eventually makes a short, steep descent to cross the north branch of Voter Brook (1.1 mi.). The trail then follows the brook downstream, keeping generally to high ground and passing interesting cascades. The trail continues, in sight of Sucker Brook, to reach its terminus at the Rattlesnake Cliffs Trail (2.2 mi.). Straight ahead, it is 0.3 mi. to the Falls of Lana Picnic Area.

SILVER LAKE TRAIL

Distance: 1.5 mi. (2.4 km)
Elevation Change: 52 ft. ascent
Hiking Time: 1 hr. (reverse ¾ hr.)

ABOUT THE TRAIL: Silver Lake and the USFS Silver Lake Recreation Area are reached by this unblazed but obvious multiuse trail.

TO THE TRAIL: A paved parking lot for this trail is on the east side of Vt. 53, 0.4 mi. south of the entrance to Branbury State Park.

DESCRIPTION: Leaving the parking lot (0.0 mi.) and following a woods road, the trail passes through a gate, climbs a short distance to the east, and soon swings to the north and ascends on easy grades. Passing under the penstock, which brings water from Silver Lake Dam to the power plant on Vt. 53 (0.3 mi.), the trail continues past unmarked spurs on the left overlooking the Falls of Lana and soon reaches a junction (0.5 mi.).

> **Junction:** Straight ahead, the Falls of Lana Trail continues a short distance across Sucker Brook to a junction, where there are trails to the picnic area, Branbury State Park, Rattlesnake Point, Mt. Moosalamoo, and Moosalamoo Campground.

Turning sharply to the right at the junction, the Silver Lake Trail continues on the woods road and ascends to the east for a short distance before resuming its northerly direction (0.6 mi.). Following easy grades, the trail passes a beaver meadow on the left (1.2 mi.) and ascends to a power line clearing (1.4 mi.). After following the power line for a short distance, the trail turns to the right (1.5 mi.) and reaches a junction a few feet northeast of the Silver Lake Dam (1.5 mi.). Leaving to the right and continuing across the dam is the Silver Lake Loop Trail, while straight ahead the Leicester Hollow Trail leads around the east shore of Silver Lake.

SILVER LAKE LOOP TRAIL

Distance: 1.7 mi. (2.7 km)
Elevation Change: minor
Hiking Time: 1 hr. either direction

ABOUT THE TRAIL: Also known as the Rocky Point Trail, this trail loops part way around Silver Lake; however, it joins with the Leicester Hollow Trail and the Goshen Trail to complete the loop.

TO THE TRAIL: This USFS trail begins just east of the Silver Lake Dam at the terminus of the Silver Lake Trail.

DESCRIPTION: From the junction (0.0 mi.), this blue-blazed trail crosses the dam and then follows the west shore of the lake, occasionally clambering onto the rocky slopes of Chandler Ridge. To the north, there are frequent views of Mt. Moosalamoo. After crossing a point and a junction with the Chandler Ridge Trail (0.5 mi.), the trail crosses a small inlet brook at the southwest corner of the lake (1.3 mi.). It continues through the woods to the southeast corner (1.5 mi.), crosses an inlet brook on a bridge (1.6 mi.), and then swings to the north. After following the east shore a short distance, the trail swings to the right and ends at a junction with the Leicester Hollow Trail (1.7 mi.).

Junction: To the north, following the Leicester Hollow Trail, it is 0.2 mi. to the Goshen Trail and 0.8 mi. back to the dam, making a total loop distance of 2.5 mi.

LEICESTER HOLLOW TRAIL

Distance: 4.6 mi. (7.4 km)
Elevation Change: 450 ft. ascent
Hiking Time: 2½ hr. (reverse 2¼ hr.)

ABOUT THE TRAIL: Cyclists, hikers, and skiers use this multi-use trail. Lying in a hollow parallel to the Chandler Ridge Trail and the Ridge Trail, it leads to primitive camping on the eastern side of Silver Lake.

TO THE TRAIL: A USFS lot, located at the end of Churchill Road (USFS Road 40), 0.7 mi. north of Vt. 73, provides limited parking near the gated southern entrance to the Green Mountain National Forest. Churchill Road leaves Vt. 73 a short distance east of the Churchill House Inn, 0.9 mi. east of the junction of Vt. 53 and Vt. 73 intersection in Forest Dale, and 4.2 mi. west of the Long Trail crossing at the summit of Brandon Gap on Vt. 73. Care should be taken not to block the road or any driveways in the area. In the winter, the road is not maintained past the one and only house.

DESCRIPTION: The Leicester Hollow Trail follows the old road north from the USFS gate (0.0 mi.) and immediately reaches an unsigned intersection where the Ridge Trail leaves to the right. Continuing on the road, the trail soon reaches a signed junction on the left (0.2 mi.) with the Minnie Baker Trail and then reaches a second signed junction on the left, this time with the Chandler Ridge Trail. The Leicester Hollow Trail remains on the well-defined old road on the valley floor and ascends northerly on easy grades, eventually making the first of numerous crossings of Leicester Hollow Brook (0.9 mi.).

Ascending deeper into the hollow past old rock slides and mossy boulders, the trail passes a gorge and pool on the left (2.9 mi.) and continues its gradual climb to a junction with the Silver Lake Loop Trail on the left (3.8 mi.). The trail then continues past a junction on the right with the Goshen Trail (4.0 mi.) and passes several campsite spurs on the left (4.2 mi.). After crossing an inlet stream on a bridge, the trail passes through the picnic area and ends at the Silver Lake Trail near the dam (4.6 mi.).

CHANDLER RIDGE TRAIL

Distance: 4.3 mi. (6.9 km)
Elevation Change: 800 ft. ascent
Hiking Time: 2½ hr. (reverse 2 hr.)

ABOUT THE TRAIL: Traversing Chandler Ridge, this trail has nice views of the Green Mountains and the Adirondacks.
TO THE TRAIL: This blue-blazed USFS trail leaves the Leicester Hollow Trail at a signed junction, 0.25 mi. north of the USFS Leicester Hollow parking lot.
DESCRIPTION: From the junction, the trail ascends southwesterly for a short distance and then swings northwesterly to slab the west slope of the ridge. After reaching the ridgeline (0.6 mi.), the trail passes views to the east of the Green Mountains (0.8 mi.) and continues past westerly views of the lower end of Lake Dunmore and the Adirondacks beyond (1.0 mi.). After passing over a bump, the trail turns to the right into a gully (1.2 mi.) and then continues northerly on the east slope of the ridge.

The trail returns to the ridge (1.8 mi.), crosses a minor bump (2.0 mi.), and then follows easy up-and-down routing west of the ridgeline before eventually reaching several limited views to the west (3.4 mi.). After passing another view (3.9 mi.), the trail returns to the ridge, and then descends to reach its terminus at a junction with the Silver Lake Loop Trail (4.3 mi.) on the west shore of the lake.

Junction: To the left, it is 0.5 mi. to the Silver Lake dam and northern terminus of the Leicester Hollow Trail. To the right, via the Silver Lake Loop Trail, it is 1.2 mi. to the Leicester Hollow Trail, which leads 3.8 mi. back to the parking area. Or, via the Silver Lake Loop Trail, Leicester Hollow Trail, and the Goshen Trail, it is 1.8 mi. to the Ridge Trail, which leads 3.9 mi. to the parking lot.

RIDGE TRAIL

Distance: 3.9 mi. (6.3 km)
Elevation Change: 700 ft. ascent
Hiking Time: 2¼ hr. (reverse 2 hr.)

ABOUT THE TRAIL: Maintained on national forest land by the Churchill House Inn, this ski trail is marked with blue diamonds and generally parallels the Leicester Hollow Trail but follows higher ground to the east.

TO THE TRAIL: The trail leaves the Leicester Hollow Trail about 50 ft. north of the U.S. Forest Service gate at the southern end of the Leicester Hollow Trail.

DESCRIPTION: From the unsigned junction (0.0 mi.), the trail ascends southerly on an old woods road for some distance, and then assumes a more easterly direction. Eventually swinging sharply to the north (0.5 mi.), the trail crosses a wide, grassy forest service road (0.6 mi.) and continues its ascent toward the ridge, but does not cross it. Bearing to the left at all junctions and briefly following reddish orange blazes beyond the Glade Trail junction (1.8 mi.), the trail eventually reaches a junction with the Goshen Trail (3.9 mi.), 0.4 mi. east of its junction with the northern end of the Leicester Hollow Trail.

MINNIE BAKER TRAIL

Distance: 1.2 mi. (1.9 km)
Elevation Change: 450 ft. ascent
Hiking Time: 50 min. (reverse 35 min.)

TO THE TRAIL: This multipurpose U.S. Forest Service trail starts at a parking area on the east side of Vt. 53, 1.7 mi. north of its junction with Vt. 73 in Forest Dale.
DESCRIPTION: From the parking area gate (0.0 mi.), the Minnie Baker Trail follows a woods road northeasterly, bears to the right at a woods road junction (0.2 mi.), and ascends to cross the ridge (0.8 mi.). It then descends to reach its terminus at a junction (1.2 mi.) with the Leicester Hollow Trail, 0.2 mi. north of the Leicester Hollow parking area and a short distance south of the start of the Chandler Ridge Trail.

GOSHEN TRAIL

Distance: 0.6 mi. (0.9 km)
Elevation Change: 270 ft. descent
Hiking Time: ¼ hr. either direction

TO THE TRAIL: Marked with blue blazes, this USFS trail begins at a parking area at the end of USFS Road 27. From Vt. 73, 1.6 mi. east of Forest Dale, follow the Goshen-Ripton Road (USFS Road 32) north for 2.3 mi. to a crossroads. Turn left onto USFS Road 27 and continue north to the end of the road (4.3 mi.) and the parking area.
DESCRIPTION: From the parking area (0.0 mi.), the trail crests a low ridge and crosses a power line (0.1 mi.). Descending through the woods, the trail reaches a junction on the left with the Ridge Trail (0.2 mi.), crosses a small stream in a hollow (0.3 mi.), and rises to join an old road (0.4 mi.). The trail then descends to its terminus near the northern end of the Leicester Hollow Trail (0.6 mi.).

ROBERT FROST INTERPRETIVE TRAIL

Distance: 1.0 mi. (1.6 km)
Elevation Change: minor
Hiking Time: ½ hr. either direction

ABOUT THE TRAIL: The first part of this loop trail is handicap accessible, while the remainder uses boardwalks, gravel paths, and an unimproved dirt footbed. Several of Robert Frost's poems are posted along the trail so they can be enjoyed in appropriate settings.

TO THE TRAIL: About 1.0 mi. long, this USFS trail loop begins at a parking area on the south side of Vt. 125, 2.0 mi. east of Ripton and 3.8 mi. west of Middlebury Gap (USGS East Middlebury).

DESCRIPTION: From the parking area, the trail passes through woods and old clearings. A spur trail from the loop connects to the Water Tower Trails, which are not described in this guide. The U.S. Forest Service maintains all the old fields along this trail with prescribed fire to preserve the scenic open appearance of the area.

SILENT CLIFF

Distance: 0.8 mi. (1.3 km)
Elevation Change: 520 ft. ascent
Hiking Time: ¾ hr. (reverse ½ hr.)

TO THE TRAIL: This trail is reached via the Long Trail from its crossing on Vt. 125, 10.1 mi. east of the junction of Vt. 125 and U.S. 7 (3.8 mi. south of Middlebury). The crossing is 6.4 mi. west of Vt. 100 in Hancock. A large parking area is on the south side of the road.

DESCRIPTION: From Vt. 125, the Long Trail rises rapidly to a junction with the Silent Cliff Trail (0.4 mi.), which departs to the east (right). From here the Silent Cliff Trail ascends easterly to Silent Cliff and Silent Cave (0.8 mi.), where there is an excellent view south to Middlebury Gap with Monastery Gap and the Green Mountains beyond (see USGS Bread Loaf).

• • • • • • • • • • • • • • • •

SNAKE MOUNTAIN

Distance: 1.8 mi. (2.9 km)
Elevation Change: 900 ft. ascent
Hiking Time: 1½ hr. (reverse 1 hr.)

ABOUT THE TRAIL: Snake Mtn. is on the Addison-Weybridge town line (USGS Port Henry) and derives its name from the serpentine shape of its long ridge. When a hotel was established near the summit sometime after 1870, the name changed to Grand View Mtn. The new name, however, lasted only slightly longer than the hotel. An open spot at the hotel's former site offers excellent views of the Champlain Valley and the Adirondacks. Much of the mountain is part of the 999-acre Snake Mountain Wildlife Management Area; however, the summit and the lower end of the trail are on private property. The route to the summit is part of an extensive network of logging roads on the mountain. Hikers should stay on this well-traveled route.

TO THE TRAIL: From the junction of Vt. 22A and Vt. 17 at Addison Four Corners (0.0 mi.), follow Vt. 17 east to a junction on the right with Mountain Road (0.8 mi.). Follow this road south past the Whitford Road to a small parking lot on the right, about 500 yds. north of the junction with Willmarth Road (3.5 mi.). The trailhead is on the east side of the road junction. Special care should be taken to park only in the designated lot, and not alongside the road in the vicinity of the trailhead.

DESCRIPTION: From the junction of Mountain Road and Willmarth Road (0.0 mi.), the trail follows a gated woods road east to a junction, where the old summit carriage

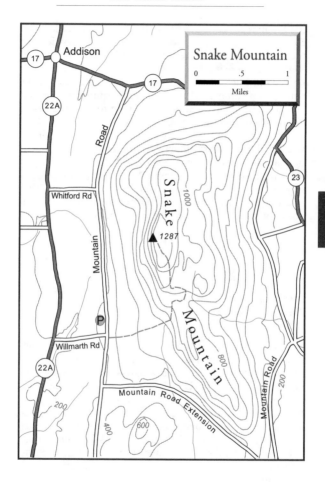

road comes in from the right (0.5 mi.). Bearing left and continuing more steeply to the north, the trail swings to the east onto the ridge and reaches another junction (0.9 mi.), where it takes the right-hand fork and continues up the old blue-blazed carriage road. The trail eventually reaches an unmarked but obvious spur on the left (1.7 mi.), which leads 500 ft. southwest to tiny Red Rocks Pond, where there is a view to the west.

From the spur trail junction, the main trail continues straight ahead a short distance to reach a concrete foundation at the former hotel site (1,250 ft.) (1.8 mi.) just southwest of the true summit (1,287 ft.). Although a snowmobile trail blazed with orange diamonds continues past the hotel site, hikers should not follow it because it does not present any loop hike possibilities.

• • • • • • • • • • • • • • • • •

ABBEY POND

Distance: 2.3 mi. (3.7 km)
Elevation Change: 1,260 ft. ascent
Hiking Time: 1¾ hr. (reverse 1¼ hr.)

ABOUT THE TRAIL: Located in the northwest corner of Ripton, this attractive wilderness pond is reached by a blue-blazed USFS trail, which follows old woods roads along or near the outlet brook (USGS South Mtn.). From the pond, there is a view of the twin peaks of Robert Frost Mtn.

TO THE TRAIL: The trail begins on the east side of Vt. 116 at a road junction (Abbey Pond Road) and USFS trail sign located 4.3 mi. north of Vt. 125 in East Middlebury. Limited roadside parking is available at the trailhead, and caution should be taken not to block the forest service road, which may be used by gravel trucks.

DESCRIPTION: From the highway (0.0 mi.), the trail bears left at a fork in the road and follows occasional blue blazes

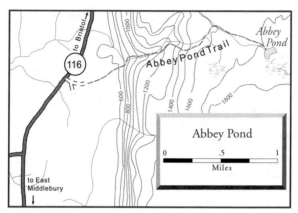

past a series of active gravel pits. Turning to the left just beyond the last pit (0.3 mi.), the trail ascends an old woods road and crosses the outlet of Abbey Pond just below a series of cascades (0.6 mi.). Soon swinging to the right and climbing steadily, the trail recrosses the brook (1.0 mi.) and bears to the left at a fork (1.3 mi.) before continuing on easy grades to a third and final brook crossing (1.6 mi.). After bearing away from the brook (1.8 mi.), the trail ascends gradually through occasional wet areas to reach the pond near its outlet (2.3 mi.).

• • • • • • • • • • • • • • • •

BRISTOL CLIFFS WILDERNESS

ABOUT THE TRAIL: Part of the Green Mountain National Forest, the Bristol Cliffs Wilderness consists of more than 3,700 acres in the South Mtn. area southeast of Bristol (USGS South Mtn.). Permits are not required for entry into the area, and there are no marked trails or established campsites in the wilderness. However, there are several natural attractions, including the cliffs and jumbled talus slopes for which the area is named. These cliffs rise 1,500 ft. above the Champlain Valley and provide a spectacular view of Lake Champlain and the Adirondack Mountains. For further information, including a map of the area, contact the U.S. Forest Service, Middlebury Ranger District. A USGS map and a compass are essential for exploration of this area.

To the Trail: From the village of Bristol, follow Vt. 17 east for about 3.0 mi. to the hamlet of Rocky Dale and turn south onto Lincoln Road. Continue for about 2.0 mi. to the village of West Lincoln, and turn south onto York Hill Road. Parking is at a signed lot 1.7 mi. from West Lincoln, from which point a footpath leads into the wilderness.

• • • • • • • • • • • • • • • •

Bristol Ledges

Distance: 1.0 mi. (1.6 km)
Elevation Change: 960 ft. ascent
Hiking Time: 1 hr. (reverse ¾ hr.)

About the Trail: From the ledges on the southwest side of Hogback Mtn. (USGS Bristol), there are good views of Bristol Village and the lower Champlain Valley. The ledges are reached by following an unmarked woods road westerly from the Bristol Reservoir.

To the Trail: From Main Street (Vt. 116), a short distance east of the shopping district in Bristol Village, turn north onto Mountain Street. Turn right almost immediately onto Mountain Terrace, then bear right again at the next fork and continue to the end of the street, where limited parking is available.

Description: From the end of the street (0.0 mi.), the trail follows a winding jeep road easterly to the Bristol Reservoir (0.3 mi.). Just before reaching the reservoir clearing, a woods road forks to the left and continues straight ahead uphill. Soon turning sharply to the left (0.4 mi.), the trail ascends easily in a northerly direction, meets a cutoff spur from the reservoir junction on the left (0.5 mi.), and then climbs fairly steadily to the rock ledges (1.0 mi.).

•••••••••••••••••

RAMBLES

HUBBARDTON BATTLEFIELD

ABOUT THE TRAIL: In the summer of 1777, after a British force captured Mt. Independence and Fort Ticonderoga, the American army hastily retreated through Hubbardton. The only Revolutionary War battle fought in Vermont occurred here on July 7, 1777 when Seth Warner's Green Mountain Boys staged a rear-guard action against General Burgoyne, checking the British advance and allowing the main American force time to escape. A small visitors center, with a diorama and period artifacts, gives a good overview of the battle and the terrain. An easy path encircles Monument Hill, the site of the Battle of Hubbardton.
TO THE TRAIL: Leave U.S. 4 at exit 5 near Castleton, and turn north onto the paved East Hubbardton Road. The visitor center is on the left, about 7.0 mi. north of U.S. 4.
DESCRIPTION: The trail begins at the visitors center parking lot (0.0 mi.) and follows a mowed strip through open fields. Turning right at a fork (0.1 mi.) and then left, the trail follows the northern edge of the field and reaches a small hill. Passing to the west of a small slate house, the

trail descends in an easterly direction to a junction at a small bridge (0.4 mi.). The trail follows the right fork to a small loop around the Selleck Cabin Site (0.5 mi.), before recrossing the bridge and gently ascending Monument Hill. Passing to the south of the visitors center, the trail reaches the monument dedicated to the battle before returning to the parking lot (0.7 mi.).

PITTSFORD RECREATION AREA

ABOUT THE TRAIL: This system of trails is located in the town-owned Pittsford Recreation Area and consists of a half-dozen interconnecting paths, blazed in different colors and totaling about 3.0 mi. in length. The 200-acre recreation area lies to the north and east of U.S. 7 and is roughly bounded on the north by Plains Road, which leaves U.S. 7 about 0.25 mi. north of the Pittsford village green, and on the south by Furnace Road, which leaves U.S. 7 about 0.75 mi. south of the same spot.

The trail network, designated for foot travel only, is open to the public year-round without charge and leads through abandoned pastures, woodlands, and wetlands. A flyer, containing a map of the trails as well as brief descriptions, is available at the town offices on Plains Road, about 0.75 mi. from the junction with U.S. 7.

TO THE TRAIL: The main entrance to the recreation area is on Furnace Road, about 0.5 mi. from U.S. 7. This entrance is near the area's day-use facilities, which include picnic areas and a swimming pond (a fee is charged in-season).

DESCRIPTION: Convenient access to the network may be gained from two of the trails. The Blue Trail traverses most of the recreation area and starts behind the Pittsford town offices. The trail leads south and east to the main entrance of the Pittsford Recreation Area on Furnace Road. The White Trail starts behind the Pittsford Congregational Church near the village green and leads into the recreation area and a junction with the Blue Trail.

GIFFORD WOODS STATE PARK

ABOUT THE TRAIL: Camping facilities are available, and a day-use fee is charged in-season. The Appalachian Trail passes through the park about 1.9 mi. east of its departure from the Long Trail at Maine Junction at Willard Gap. These trail systems are described in the GMC's *Long Trail Guide* and in a brochure available at the park contact station.

Across Vt. 100 from the park gates lies Gifford Woods Natural Area, a seven-acre, old-growth virgin hardwood stand containing many grand trees with an understory of native wildflowers. The area contains no formal trails nor development of any kind and is designated both as a National Natural Landmark and a State Fragile Area.

TO THE TRAIL: Gifford Woods State Park is on Vt. 100, 0.5 mi. north of its junction with U.S. 4 in Killington.

DESCRIPTION: Within the park, the Kent Brook Trail follows gentle terrain to make a counterclockwise loop of the camping area through a northern hardwood forest. Starting near the park entrance (0.0 mi.), the yellow-blazed trail follows a well-defined footpath to the north through the day-use area. The hiking trail crosses a blue-blazed cross-country ski trail and descends to cross the Appalachian Trail west of the campground before ending on a road at the south end of the park (0.7 mi.).

TEXAS FALLS NATURE TRAIL

ABOUT THE TRAIL: Texas Falls lies in a dramatic ravine; several observation points and a bridge overlook the ravine.

TO THE TRAIL: From Vt. 125, 3.2 mi. east of Middlebury Gap and 3.1 mi. west of Vt. 100 in Hancock, a paved road leads north 0.5 mi. to a parking area on the left.

DESCRIPTION: From the parking area, a self-guided nature trail (descriptive brochure available at the site) crosses a rustic bridge over Texas Falls and follows Hancock Brook upstream for 0.3 mi. toward the Texas Falls Picnic Area.

Bear right just before crossing the paved road at the picnic area to reach the upper section of the nature trail, which leads 0.9 mi. back to the falls. The complete loop is 1.2 mi. (1.9 km) and will take about ½ hr. to hike.

BUTTON BAY STATE PARK

ABOUT THE TRAIL: Located in Vergennes, Button Bay State Park occupies a 253-acre former farm site on a bluff overlooking Lake Champlain. The park is named for the button-like concretions formed by clay deposits that are found along the shoreline. Overnight camping and day-use facilities are available, with a fee charged in-season. Button Point Natural Area, a 13-acre peninsula forming the western end of the park, contains fossils, an old-growth forest stand, and several rare or endangered plant species.

TO THE TRAIL: From the traffic light in the city of Vergennes, continue south about 0.5 mi. on Vt. 22A then turn west on Panton Road. Following the state park signs, it is about 6.5 mi. northwest, then south over local roads to the state park entrance.

DESCRIPTION: A 0.5-mi. gated gravel road (no motor vehicles) leads west from the park picnic area to the natural area and the nature center, where a guide and pamphlet describing the interesting geology of this area are available. In-season, a park naturalist runs daily nature programs for adults and children; call ahead for details: (802) 475-2377. From the center, the 0.5-mi. Champlain Nature Trail explores the hardwood forest and bluffs above the lake.

KINGSLAND BAY STATE PARK

ABOUT THE TRAIL: Located in the town of Ferrisburg, Kingsland Bay State Park currently offers only day-use facilities. Occupying 264 acres along the shores of Lake Champlain that was formerly the site of an exclusive girls camp, this striking area was also home to one of the earliest settlements in Ferrisburg.

TO THE TRAIL: From its junction with Vt. 22A near Vergennes, proceed north on U.S. 7 about 0.5 mi. and turn west onto Tuppers Crossing Road (0.0 mi.), just past a sign for Kingsland Bay State Park. Turn right onto Botsford Road as indicated by a second state park sign, and continue straight through a crossroads (1.1 mi.) onto Hawkins Road. Follow this road for a distance along Little Otter Creek to Kingsland Bay State Park Road and the entrance to the state park on the right (4.5 mi.).

DESCRIPTION: A level trail, about 1.0 mi. in length, leaves the northern end of the parking area and parallels the shoreline around the peninsula. The trail follows a wooded route before breaking onto the shoreline, offering intimate lake views of sailboats on Kingsland Bay and more sweeping vistas across the lake into the Adirondacks.

WILLIAMS WOODS

ABOUT THE TRAIL: In 1996, the Nature Conservancy acquired this 63-acre wooded tract located in the town of Charlotte. It is an exceptional example of mature Vermont bottomland. Within its gently rolling terrain, unlogged stands of hemlock and oak closely resemble the forest seen by the first settlers of the Champlain Valley. The nature preserve is open to the public for foot travel over a white-blazed, 1.5-mi. trail loop.

TO THE TRAIL: From its junction with U.S. 7 (0.0 mi.), follow Ferry Road west to Charlotte and a four-way intersection (0.3 mi.). Turn south onto Greenbush Road, and proceed straight through a staggered intersection (2.3 mi.) where roads leave to the right, then left. The trailhead is soon reached on the right at a sign (3.2 mi.). Limited parking is available on the shoulder of the road, and care should be taken to park vehicles off the traveled surface.

DESCRIPTION: From the trailhead at the sign (0.0 mi.), an access trail leads southwest to a register box (0.3 mi.) containing a logbook and map of the area. The access trail then crosses two wooden bridges to reach a junction with the trail loop. Following an arrow to the right, this trail makes about a 1.0-mi. counterclockwise circuit around the preserve, returning to the junction with the access trail.

A conspicuous feature of the preserve's forest is the profusion of downed trees, many blown down because only a shallow layer of topsoil covers the bedrock. The trail is challenging due to many protruding roots and occasional wet areas.

MOUNT PHILO STATE PARK

ABOUT THE TRAIL: Occupying 168 acres in the town of Charlotte, Mount Philo State Park was established in 1924 and is the oldest park in the state system. A limited number of campsites are available atop the mountain and on its north side. Some very fine views of the Adirondacks and nearly the entire length of Lake Champlain can be seen from the north- and west-ledge lookouts of this 980-ft.-high mountain (USGS Mt. Philo).

TO THE TRAIL: From its junction with Ferry Road, proceed south on U.S. 7 for 3.0 mi. to reach a junction on the left with State Park Road. The same point may be reached from the south by following U.S. 7 north for about 7.5 mi. from its junction with Vt. 22A near Vergennes. Turn east onto State Park Road and continue 0.6 mi. to the park entrance, located at a four-way intersection. A paved state park road ascends to the summit area.

DESCRIPTION: About 100 yds. from the park gate, a blue-blazed trail departs the road to the left (0.0 mi.) and ascends the northwest side of the mountain. After crossing a park road (0.4 mi.), the trail soon reaches a junction at the base of a rocky outcrop.

Junction: Here, a blue-blazed trail departs to the right and skirts an interesting area along the base of the cliffs, leading south and eventually terminating on the park access road (0.5 mi.). From this point it is 0.7 mi. downhill along the road back to the park entrance, or about 0.3 mi. up the road to the contact station atop the mountain.

Bearing left at the junction, the main trail climbs to the top of the ledges and soon arrives at a second junction (0.5 mi.), where a blue-blazed trail departs to the left and leads 0.25 mi. to a camping area low on the mountain's north flank. The main trail continues straight ahead and soon reaches the first of several outstanding vistas atop the mountain (0.6 mi.). Near the top of the cliff, the blazes soon end, and the trail skirts the summit picnic area before following an old carriage road through the woods (0.7 mi.). The trail ends on the summit access road on the western side of the mountain (1.0 mi.), a short distance below the contact station.

In 1924 to 1926, the summit of Mt. Philo became a fire lookout station. In 1938 to 1940, the CCC constructed a steel tower on the mountain, which remained an active outpost until the 1950s. During the 1970s, the tower was removed.

Green Mountain Audubon Nature Center

About the Trail: Owned by the Green Mountain Audubon Society, the Green Mountain Audubon Nature Center is a 255-acre sanctuary that includes a great diversity of natural habitats, a working sugarbush, and a Native American longhouse. There is no admission fee, but contributions are accepted. Green Mountain Audubon also offers a variety of natural history programs for adults and children. For information, contact 255 Sherman Hollow Road, Huntington, Vermont 05462; (802) 434-3068.

To the Trail: The nature center is on the Richmond-Huntington Road, about 5.0 mi. south of Richmond village and about 1.0 mi. north of Huntington village. There is a visitor's center with parking on Sherman Hollow Road about 0.25 mi. west of the highway.

A 5.0-mi. network of trails, open every day from dawn to dusk, crisscrosses the property. These trails lead to a variety of wildlife habitats and offer views of the neighboring mountains, with Camel's Hump the most spectacular. A map, available at the nature center, is invaluable for locating and identifying the numerous trails found on both sides of Sherman Hollow Road.

REGION 4
East Central Vermont

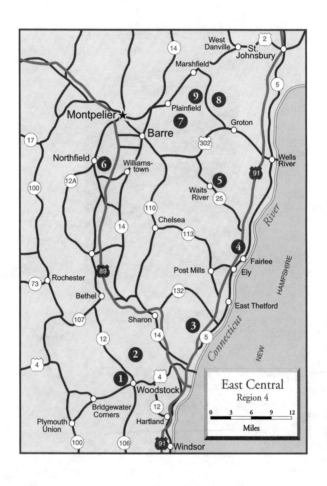

West
Danville
St.
Johnsbury

14

2

Marshfield

5

9

8

Plainfield

7

Groton

Montpelier ★

Barre

302

17

Wells
River

Northfield

6

Williams-
town

91

12A

5

Waits
River

100

25

110

Chelsea

14

113

4

Fairlee
Ely

Post Mills

Rochester

89

73

132

Bethel

East Thetford

107

3

Sharon

14

5

12

2

4

1

Woodstock

Bridgewater
Corners

12

Hartland

Plymouth
Union

91

Windsor

100

106

NEW HAMPSHIRE

Connecticut River

East Central
Region 4

0 3 6 9 12

Miles

REGION 4
East Central Vermont

Most of the hiking trails in the region are dispersed as single trails up prominent peaks. Along the western edge of this section, the easternmost of three ranges of the Green Mountains runs from the Braintree Mountains in the south northward to the Northfield Mountains.

This region is home to Vermont's only national park. The Marsh-Billings-Rockefeller National Historic Park in Woodstock is popular for its historic significance and its network of walking trails and old carriage roads.

East of Barre is a discontinuous range sometimes called the Granite Hills that extends north for some distance. This area of the state is similar geologically to New Hampshire. Several peaks reach elevations in excess of 3,000 ft. in the Orange-Groton area. Vermont's largest state forest is located here. With 25,000 acres, Groton State Forest includes lakes, bogs, inspiring summits, and plenty of land for hiking and camping.

WOODSTOCK AREA

R ising above the village of Woodstock to the northwest of the Ottauquechee Valley, Mt. Tom (USGS
Woodstock North, Woodstock South) is the site of more
than 20 mi. of trails, cross-country ski trails, logging roads,
and carriage roads. The main natural features in the area
are Mt. Tom, the Pogue (a pond tucked into the cleft of a
mountain), and many large, old trees. Mt. Peg is also in
the area and makes a great walk for children.

The Billings Museum, the Rockefeller home, and
Mt. Tom lands were incorporated in the Marsh-Billings-
Rockefeller National Historic Park in 1998. George
Perkins Marsh (1801–1882), an early conservationist, first
owned the farmlands later purchased by Frederick Billings
(1823–1890). Billings developed his farm as a model of
wise agricultural stewardship. After his death, his wife,
Julia, and their three daughters sustained his plan. Later,
Billing's granddaughter, Mary French, and her husband,
Laurance S. Rockefeller, continued this commitment to
stewardship, eventually gifting the farm to establish Vermont's first national park.

The park includes the Billings Farm and Museum, a
working dairy farm with a museum of agricultural and
rural life, as well as carriage roads and walking trails, and a
visitor center with displays in the Carriage House. A trail
map issued by the national park is invaluable for exploring
the area. During the winter, the Woodstock Ski Touring
Center grooms the trails for cross-country skiing, and
walking on the trails is not allowed. For more information,
contact the national park at Marsh-Billings-Rockefeller
National Historic Park, P.O. Box 178, Woodstock, Vermont 05091; (802) 457-3368; www.nps.gov/mabi. Trails
are accessed via the national park main entrance, from
Faulkner Park, or from Prosper Road.

4

MOUNT TOM

Distance: 1.6 mi. (2.6 km)
Elevation Change: 550 ft. ascent
Hiking Time: 1 hr. (reverse ¾ hr.)

ABOUT THE TRAIL: The graded pathway, long and winding switchbacks, and park benches along the route make this trail a Vermont rarity. The unblazed but obvious trail, known as the Faulkner Trail, begins in Faulkner Park.

TO THE TRAIL: From the Woodstock village green, cross U.S. 4 to reach Mountain Avenue and drive or walk through the covered bridge across the Ottauquechee River. Bear left on Mountain Avenue where it crosses River Street, and continue a short distance west to Faulkner Park on the right. Roadside parking is available.

DESCRIPTION: Follow the asphalt path along the stone wall, which forms the eastern boundary of the park, to where the trail enters the woods just below a large boulder (0.0 mi.). The path promptly begins a zigzag climb on very gradual grades, where hikers should avoid the temptation to follow rogue paths between the switchbacks. The path soon reaches a junction (0.5 mi.) on the right with the Lower Link Trail, which follows easy grades for 0.2 mi. to a terminus on the North Peak Trail. Past this junction, the Faulkner Trail continues a zigzag climb to reach another junction (1.2 mi.) on the right, this time with the Upper Link Trail, which also leads 0.2 mi. to the North Peak Trail. From this junction, the Faulkner Trail proceeds straight ahead to ascend to a knoll (1.5 mi.) where there are views to the south and east.

The trail then drops into a shallow sag before beginning a moderately steep climb over the rocks, meeting the end of a carriage road on the south peak (1,250 ft.) of Mt. Tom (1.6 mi.). Here there are fine views to the south of Woodstock and Okemo Mtn. (Ludlow Mtn.) and to the Ottauquechee River in the east.

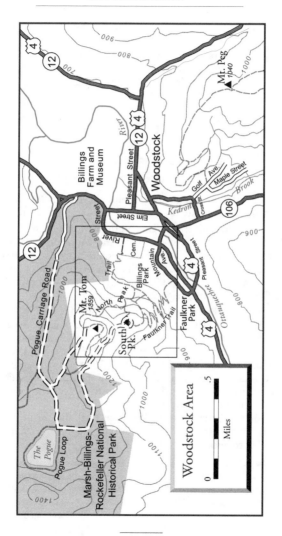

Woodstock Area

0 .5

Miles

About 125 ft. to the right, at the communication poles, the Precipice Trail descends a short distance to a rock lookout, where there are impressive views. The carriage road atop the south peak forms a short circular loop, which affords views in all directions and also leads northwest to the Pogue.

NORTH PEAK TRAIL

Distance: 1.1 mi. (1.8 km)
Elevation Change: 650 ft. ascent
Hiking Time: 1 hr. (reverse ¾ hr.)

ABOUT THE TRAIL: With other trails, the North Peak Trail provides an alternate route up Mt. Tom and to the Pogue.

TO THE TRAIL: This trail begins on the east side of the River Street Cemetery, reached from the Woodstock village green by following Mountain Avenue across a covered bridge, turning right at the first intersection onto River Street, and proceeding 0.2 mi. to the cemetery on the left. A Billings Park trails sign marks the trailhead.

DESCRIPTION: From River Street (0.0 mi.), the trail follows an old road used as a bridle and ski touring trail, on an easy winding ascent. Soon after passing a cabin on the left (0.3 mi.), the trail turns sharply left, leaving the old road and now following yellow blazes. After several hundred feet, there is a junction with the Lower Link Trail, which continues straight ahead 0.2 mi. to the lower end of the Faulkner Trail.

Following a sign for the Precipice Trail, the North Peak Trail turns sharply to the right at the junction and ascends steadily to another junction (0.4 mi.).

Junction: Turning off to the left here are the yellow-blazed Middle and Upper Link Trails, which coincide for about 200 ft. before diverging at a fork. The Middle Link Trail bears left and joins the Lower Link Trail about 0.1 mi. from the Faulkner Trail. The Upper Link Trail bears right and

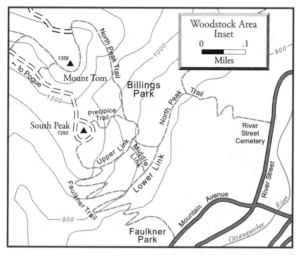

follows higher ground for 0.2 mi. to its junction with the Faulkner Trail, 0.4 mi. below the south peak of Mt. Tom.

Turning to the right at the junction, the North Peak Trail descends into a sag, climbs steadily for a short distance, and reaches a junction (0.5 mi.) marked by a yellow-blazed boulder. To the right, an obvious path leads to a series of unblazed trails and woods roads. Bearing sharply left at the junction, the trail climbs to an open rock area, offering limited views of the village and reaches yet another junction (0.6 mi.). It is here that the Precipice and North Peak Trails diverge.

Junction: The Precipice Trail continues straight ahead from the open area, along a narrow, but well-defined, path. Bordered along the edge by protective cabling, it traverses exceptionally beautiful ledges and boulder fields covered in lichen, sphagnum, and polypody. The trail ascends past an impressive rock lookout near the summit to reach the south peak of Mt. Tom in 0.3 mi. at a carriage road.

From the junction in the open area, the North Peak Trail turns sharply right and ascends steadily to a shoulder of the south peak (0.7 mi.). The trail continues on easier grades before turning sharply to the left (0.8 mi.) and ascending easily around the north summit of Mt. Tom. Passing a large boulder on the left where there are views to the south and east, the trail then descends past a junction on the right with the former Back Loop Trail (1.0 mi.), now a carriage road.

From the junction, the North Peak Trail descends to the old carriage road (1.1 mi.). To the left via this carriage road it is 0.3 mi. to the upper end of the Faulkner Trail at the south peak of Mt. Tom. Following this carriage road to the right, it is 0.7 mi. to the Pogue.

Note: Care should be taken to descend the North Peak Trail following exactly the reverse directions. New, but obvious, trail work and yellow blazing in the area may prove confusing and lead the hiker onto dead-end spurs and trails under construction.

THE POGUE

Distance: 1.1 mi. (1.8 km)
Elevation Change: 80 ft. descent
Hiking Time: 35 min. either direction

ABOUT THE TRAIL: This small pond, located northwest of Mt. Tom, is reached by following a carriage road on very easy grades. There are several ways to reach the Pogue, from Prosper Street, from the Billings Farm and Museum, or from one of the trails at the summit of Mt. Tom (described earlier). Only the description from the south peak of Mt. Tom is described here. To follow the other routes, obtain the national park brochure.
TO THE TRAIL: From Faulkner Park, hike to the south peak of Mt. Tom via the Faulkner Trail described on page 216.
DESCRIPTION: Leaving the Faulkner Trail at the south peak of Mt. Tom (0.0 mi.), an unblazed carriage road ascends

to the northwest, passes two signs for the North Peak Trail (0.3 mi.), and bears to the left at a junction where an unmarked trail turns right (0.5 mi.). Continuing through the woods for some distance, the road bears right in a large clearing (0.8 mi.), where there are extensive views to the west. The road then descends to a large meadow and turns right to follow its margin, shortly reaching a four-way junction (1.0 mi.).

> **Junction:** The road to the left reaches the southeast corner of the Pogue in about 400 ft. and continues on to circle the small pond, making a loop about 0.75 mi. long and returning via the path lying straight ahead. To the right at the four-way junction, another carriage road makes a very gradual descent, eventually reaching a fork. To the right at this junction, a ski trail leads back to the North Peak Trail near the River Street Cemetery; to the left a steeper trail descends to Vt. 12 at the Billings Farm and Museum about 0.5 mi. north of the village green.

Mount Peg

Distance: 0.5 mi. (0.8 km)
Elevation Change: 320 ft. ascent
Hiking Time: ½ hr. (reverse ¼ hr.)

About the Trail: This is a pleasant walk, especially good for children, up Mt. Peg. For a longer return hike, take the alternate route described.

To the Trail: Located in the southern part of the village, the unblazed, graded path to the summit (1,080 ft.) begins at the intersection of Golf Avenue and Maple Street (USGS Woodstock South). From the village green, follow South Street (Vt. 106) south for about 0.1 mi., past the Woodstock Inn. Turn left onto Cross Street, continue past Court Street on the left to cross Kedron Brook, then turn right onto Golf Avenue at the next intersection. Continue for a short distance to another intersection with Maple Street. Just before the Maple Street sign is a three-car parking lot on the left. The trail enters the woods from a driveway behind the parking lot on the left-hand side of Golf Avenue. A sign marks the beginning of the trail.

DESCRIPTION: From the sign (0.0 mi.), the trail climbs on switchbacks through the woods. At the first switchback, a partially overgrown abandoned trail enters from the left, while the main trail stays to the right. The route soon reaches a junction (0.1 mi.) where an alternate trail departs to the right. Taking the left fork, the main trail climbs to the north, turns back to the right (0.3 mi.), and then descends very gradually to the south. It soon reaches another junction (0.4 mi.) where the alternate route rejoins the main trail from the right, and bears left at this convergence to continue the ascent to the summit.

The trail continues a short distance uphill to a junction with a small loop trail that leads around the summit. The trail turns left into the loop and then immediately turns right at a junction where a spur trail leads north to Slayton Terrace. The summit loop climbs southward to a small picnic area on the viewless summit of Mt. Peg (0.5 mi.) before reaching a junction where a side trail departs to the left (description follows). The summit loop then swings to the north and descends to rejoin the start of the circuit.

ALTERNATE RETURN ROUTE: From the southeastern corner of the summit loop (0.0 mi.), a side trail departs to the south and is soon marked first by red arrows on trees and then diamond-shaped metal markers or red blazes. The trail passes through a wooded area, crosses a power line on private property, and then reaches the end of an old field. Turning left, the trail then ascends steadily in the open past extensive views to the east, north, and west. After reaching the woods on a ridge (0.4 mi.), cross-country ski paths and bridle trails lead south to the Woodstock Country Club/Ski Touring Area. While hiking is encouraged along the trails in warmer weather, during the winter these trails are maintained for skiing only, and an access fee must be paid at the touring center. The red-blazed trail continues

ntry Club's golf course and even-
e Health and Fitness Center. A
ng the shoulder of Vt. 106 leads
back to Woodstock. A return to Mt.
be made via other ski trails or paths, using
ssued by the touring center.

•••••••••••••••

AMITY POND NATURAL AREA

Distance: 2.9 mi. (4.7 km) loop
Elevation Change: 660 ft. ascent
Hiking Time: 1¾ hr. either direction

ABOUT THE TRAIL: Located in the northwest corner of Pomfret, the Amity Pond Natural Area (USGS Woodstock
North) consists of woodlands and upland pastures donated to the state for nonmotorized and nonwheeled outdoor recreation. The area is circled by a loop trail that
coincides for a distance with the Sky Line cross-country ski
trail. The ski trail, which travels between Woodstock and
Pomfret, is marked with blue-and-orange markers. It is
possible to walk a shorter 1.4-mi. loop using the Crossover
Trail. The longer 2.9-mi. loop described involves a pleasant 0.3-mi. walk on the gravel Broad Brook Road.

TO THE TRAIL: From U.S. 4 in Woodstock, follow Vt. 12
north 1.2 mi. to a fork, and turn right onto South Pomfret Road. At the South Pomfret post office (3.3 mi.), bear
right at a fork and continue north through the village of
Pomfret to the hamlet of Hewetts Corners (7.9 mi.).
Reaching a junction, bear right, staying on the paved road,
then take an immediate left onto another paved road,
where signs point to I-89 and Sharon. Continue a short
distance to a gravel road on the left (8.5 mi.). Bear left
onto the gravel Allen Hill Road, and continue uphill to a
wide spot at a height of land (10.8 mi.). On the right side
of the road is a small parking area for five cars.

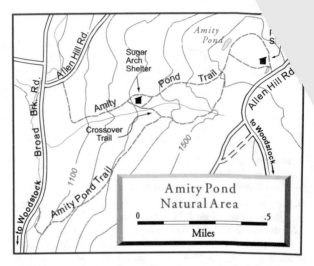

DESCRIPTION: Across the road to the west is the signed entrance to the Amity Pond Natural Area. Two trails leads from here. The most obvious trail is a side trail that leads from the sign straight ahead a short distance to Amity Pond Shelter. From the shelter, this trail passes to the right of a small pond, ascends a bank, and crosses a field to join the main trail just below Amity Pond.

The beginning of the main trail is more difficult to spot. From the sign (0.0 mi.), the Amity Pond Trail departs to the right and parallels the road for a short distance before ascending through a wooded area. The trail breaks into the open to reach a height of land (0.2 mi.), where there are views to Mt. Ascutney, Killington, and Pico Peak. Amity Pond, named to commemorate the lifelong friendship of two area women who met frequently at this spot, is located in the meadow to the west of the trail. The small pond has all but disappeared behind trees growing near the trail at the height of land.

The trail then begins a gentle descent and near a large rock is joined on the left by the side trail from Amity Pond Shelter. Descending to a well-marked junction at the head of a large loop (0.3 mi.) the trail bears to the right and crosses the rest of the open field before reentering the woods. After crossing a stone wall, the trail descends to a junction (0.6 mi.) with the north end of the Crossover Trail.

Junction: To the left, this trail leads a short distance to Sugar Arch Shelter, then continues a short distance beyond to rejoin the Amity Pond Trail on its return leg to the parking lot.

Bearing right at the junction, the Amity Pond Trail passes through a small clearing (0.7 mi.) and descends through the woods to cross a power line (0.8 mi.). After descending steadily on an abandoned road, the trail turns to the right just before a fenced field (0.9 mi.) and follows the fence line along the edge of the woods. The trail keeps to the right of a fenced horse pasture and barn. The trail then crosses a small footbridge just above the house and crosses a field to the Allen Hill Road, a gravel-surfaced town road. Turn left and follow this road to its intersection with Broad Brook Road (1.1 mi.) by the East Barnard Cemetery.

The Amity Pond Trail turns left onto Broad Brook Road and crosses the Broad Brook on a concrete bridge (1.4 mi.). Immediately after this bridge, the trail turns off the town road to the left, fords the brook, and follows an old woods road along Broad Brook. The trail then makes a sharp left turn (1.5 mi.), begins a winding climb, and crosses a small brook (1.7 mi.). Near an old moss-covered stone wall (2.0 mi.), the trail makes another sharp left turn to parallel the orange-marked boundary line and crosses a small drainage on a log bridge.

Ascending, the Amity Pond Trail reaches a junction on the left with the south end of the Crossover Trail (2.2 mi.), leading from Sugar Arch Shelter, and then crosses a

4

powerline (2.4 mi.). The trail drops down to a brook crossing (2.5 mi.), and after climbing steadily for a short distance, it leaves the woods and continues uphill through a field. The trail quickly reaches the junction marking the beginning of the loop and then turns right to pass Amity Pond again before returning to the parking area (2.9 mi.).

•••••••••••••••••

GILE MOUNTAIN

Distance: 0.7 mi. (1.1 km)
Elevation Change: 390 ft. ascent
Hiking Time: ½ hr. (reverse 20 min.)

ABOUT THE TRAIL: Located in a municipal forest in the northwest corner of the town of Norwich, Gile Mtn. (USGS South Strafford) boasts a well-maintained fire tower on its summit (1,873 ft.), from which there are panoramic views. An easy ascent along an obvious, well-trodden trail makes this a good hike for young children.

TO THE TRAIL: From the junction in the village of Norwich where U.S. 5 turns to the east off Main Street (0.0 mi.), continue north along Main Street for a short distance before turning left onto Turnpike Road (0.6 mi.). Continue past the end of the pavement (2.5 mi.) and ascend through a sheltered valley to the signed parking area on the left (5.2 mi.), just before a farmhouse on the right.

DESCRIPTION: From the back of the parking lot (0.0 mi.), the trail follows the tower trail sign to a logging road (0.1 mi.) on the left, which it follows along blue blazes. The trail soon leaves the road to the right (0.2 mi.), crosses a log bridge, and ascends to cross an open swath beneath a power line (0.3 mi.), where there is a fine view of the neighboring New Hampshire hills. Entering the woods again at a stand of old birches, the trail follows easy switchbacks to ascend to a cabin (0.7 mi.), just below the fire tower, where from the observation platform there are spectacular views in all directions. To the east, over the nearby Connecticut River Valley, lie the White Mountains, while Mt. Ascutney's bulk dominates the southern horizon. To the west, the spine of the Green Mountains is visible in the distance.

•••••••••••••••

THE PALISADES

Distance: 0.75 mi. (1.2 km)
Elevation Change: 350 ft. ascent
Hiking Time: ½ hr. either direction

ABOUT THE TRAIL: Rising dramatically west of the Connecticut River, the Palisades are a series of cliffs along the east side of Morey Mtn. A trail created by the Lake Morey Trails Association ascends to the edge of the precipice from the west. In recent years, the rocky outcrops have become a nesting site for peregrine falcons, which are legally protected from human disturbance during the breeding season. Pursuant to state of Vermont and federal laws, a clearly marked area near the cliff top is off-limits to hikers between March 15 and August 1. Since the ascent to the edge of the nesting area is fairly short, it is recommended this hike be reserved for the fall season when the cliff top is accessible.

TO THE TRAIL: From I-91 exit 15, a short distance west of U.S. 5, turn west onto Lake Morey Road. Turn right almost immediately at a four-way intersection, and then turn right again into the parking lot of the Fairlee Fire Department across from the Lake Morey Country Club. Ample parking is available, but care should be taken to leave vehicles on the right side of the lot as far from the fire station entrance as possible.

DESCRIPTION: The obvious trail, which is sporadically marked by yellow metal squares of the Lake Morey Trails Association, begins in the back of the parking lot at the corner nearest the interstate (0.0 mi.). Bearing north, the trail follows the east side of a chain-link fence and passes to the right of several old crab apple trees before making abrupt turns to the left then right. Now an obvious path in the woods, the trail winds steeply for a few hundred feet, still heading north, parallel to the interstate. Passing through a mixed hardwood-softwood forest, the trail follows a fence on the left and soon arrives at a sign warning of the peregrine falcon nesting area ahead.

The trail levels off briefly (0.1 mi.), and then resumes its climb, but less steeply. It passes through an opening in the fence, levels off, and then ascends gradually before making jogs to the left and then right (0.2 mi.). Passing another trail on the left, the path crosses a seasonal stream and then reaches a power line. There is no trespassing past this point during the peregrine falcon nesting season from March 15 to August 1; the area is regularly patrolled. From this cut there are views to the south to Fairlee, the Connecticut River, and Mt. Ascutney. The trail continues straight across the swath cut by the power line and reenters the woods, winding along granite ledges to a level ridge that leads to the open area above the Palisades (0.7 mi.). There are many spots from which to enjoy pastoral views of farms, church steeples, and white clapboard houses on the river at Orford, New Hampshire.

•••••••••••••••••

WRIGHT'S MOUNTAIN

Distance: 1.0 mi. (1.6 km)
Elevation Change: 415 ft. ascent
Hiking Time: ¾ hr. (½ reverse)

ABOUT THE TRAIL: Located in the northeast corner of Bradford, Wright's Mtn. offers good views to the north, west, and southwest from a rock lookout west of the summit

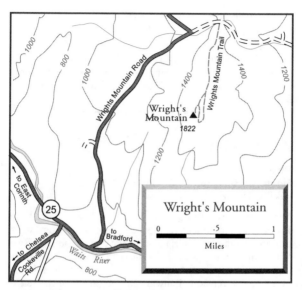

Wright's Mountain

0   .5   1

Miles

(USGS East Corinth). The unblazed, but obvious, trail is owned by the town of Bradford and maintained by the Friends of Wright's Mtn. volunteers.

TO THE TRAIL: The trail begins on Wright's Mountain Road, 2.3 mi. from its junction with Vt. 25. From Vt. 25 (0.0 mi.), follow Wright's Mountain Road north. Stay on the main road past the fork intersection with Fulton Road (2.1 mi.). At the crest of the hill, there is an abandoned road on the left and a wooden gate on the right (2.3 mi.). Parking is on the abandoned road.

DESCRIPTION: From Wright's Mountain Road (0.0 mi.), the trail passes through the gate and follows a woods road south on easy grades. The trail reaches a fork (0.4 mi.) where two routes lead to the lookout. Bearing right, the main trail climbs steeply to the junction with the other end of the alternate route (0.9 mi.).

Junction: The left-hand alternate route is a gentler climb to its junction with the main trail.

The two trails continue up to the end of the woods road. The trail then turns right and descends through the woods to an abandoned camp; just beyond is a large open rock area overlooking the Waits River Valley (1.0 mi.).

●●●●●●●●●●●●●●●●●

PAINE MOUNTAIN

Distance: 2.8 mi. (4.5 km)
Elevation Change: 1,198 ft. ascent
Hiking Time: 2½ hr. (reverse 1½ hr.)

ABOUT THE TRAIL: Paine Mtn. (2,411 ft., USGS Barre West, Brookfield, Northfield, Roxbury) is the southernmost extremity of a range of hills rising to the east of the Dog River Valley in the town of Northfield. The area was largely cleared of forest in the last century to provide fuel for the new Central Vermont Railway, but like much of the rest of Vermont, it has now mostly reverted to woodland. There remains much evidence of human activity, including a network of old roads and many rusted and broken pipes that once carried water west to Northfield. The ascent described, known informally as the Clark Route, follows old town roads that now form a multiuse trail system on the lands of the town of Northfield, Norwich University, and the Northfield Telephone Company. An alternate descent route is given in the description. Additional trails on the mountain, as well as the natural and cultural history of the area, are described in the *Paine Mountain Guidebook*, written by GMCer Bill Osgood. The book is available from the GMC.

TO THE TRAIL: From the common in the village of Northfield (0.0 mi.), proceed south on Vt. 12 and turn left onto Vt. 64 (2.1 mi.). Proceed eastward on Vt. 64, ascending to reach an intersection on the left with Barrows Road (3.4 mi.).

Turning north onto this road and ignoring a dead-end fork to the left, there is parking for eight to ten vehicles along the roadside at the junction. (Note: Although it is tempting to drive on Barrows Road beyond this point, there is no parking further along the road and cars will be towed.)

DESCRIPTION: From the parking area (0.0 mi.), follow Barrows Road in an easterly direction. A junction is quickly reached near a house (0.3 mi.) where an old town road forks to the left and the Barrows Road curves right. Bearing to the left along the eroded roadway, the unblazed but obvious trail ascends to the north, eventually reaching an open meadow (0.9 mi.) where there are views back down the Robinson Brook Valley. The Clark family, for whom this route is named, formerly operated a hill farm in this area.

While still in the meadow, the trail meets and crosses a snowmobile trail, which it ignores. Bearing left out of the meadow and climbing steeply at first, the trail continues on more moderate grades through a dense growth of young sugar maple trees. Slightly farther along, the trail passes through an old apple orchard and descends to a brook crossing (1.7 mi.) before reaching a conifer plantation established in the 1930s as part of the Norwich Town Forest. At a fork (1.8 mi.), the trail bears to the right and continues uphill, then follows a sharp switchback, which veers to the south. After the grade moderates, the trail reaches another junction (2.3 mi.). Here the trail turns sharply to the left and ascends a spur to a bronze survey marker at the wooded summit (2.8 mi.) of Paine Mtn. At the summit, evidence of the severe damage caused by the 1998 ice storm is apparent. The storm broke off the crowns of the trees, opening the understory below to sunlight.

ALTERNATE RETURN ROUTE: A slightly different route offers substantial views of the two mountain ranges to the west. At the junction below the summit (0.0 mi.), proceed straight, past the trail on the right used for the ascent. Known informally as the Hawk Watch Trail, this route soon reaches a semiopen pasture with a shelter (0.1 mi.),

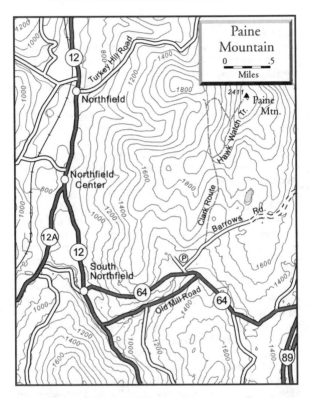

where there are excellent views west over the Dog River Valley. By moving about the clearing, it is possible to gain views over the closer third range of the Green Mountains (known as the Northfield Mountains south of the Winooski River) to the more distant main range of the Green Mountains. The view extends almost unbroken from Camel's Hump south to Lincoln Gap, with Killington and Pico visible in the southwest. To the south, stands the monadnock of Mt. Ascutney. Hawk watches are staged in this clearing in the spring and fall, as Paine Mtn. falls in the line of a major migratory route. A footpath, indistinct at times, leads south from the clearing, then veers to the west through a young hardwood forest and raspberry canes to rejoin the Clark Route (0.4 mi.) in the old apple orchard described in the ascent route.

•••••••••••••••••

Spruce Mountain

Hiking Time: 2.2 mi. (3.5 km)
Elevation Change: 1,180 ft. ascent
Hiking Time: 1¾ hr. (reverse 1 hr.)

About the Trail: Located in the town of Plainfield, the summit (3,037 ft., USGS Barre East, Knox Mtn.) is the site of a preserved fire tower, from which there is a panoramic view of north central Vermont and western New Hampshire. The occasionally blue-blazed but obvious trail to the summit is partly located in the L. R. Jones State Forest and partly in Groton State Forest.

To the Trail: From its junction with Vt. 110 in East Barre, follow U.S. 302 east 1.1 mi. and turn north onto Reservoir Road (0.0 mi., called Brook Road when it enters Plainfield). After reaching the end of the pavement (4.9 mi.), continue to a junction (5.6 mi.) and turn right onto East Hill Road. Proceed uphill, and turn right again onto Spruce Mountain Road (6.5 mi.). At the next junction (6.8 mi.), turn left as indicated by signs reading "Summit Trail ½ M" and follow the narrow and winding road to a parking area at the start of the trail (7.5 mi.).

Description: From the parking area, the trail passes through a set of gateposts and turns right to pass a second set of gateposts (0.1 mi.) before following a wide woods road to the southeast. The trail follows the old road on

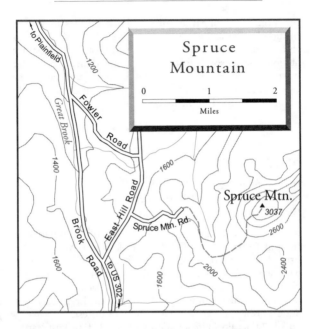

easy grades for some distance before beginning a gradual ascent, offering occasional views to the summit tower on the left. Gradually swinging to the east, the trail reaches the end of the well-defined road at a clearing (1.0 mi.). Continuing straight ahead, the trail then passes through several wet areas, where long-ago fire tower lookouts placed stepping stones and built up the footbed with gravel fill. The trail soon crosses a small stream bridged by a pair of cut logs (1.3 mi.) before continuing along more raised trail bed.

Following a northeasterly course in deep woods, the trail begins a moderately steep climb (1.5 mi.), bearing north through spruce forest. Passing two large boulders split from the bedrock (1.6 mi.), the trail then climbs somewhat less steeply over granite slabs for some distance. Resuming a steady ascent (1.9 mi.), the trail passes through a fern-filled clearing and then continues on easier grades to the summit and the tower (2.2 mi.). The cellar hole from the caretaker's cabin is nearby.

Spruce Mtn. was first used as a fire lookout about 1919, when a summit trail, cabin, telephone line, and tower were built. In 1931, the original tower was replaced, then in 1943 to 1944, the tower from Bellevue Hill in St. Albans was transferred to the summit. The site was abandoned as a fire lookout in 1974. In 1994, the tower was placed on the National Historic Lookout Register.

• • • • • • • • • • • • • • • •

GROTON STATE FOREST

With 25,000 acres to its name, Groton State Forest is the second-largest contiguous block of land owned by the state of Vermont. Located in the towns of Groton, Peacham, Marshfield, Orange, and Topsham (USGS Groton, Barnet, Marshfield), the forest is generally bounded on the north by U.S. 2, north of Marshfield, and on the south by U.S. 302, west of Groton. Vt. 232 bisects the forest. Along this road lie five state park campgrounds; from south to north they are Ricker, Stillwater, Big Deer, Kettle Pond, and New Discovery. Day-use facilities are available on Lake Groton.

The campgrounds and many of the area's bodies of water and mountains are linked by a network of hiking and multiuse trails, which are shown in the Department of Forests, Parks, and Recreation's "Groton State Forest Guide," available free at various contact stations. A second department pamphlet, the "Groton State Forest History Guide," may be obtained in-season at the Groton Nature Center, located near the north end of Lake Groton on the Boulder Beach access road. Groton's geology is more similar to the

White Mountains of New Hampshire than Vermont's Green Mountains. The exposed granite bedrock makes for a rocky, rough topography.

Logging is common in Groton State Forest and may disrupt portions of the trail system, so hikers should obtain current trail information from park personnel. In some cases, trees have been marked for cutting with blue paint. Be especially careful to follow the trail in these areas. Primitive camping is allowed within designated areas of the forest, including many backcountry lean-tos. Check with park personnel before camping away from the established campgrounds.

BIG DEER MOUNTAIN

Distance: 1.4 mi. (2.3 km)
Elevation Change: 380 ft. ascent
Hiking Time: 50 min. (reverse 40 min.)

TO THE TRAIL: The New Discovery Campground is on the east side of Vt. 232, 4.4 mi. south of its junction with U.S. 2 east of Marshfield. From the entrance to the campground, follow the access road 0.2 mi. to a junction and bear left through a gate toward Peacham Pond. Limited roadside parking is available just past the trailhead, which is on the right side of the road, 0.5 mi. from the campground entrance.

DESCRIPTION: Leaving the road (0.0 mi.), the occasionally blue-blazed Big Deer Mountain Trail descends through a red pine plantation and a logged area to a CCC-era lean-to (0.7 mi.). Passing to the left of the shelter, the trail then ascends gently to a junction (1.1 mi.) with the Osmore Pond/Big Deer Mountain Trail. Bearing left at the junction, the trail begins a steeper ascent to reach the crest of Big Deer Mtn. (1,992 ft.) (1.3 mi.), then follows the ridge on gentle grades among giant boulders to reach a rock outcrop with a stunning view south to Lake Groton (1.4 mi.).

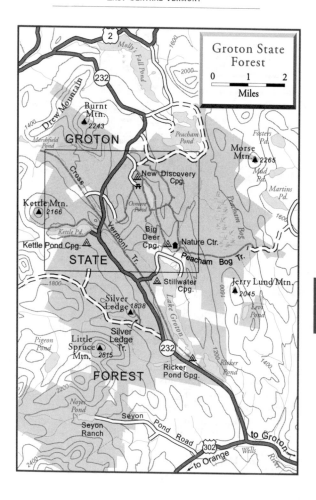

Groton State Forest

0 1 2
Miles

Molly's Fall Pond

Drew Mountain

Burnt Mtn. 2243

GROTON

Marshfield Pond

Peacham Pond

Fosters Pd.

Morse Mtn. 2265

Mud Rd.

Martins Pd.

New Discovery Cpg.

Cross

Kettle Mtn. 2166

Osmore Pond

Peacham Bog

Kettle Pd.

Kettle Pond Cpg.

Vermont Tr.

Big Deer Cpg.

Nature Ctr.

Peacham Bog Tr.

STATE

Stillwater Cpg.

Lake Groton

Jerry Lund Mtn. 2045

Levi Pond

Silver Ledge 1838

Pigeon Pond

Little Spruce Mtn. 2615

Silver Ledge Tr.

FOREST

Ricker Pond Cpg.

Ricker Pond

Noyes Pond

Seyon Pond Road

Seyon Ranch

to Groton

to Orange

Wells River

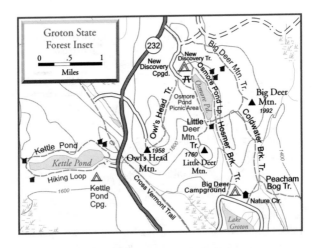

NEW DISCOVERY/OSMORE POND TRAIL

TO THE TRAIL: From the entrance to the New Discovery Campground, where some parking is available, follow the access road 0.2 mi. to a junction.

DESCRIPTION: The blue-blazed New Discovery/Osmore Pond Trail begins across the road junction to the left of the bathhouse and descends steadily through a spruce-fir stand to cross a logging road (0.3 mi.). The trail then passes through an old firewood cutting area before arriving at its terminus on the north shore of Osmore Pond at a junction with the Osmore Pond Hiking Loop.

OSMORE POND HIKING LOOP

Distance: 1.8 mi. (2.9 km)
Elevation Change: 150 ft. ascent
Hiking Time: 1 hr. either direction

To the Trail: This blue-blazed trail begins at the Osmore Pond picnic shelter, accessed through the New Discovery Campground off Vt. 232.

Description: From the shelter (0.0 mi.), the trail descends to the shore and continues southerly through the picnic area. After following the shore for some distance and passing views across the pond to Big Deer Mtn., the trail bears away from the pond and reaches a junction on the right (0.4 mi.) with the Little Deer Trail in a power line clearing. Continuing straight ahead and returning to the woods, the trail first crosses the outlet of Osmore Pond on a plank bridge, passing a spur path to the left that leads to a shoreline lean-to. The trail then passes through a wet area on puncheon built by the Vermont Youth Conservation Corps in 1997, before reaching a four-way junction (0.5 mi.).

> **Junction:** From this junction, the Osmore Pond/Big Deer Mountain Trail leads straight ahead 1.0 mi. to a vista near the summit of Big Deer Mtn. The Hosmer Brook Trail departs to the right, leading about 1.3 mi. south to the Boulder Beach access road at the north end of Lake Groton.

4

Turning to the left at the junction, the Osmore Pond Loop passes through open forest for some distance before entering deep woods and passing two lean-tos (1.0 mi., 1.4 mi.). At the north end of the pond, the trail reaches a junction on the right (1.5 mi.) with the New Discovery Campground/Osmore Pond Trail before following the shoreline back to the picnic shelter (1.8 mi.).

LITTLE DEER MOUNTAIN

Distance: 0.5 mi. (0.8 km)
Elevation Change: 280 ft. ascent
Hiking Time: 25 min. (reverse 20 min.)

To the Trail: This blue-blazed trail leaves the Osmore Pond Hiking Loop in a power line clearing, 0.4 mi. south of the picnic shelter.

DESCRIPTION: From the junction (0.0 mi.), the trail follows a power line for a short distance before bearing to the right and climbing easily through the woods. At a sharp left turn (0.2 mi.), the trail begins a steady climb to the wooded summit of Little Deer Mtn. (1,760 ft.) (0.5 mi.). The trail then continues 50 yds. further to a rock outcrop, where there is a good view to the south over Lake Groton.

OSMORE POND/
BIG DEER MOUNTAIN TRAIL

Distance: 1.0 mi. (1.6 km)
Elevation Change: 510 ft. ascent
Hiking Time: ¾ hr. (reverse ½ hr.)

DESCRIPTION: Marked with blue blazes, this trail leaves a four-way junction with the Osmore Pond Hiking Loop and Hosmer Brook Trail at the south end of Osmore Pond (0.0 mi.). The trail climbs steadily to a low ridge (0.2 mi.), crosses a wet sag on puncheon, and soon reaches a junction on the right (0.4 mi.) with the Coldwater Brook Trail from Lake Groton. The trail then slabs northerly up the mountain to arrive at its terminus at a junction (0.7 mi.) with the New Discovery/Big Deer Mountain Trail. To the right, it is a short steep climb over Big Deer Mtn. to the scenic vista south of the summit (1.0 mi.).

HOSMER BROOK TRAIL

Distance: 1.3 mi. (2.1 km)
Elevation Change: 370 ft. ascent
Hiking Time: 1 hr. (reverse ½ hr.)

ABOUT THE TRAIL: This trail provides a link between the Big Deer Campground at the north end of Lake Groton and Osmore Pond, near the New Discovery Campground. The southern trailhead is found on the Boulder Beach access

road, which leaves the east side of Vt. 232 near the north end of Lake Groton, about 5.5 mi. north of U.S. 302 and 0.3 mi. north of the entrance to the Stillwater Campground.
To the Trail: From Vt. 232 (0.0 mi.) follow the Boulder Beach access road east past the trailhead (1.3 mi.) to the Groton Nature Center (1.6 mi.) and parking.
Description: From the trailhead on the Boulder Beach access road (0.0 mi.), this blue-blazed trail bears north and gradually ascends through open forest on a woods road. Upon reaching Hosmer Brook (0.5 mi.), the trail follows its east bank upstream to a four-way junction (1.3 mi.).

> **Junction:** From this junction, the Osmore Pond/Big Deer Mountain Trail departs to the right and leads 1.0 mi. to a vista near the summit of Big Deer Mtn. To the left, the west branch of the Osmore Pond Hiking Loop leads about 0.5 mi. to the Osmore Pond Picnic Area. Straight ahead, the east branch of this trail leads 1.3 mi. around the north end of the pond to reach the same spot.

COLDWATER BROOK TRAIL

4

Distance: 2.0 mi. (3.2 km)
Elevation Change: 489 ft. ascent
Hiking Time: 1¼ hr. (reverse 1 hr.)

About the Trail: This trail follows Coldwater Brook north and links the north end of Lake Groton and the south end of Osmore Pond near Big Deer Mtn. The trailhead is found at the Groton Nature Center.
To the Trail: The Groton Nature Center is a short distance past the Big Deer Campground on the Boulder Beach access road, which leaves Vt. 232 near the north end of Lake Groton, about 5.5 mi. north of U.S. 302. The area provides access to the Coldwater Brook Trail, Hosmer Brook Trail, and Peacham Bog Trail. In addition, the center has two short loop trails, the 0.6-mi. Nature Trail and the 0.9-mi. Little Loop Trail.

DESCRIPTION: The blue-blazed Coldwater Brook Trail initially coincides with the Peacham Bog Trail, beginning at a signpost in the northeast corner of the nature center parking lot (0.0 mi.). At a junction (0.4 mi.), the Peacham Bog Trail bears right, while the Coldwater Brook Trail bears left to slab around a low knoll before passing two large boulders on the left (0.6 mi.). The trail ascends gradually through several boggy areas (0.7 mi.) and crosses two streams before reaching the stonework of an old sawmill (1.1 mi.), one of several that once used the waters of Coldwater Brook.

From the sawmill site, the trail ascends to a junction (1.2 mi.), where an unmaintained spur leads to the right. Bearing left and ascending on easy grades over occasional wet areas and rough footing, the trail reaches its terminus (2.0 mi.) on the Osmore Pond/Big Deer Mountain Trail.

Junction: To the right, the Osmore Pond/Big Deer Mountain Trail leads about 0.6 mi. to a vista near the summit of Big Deer Mtn., while to the left, it leads 0.4 mi. to a junction with the Hosmer Brook Trail. By this trail it is then 1.3 mi. south to the Boulder Beach access road and a short distance east to the nature center.

OWL'S HEAD MOUNTAIN

Distance: 1.9 mi. (3.1 km)
Elevation Change: 360 ft. ascent
Hiking Time: 1¼ hr. (reverse 1 hr.)

ABOUT THE TRAIL: Although not high, this mountain with its rocky summit offers outstanding panoramic views. A 1.9-mi. foot trail leads to the summit, while a 1.0-mi. auto road, open to cars only in summer, leads to a parking area and summit trail 0.25 mi. from the top. A drive up the road and the short walk to the summit make a perfect hike for children. Alternatively, a loop a little longer than 4.5 mi.

may be hiked using the trail described, the auto road, and a 1.5-mi. walk on Vt. 232 and the trailhead access road.

To the Trail: This blue-blazed trail begins on the road to the Osmore Pond picnic shelter. From the entrance to the New Discovery Campground on Vt. 232, continue south on the highway a short distance to the second left-hand turn. Follow the dirt road east, bearing right at a fork after 0.25 mi., before reaching the trailhead on the right, about 0.5 mi. from Vt. 232. Limited roadside parking is available.

Description: From the access road (0.0 mi.), the trail follows an old road that linked the picnic shelter with the maintenance area to the north and turns left (0.1 mi.) into the woods just before reaching the maintenance area. The trail then follows a level path under a power line (0.3 mi.) before starting a gentle ascent. Climbing steadily and then more steeply to attain the ridgeline (1.2 mi.), the trail passes over a rock ledge, descends to the west into a small dip, and then ascends to the Owl's Head picnic area parking lot (1.6 mi.). The trail then climbs rock stairs on steep terrain to the open summit (1,958 ft.) (1.9 mi.) with its airy stone shelter. From the summit, there are good views of Lake Groton, Kettle Pond, the White Mountains, and Green Mountains. No camping is allowed on Owl's Head.

Kettle Pond Hiking Loop

Distance: 3.2 mi. (5.2 km)
Elevation Change: minor
Hiking Time: 1½ hr. either direction

To the Trail: This trail begins at the large Kettle Pond parking area on the west side of Vt. 232, 7.1 mi. north of U.S. 302 and 4.0 mi. south of U.S. 2. Although there is a sign for the parking area, no sign indicates the presence of the trailhead.

Description: This blue-blazed trail begins at the northwest corner of the parking lot (0.0 mi.). Following a level grade, the trail divides (0.2 mi.) a short distance before reaching the pond. At the junction, a spur to the left leads a short distance to the pond's edge. Bearing right at the junction, the trail follows the north side of the pond, passes two lean-tos, and continues through the woods to a left turn (0.5 mi.). The trail then passes through a wet area to the shore. The trail continues along the shoreline, passing through an area with large boulders at the site of an old camp (0.8 mi.) and past a lean-to (1.2 mi.).

The trail then bears right and shortly passes another lean-to (1.7 mi.). Circling the west end of Kettle Pond, the trail traverses some wet and rocky areas. After passing a private camp, the trail climbs over and around some large boulders and reaches another lean-to. The trail remains in the vicinity of the shoreline for a distance, before reaching its terminus at the Kettle Pond Group Camping Area (3.0 mi.). Straight ahead via the access road, it is a short distance back to Vt. 232, then a short distance north to the Kettle Pond parking area.

PEACHAM BOG

Distance: 2.8 mi. (4.5 km)
Elevation Change: 433 ft. ascent
Hiking Time: 1 hr. 40 min. (reverse 1 hr. 25 min.)

ABOUT THE TRAIL: The Peacham Bog natural area contains a 125-acre peat bog, the second largest in the state and one of two documented raised (or domed) bogs in Vermont. Because of the fragile nature of the bog environment, to say nothing of the possibility of losing one's way, the hiker should remain on the trail in the bog. Follow directions to the Groton Nature Center described in the Coldwater Brook Trail on page 241.
DESCRIPTION: Marked with blue blazes, the Peacham Bog Trail begins at a signpost in the northeast corner of the na-

ture center parking area, and coincides with the Coldwater Brook Trail for a short distance. From the sign (0.0 mi.), the trail climbs a steep embankment and then descends gradually through the woods to a junction (0.4 mi.) where the Coldwater Brook Trail departs to the left.

Bearing right at the junction, the Peacham Bog Trail soon crosses Coldwater Brook on a bridge, before following it downstream for a short distance. Resuming an easterly direction, the trail begins an easy ascent, crosses a logging road (0.7 mi.), and continues along on variously rocky and wet footing. After crossing a small stream (1.5 mi.) and cresting a low ridge, the trail descends on easy grades into a shallow sag (2.4 mi.). The trail then passes by a leg of the bog, which has been dammed by beavers (2.6 mi.), and returns to the woods briefly before reaching the bog itself (2.8 mi.). The trail crosses the southeast corner of the bog on a boardwalk and bridge for about 250 yds. before entering the woods again and reaching its terminus at a junction with a multipurpose trail. This trail, not maintained for hiking, leads about 1.5 mi. east to exit Groton State Forest and ends on a public road near Martin's Pond, south of the hamlet of Green Bay.

4

SILVER LEDGE TRAIL

Distance: 0.6 mi. (0.9 km)
Elevation Change: 500 ft. ascent
Hiking Time: ¾ hr. (reverse ½ hr.)

ABOUT THE TRAIL: Marked with blue blazes, the trail begins on a logging road that leaves the west side of Vt. 232 1.0 mi. north of the Ricker Pond Camping Area and 3.5 mi. south of the Kettle Pond parking area. The trailhead is on the right side of the logging road, 0.7 mi. from Vt. 232. A grassy pull-off can accommodate two vehicles, while additional parking is available along the roadside.
DESCRIPTION: From the logging road (0.0 mi.), the Silver

Ledge Trail bears right into the woods, quickly crosses Beaver Brook, and then begins a winding climb through a mixed hardwood-softwood forest. After passing a ledge (0.5 mi.) with a vista of Lake Groton with the White Mountains in the distance, the trail quickly reaches the summit of Silver Ledge (1,838 ft.) (0.6 mi.). Two large boulders are found nearby, and there is a limited view of Lake Groton through the trees.

•••••••••••••••••

CROSS VERMONT TRAIL

When completed, the Cross Vermont Trail (CVT) will be Vermont's first west-to-east, long-distance, multiuse trail—spanning 75 mi. from Lake Champlain in Burlington to the Connecticut River in Wells River. Trail founders envision the trail as a safe, scenic link between villages, public places, schools, playgrounds, and state parks.

West of Montpelier, the trail will follow existing and future bike and recreation paths as well as on-road routes. Portions of the former Montpelier and Wells River Railroad bed will be used to develop the trail east of Montpelier.

The 10-year-old Cross Vermont Trail Association, a grassroots nonprofit organization, has completed and designated 28 mi. of the trail. The three best sections for walking are outlined here. For more information, contact the Cross Vermont Trail Coordinator, c/o Cross Vermont Trail Association, 81 East Hill Road, Plainfield, Vermont 05667; georges@together.net.

EAST MONTPELIER

This signed and designated 1.6-mi. section of the CVT passes through land the Montpelier–Wells River Railroad once traveled. Walkers, cyclists, horseback riders, nordic skiers, snowshoers, and snowmobilers enjoy the trail. Trail users should yield to snowmobiles and horseback riders. The trailhead is on the east side of Vt. 14, 0.8 mi. south of its junction with U.S. 2 in East Montpelier. The trail ends at the East Montpelier/Plainfield town line, where there is a gate with no trespassing signs on it.

GROTON STATE FOREST

This 9.2-mi. section of the CVT can be accessed from several places in Groton State Forest. Parking areas are at Ricker Pond and Kettle Pond, found on the east and west sides of Vt. 232, respectively.

The trail is shown as a class 4 road on USGS quads and in DeLorme's *Vermont Atlas & Gazetteer*. The signed and designated segment of the trail reverts to private ownership at either end of the state forest, where the boundaries are clearly marked. Walkers, cyclists, horseback riders, nordic skiers, snowshoers, and snowmobilers enjoy the trail. During winter, trail users should yield to snowmobiles; during summer, trail users should yield to horseback riders.

As it travels through the state forest, the trail passes by historic railroad markers, through a boreal-transitional forest, and along glacial ponds and lakes, including Marshfield Pond, Kettle Pond, Lake Groton, and Ricker Pond. The Lake Groton Nature Center can be accessed via a side road. One of the highlights of the trail is a view of Big Deer Mtn. with its sheer granite cliffs.

Southeast of the state forest boundary, the trail continues as a bicycling route south on Vt. 232, then east on U.S. 302. After passing the Upper Valley Grill, the trail leaves the highway at Little Italy Road, where the route rejoins the old rail bed. For the next 3.0 mi., the Cross Vermont Trail passes through a mixed spruce, birch, and beech forest, with views of farms, ponds, and bogs. The route ends at the Mills Memorial Ballfield in South Ryegate, where there is ample parking.

WELLS RIVER

Newbury and Wells River host 1.75 mi. of the CVT. Two points on U.S. 302 provide access to the trail. A western (recommended) trailhead with ample parking is on the Ryegate-Newbury town line on the north side of U.S. 302, next to the Curious Cow, Too gift shop. Eastern access is just west of the state fishing access, where the Wells River comes closest to U.S. 302.

The Wells River CVT is remarkably diverse along its short length, passing through a large white pine and eastern hemlock stand, as well as wetlands and bogs with viewing benches and wildlife habitat boxes. The trail segment is divided in the middle by the I-91 bridge over the Wells River. Travel under the bridge is rough going (similar to a steep talus slope), but a path suitable for bicycles is scheduled to be constructed in 2002.

Two trails in the area intersect with the CVT. West of the I-91 bridge is the Boltonville Nature Trail, approximately 1.0 mi. in length. It explores the upland slopes and riparian floodplain of the Wells River. This trail makes a junction with the CVT at two points from the north. East of the I-91 bridge is the Blue Mountain Nature Trail, which is also approximately 1.0 mi. in length and which joins the CVT from the north. This trail passes through upland hemlock and spruce-fir forest and offers beautiful views of the Wells River via cliffs and ledges.

REGION 5

Northwest
Vermont

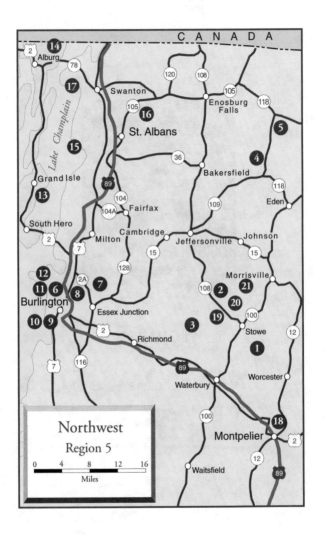

CANADA

Alburg
2
14
78
120
108
105
118
17
Swanton
105
16
Enosburg
Falls
5
St. Albans
36
4
Bakersfield
15
Grand Isle
89
118
Eden
13
104
104A
Fairfax
109
South Hero
Cambridge
Johnson
2
Milton
Jeffersonville
7
15
15
Morrisville
21
128
12
2A
7
108
2
11
6
8
20
10
9
Essex Junction
19
3
Stowe
1
2
Richmond
12
7
116
89
Waterbury
Worcester
18
Montpelier
Northwest
Region 5
100
2
0   4   8   12   16
Miles
12
Waitsfield
89

Lake Champlain
Burlington

REGION 5
Northwest Vermont

This region is a land of contrasts, featuring Lake Champlain in the west and the Worcester Range in the east. Lake Champlain, with its scenic shoreline and islands, reaches its greatest width in northern Vermont. Along or near the shore are numerous low hills, where fossil remains and traces of old shorelines are reminders of glacial times when a deeper and wider Lake Champlain was an arm of an inland sea. Farther east, along the valley floor, is a fragmented chain of low mountains, which were once part of the Green Mountains. To the south, in Addison County, these hills become more organized and form the first range of the Green Mountains.

The northern Green Mountains run south to north near the eastern margin of the region. In approximately 20 mi., they rise from their lowest point (326 ft.) at a water gap cut by the Winooski River to their highest elevation (4,395 ft.) at the Chin of Mt. Mansfield. In the northern part of the region, the main range continues from the Lamoille River northward into Quebec, becoming the Sutton Mountains. A significant subrange, called the Cold Hollow Mountains, parallels the main range on the west from the Waterville area northward for several miles.

The third range of the Green Mountains lies to the east of Vt. 100. After originating in the Sherburne-Stockbridge area, the range is known as the Northfield Mountains south of the Winooski River, continues as the Worcester Mountain Range north of the Winooski, and is known as the Lowell Mountains north of the Lamoille River.

WORCESTER MOUNTAINS

The Worcester Mountain Range is a prominent ridge rising to the east of the main range of the Green Mountains. Geographically, it is the third range of the Green Mountains (USGS Montpelier, Middlesex, Stowe, Mt. Worcester, Morrisville). Of the dozen or so prominent peaks in the range, Mt. Hunger (3,586 ft.) is the most conspicuous and best known—perhaps because of its bald south summit. However, the highest point (3,642 ft.) is a nameless peak sometimes referred to as Mt. Putnam, located about 2.8 mi. north of Mt. Hunger's south summit

From White Rock Mtn. north, much of the range is included in Putnam State Forest, while the northernmost peak, Elmore Mtn., is in Elmore State Park. The Vermont Department of Forests, Parks, and Recreation along with the Vermont Youth Conservation Corps have made major improvements and additions to the Worcester Range hiking trails in recent years, linking the Mt. Hunger summits with Stowe Pinnacle and Worcester Mtn. to the north.

Once a well-kept secret, the range now is almost as popular as the more prominent peaks in the Green Mountain Range. To minimize erosion along the fragile high-elevation terrain of the range, the Worcester Mountain Range trail system is closed by the state of Vermont between mid-April and Memorial Day.

5

ELMORE MOUNTAIN

Distance: 2.1 mi. (3.4 km)
Elevation Change: 1,450 ft. ascent
Hiking Time: 1¾ hr. (reverse 1 hr.)

ABOUT THE TRAIL: Although it is one of the lowest peaks in the Worcester Mountains, Elmore Mtn. (USGS Morrisville) may offer the most varied and interesting views, due to its isolated location at the north end of the range and its commanding view of the pastoral Lamoille River valley. A trail to the summit and its well-maintained fire tower begins in Elmore State Park, which has camping and day-use facilities (including a beach for an after-hike swim), with a fee charged in season.

TO THE TRAIL: The entrance to Elmore State Park is on the west side of Vt. 12, a short distance north of the village of Lake Elmore. Park in the state park campground. To reach the trailhead, walk straight ahead from the contact station along the access road to the campground.

DESCRIPTION: After passing the camping area on the right (0.0 mi.), the trail ascends along an old CCC road (0.0 mi.) and continues through a switchback. The road reaches a chained gate near a picnic shelter (0.5 mi.), where blue blazing for the Elmore Mountain Trail begins.

The trail continues on the road through the gate and ascends to the south, passing near some beaver ponds. Near the end of the road, the trail turns sharply right (1.0 mi.) at a blue arrow and sign on a tree. Following a well-worn path through open woods and climbing steadily in places, the trail reaches a grassy clearing, a short distance below the ridge (1.9 mi.). The cellar hole is from the old fire lookout's cabin. Here, overlooking Lake Elmore, there is a good view to the east.

To the right, on the west side of the clearing, the trail begins a steep and winding climb over rocks and ledges,

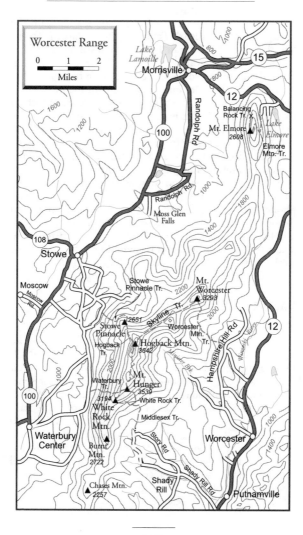

Worcester Range

0   1   2
Miles

Lake
Lamoille

Morrisville

Randolph Rd

100

15

12

Balancing
Rock Tr.

Mt. Elmore
2608

Lake
Elmore

Elmore
Mtn. Tr.

1600

1200

Randolph Rd

Moss Glen
Falls

108

Stowe

Moscow

Moscow Rd

Stowe
Pinnacle Tr.

Mt.
Worcester
3293

Skyline Tr.

2651

Stowe
Pinnacle

Worcester
Mtn.
Tr.

Hampshire Hill Rd

12

Hogback
Tr.

Hogback Mtn.
3642

Waterbury
Tr.

Mt.
Hunger
3539

White Rock Tr.

3194

White
Rock
Mtn.

Middlesex Tr.

100

Waterbury
Center

Burnt
Mtn.
2722

Ston Rd

Worcester

Shady Rill Rd

1000

5

Chases Mtn.
2257

Shady
Rill

Putnamville

soon reaching a level area and a junction, where, on the right, the Balanced Rock Trail leaves to the north. To the left, the Elmore Mountain Trail continues about 100 ft. to the old fire tower on the summit (2,608 ft.) (2.1 mi.). From the tower or, to a lesser extent, from the open rocks to the south, there are impressive views of the main range of the Green Mountains from the Jay Peak area south to the Lincoln Ridge. The high ridge of the Worcester Range may be seen extending southward, with Waterbury Reservoir lying in the valley to the west. To the north lies the Lamoille River Valley; Burke Mtn. and various peaks in the Northeast Kingdom may be seen to the east.

A fire lookout station was established atop Elmore Mtn. in 1938 to 1940, with the construction of a telephone line, cabin, and the existing 60-ft. enclosed cab Aeromotor steel tower. The station remained active until 1974. In 1983, the lookout's cabin fell victim to arson. The tower was repaired and repainted in 1987 and added to the National Historic Lookout Register in 1995.

BALANCED ROCK TRAIL

The blue-blazed Balanced Rock Trail begins at a junction with the Elmore Mountain Trail just north of the Elmore Mtn. fire tower. From the junction (0.0 mi.), the trail follows easy grades just east of the ridgeline to a cleared view to the east (0.1 mi.). Continuing in the woods for some distance, the trail then crosses to the west side of the ridge (0.3 mi.) and soon reaches an open rock area (0.4 mi.), where there is an excellent view of the Stowe Valley and the Mt. Mansfield area. Quickly returning to the east side of the ridge, the trail descends through the woods to another vantage point overlooking Lake Elmore. The trail then continues a short distance further to the cigar-shaped Balanced Rock (0.5 mi.), a boulder left perched on the ridge by a long-ago glacier.

STOWE PINNACLE
STOWE PINNACLE TRAIL

Distance: 1.4 mi. (2.3 km)
Elevation Change: 1,520 ft. ascent
Hiking Time: 1½ hr. (reverse 1 hr.)

ABOUT THE TRAIL: From this prominent spur (2,651 ft.) on the northwest side of Hogback Mtn. (USGS Stowe), there are excellent views of Mt. Mansfield and other peaks in the main range of the Green Mountains, as well as of the Stowe Valley. The trail also provides links to the Hogback Trail, which ascends to the ridge of the Worcester Range.

TO THE TRAIL: From Vt. 100, about 1.5 mi. south of the village of Stowe and 8.1 mi. from I-89, turn east on Gold Brook Road just north and opposite the Nichols Farm Lodge and Gold Brook Campground (0.0 mi.). Bear left at the first fork (0.3 mi.) and follow Gold Brook upstream straight through an intersection at Covered Bridge Road (1.2 mi.). Continue on the road to a T-intersection (1.9 mi.) and turn right onto Upper Hollow Road. Continue to a small parking area on the left for several cars (2.5 mi.) where the signed trailhead is located.

DESCRIPTION: From the rear of the parking area (0.0 mi.), the blue-blazed and well-worn trail passes from an abandoned pasture into a mixed hardwood forest and soon crosses a stream (0.5 mi.). The trail begins a steeper climb over a series of wide switchbacks before reaching a junction, from which an unmarked spur trail leads left for 100 ft. to a ledge and a view of the valley below. Continuing straight at the junction, the trail soon reaches a notch just below Stowe Pinnacle (0.9 mi.), then follows the contour of the mountain to the south side of the summit. Here the trail reaches a junction with the Hogback Trail (description follows), which departs to the left to ascend 1.0 mi. to the Skyline Trail and the ridgeline of the Worcester Range. Continuing to the right on easy grades

5

over rocky outcrops and through scrub growth, the Stowe Pinnacle Trail soon reaches the open summit (1.4 mi.).

HOGBACK TRAIL

Distance: 1.0 mi. (1.6 km)
Elevation Change: 920 ft. ascent
Hiking Time: ¾ hr. (reverse ½ hr.)

ABOUT THE TRAIL: Originally, this blue-blazed trail was the northern leg of the Skyline Trail until the lengthy ridge-top section from Hogback Mtn. north to Mt. Worcester was completed. The trail provides access to the ridgeline from the northwestern side of the range.

TO THE TRAIL: The Hogback Trail starts at a signed junction on the Stowe Pinnacle Trail, about 1.0 mi. from the Stowe Pinnacle trailhead on Upper Hollow Road (page 257).

DESCRIPTION: The Hogback Trail departs the junction (0.0 mi.) to the southeast, passing through stands of hemlock and large birch to make a relatively flat approach to the high northwestern flank of Hogback Mtn. The trail then makes a steep ascent, using many switchbacks that wind between large trees and scrambles across ledges to eventually level out in a spruce-fir transition zone atop a western spur of the mountain (0.5 mi.). Resuming a steep ascent over the rocks, the trail passes limited views toward Mt. Mansfield before reaching the summit of Hogback Mtn. (0.9 mi.) and then its terminus at a signed junction with the Skyline Trail (1.0 m.). From the junction, it is about 3.0 mi. south to Mt. Hunger's southern summit, and 6.0 mi. north to Mt. Worcester.

MOUNT HUNGER

Although the north summit (3,586 ft.) of this popular mountain (USGS Stowe) is heavily wooded, the bald south summit (3,539 ft.) is famous for its excellent views of the Green Mountains and the White Mountains. There are direct routes to the south summit from the west (Waterbury Trail) and east (Middlesex Trail) and indirect routes from the north (Skyline Trail) and south (White Rock Trail). The Worcester Trail, which ascended from the northeast, has been abandoned and is no longer included in this guide.

As a result of a long-ago forest fire, the south summit has been left an exposed and barren outcrop, similar to the higher summits found to the west in the main range of the Green Mountains. Although large black spruce and balsam fir trees engulf the north summit, these same species are dwarfed on the south summit from wind exposure, in a state known as krummholz, or crooked wood.

From the summit, nearly every peak in the main range of the Green Mountains is visible, from Whiteface Mtn. in the north to Killington Peak in the south. A number of Adirondack peaks are visible to the west beyond Lake Champlain. To the east, Mt. Washington and the Presidential Range, Mt. Moosilauke, and the Franconia Range can be seen in the distance; Burke Mtn. and Bald Mtn. are among the numerous northeast Vermont mountains nearer at hand. Directly to the south are most of the other peaks in the Worcester Range.

WATERBURY TRAIL

Distance: 2.2 mi. (3.5 km)
Elevation Change: 2,290 ft. ascent
Hiking Time: 2¼ hr. (reverse 1¼ hr.)

ABOUT THE TRAIL: This blue-blazed trail starts north of Waterbury Center and ascends the western flank of the mountain to reach its south summit.

TO THE TRAIL: From I-89 exit 10, take Vt. 100 north (0.0 mi.) and turn right on Howard Avenue (2.9. mi.). Continue straight through a four-way intersection with a stop sign (3.2 mi.) to another stop sign. Turn left on Maple Street then turn right on Loomis Hill Road

(3.4 mi.). Continue uphill. Just after the pavement ends (5.3 mi.), the road forks. Bear left onto Sweet Road and continue to the signed trailhead and a parking lot on the right (6.7 mi.). Howard Avenue leaves Vt. 100 6.8 mi. from the Vt. 100/Vt. 108 junction in Stowe.

DESCRIPTION: From the trailhead at the back of the parking area (0.0 mi.), the trail begins a moderate climb through a mixed hardwood forest, passing around and over interesting rock formations. The trail passes near a stream (0.6 mi.), then continues its climb along steep grades, aided by stretches of rock stairs. The trail then enters a birch forest and levels off, following the contour of the mountain to reach a series of waterfalls (1.0 mi.). The trail makes a short ascent to the left of the falls before turning to cross the stream and then continue its steep climb along a series of switchbacks. Care should be taken when walking along the exposed rock surfaces, which can be very slippery in wet weather. Eventually, the trail crosses a stream on a primitive log bridge (1.8 mi.) before entering the spruce-fir transition zone where scrambles over rocky ledges become more common.

The trail then reaches a signed junction (2.0 mi.) where the White Rock Trail, which leads 1.0 mi. to the summit of White Rock Mtn., branches to the right. From the junction, the Waterbury Trail continues straight ahead, ascending steeply on open rocks to the south summit (2.2 mi.) and a junction with the Skyline and Middlesex Trails.

MIDDLESEX TRAIL

Distance: 2.8 mi. (4.5 km)
Elevation Change: 1,900 ft. ascent
Hiking Time: 2½ hr. (reverse 1½ hr.)

ABOUT THE TRAIL: Most of this blue-blazed trail follows the route of a carriage road built in 1877 by the proprietors of the Pavilion Hotel in Montpelier to transport guests up the mountain. A short trail, complete with wooden stairways to ease the steep climb over the ledges, connected the end of the road and the summit. This trail ascends the mountain from the east.

TO THE TRAIL: From Montpelier, follow Vt. 12 north past the Wrightsville Dam to a junction on the left with Shady Rill Road (0.0 mi.). Follow this road westerly up a long hill and straight through a junction in the hamlet of Shady Rill (1.2 mi.). Continue to an offset four corners (2.2 mi.) and turn right onto Story Road. Bear left onto Chase Road (2.6 mi.) and left again onto North Bear Swamp Road (3.4 mi.). After passing a private driveway on the right through a broad field (4.3 mi.) and a second small road to the right (4.7 mi.), a small sign points to a large parking area on the right (4.8 mi.).

DESCRIPTION: From the parking area (0.0 mi.), the trail passes through the woods for a short distance before joining a woods road and passing through an iron gate. Ascending on easy grades through a birch forest, the trail reaches a stream crossing (0.6 mi.) before turning to the west and beginning a moderate ascent. The trail climbs to a marked junction on the left with the White Rock Trail (1.6 mi.).

> **Junction:** This trail leads to a spur to the summit cone of White Rock Mtn. and to the Waterbury Trail 0.2 mi. below the Mt. Hunger summit.

At the junction, the Middlesex Trail swings to the right and ascends more steeply to an outlook (2.3 mi.). Continuing at the base of a series of ledges and coming to an apparent dead end, the trail suddenly swings sharply to the left and up a ledge (2.5 mi.). The trail then climbs steeply in the open to the south summit of Mt. Hunger, following blue blazes on rocks and trees to a signed junction with the Waterbury Trail and Skyline Trail (2.8 mi.). Care should be taken to note where the trail comes out on the summit because blazing is sometimes obscure.

5

WHITE ROCK MOUNTAIN

Distance: 1.5 mi. (2.4 km)
Elevation Change: 630 ft. ascent
Hiking Time: 1 hr. (reverse ¾ hr.)

ABOUT THE TRAIL: This blue-blazed trail leads to the summit of White Rock Mtn. (3,194 ft.) from both the Middlesex Trail (ascending the ridge from the east) and the Waterbury Trail (ascending from the west). Using these trails, it is possible to make a loop hike of Mt. Hunger. The White Rock Trail traverses a variety of terrain and can be challenging.

DESCRIPTION (FROM THE EAST): The White Rocks Trail turns left off the Middlesex Trail 1.6. mi. from the Middlesex Trail parking lot. From the junction (0.0 mi.), the White Rock Trail ascends steeply through the woods past several views to an unmarked junction (0.7 mi.).

> **Junction:** To the left, a blue-blazed spur trail leads 0.2 mi. around the south side of the peak before climbing through a short steep notch to the crown of White Rock Mtn. The elevation gain from the Middlesex Trail junction to the summit of White Rocks Mtn. is 570 ft.

The White Rock Trail takes the right fork and continues north, descending to a wet area (0.9 mi.). The trail then climbs around numerous boulders at or near the ridge to its terminus at the Waterbury Trail (1.5 mi.). To the right it is a steep 0.2-mi. ascent to the south summit of Mt. Hunger. From the Middlesex Trail to the summit of Mt. Hunger is 915 ft., the White Rocks Trail ascends 915 ft.

SKYLINE TRAIL

Distance: 9.2 mi. (14.8 km)
Elevation Change: 2,058 ft. ascent
Hiking Time: 5½ hr. (reverse 6 hr.)

ABOUT THE TRAIL: Constructed by the Vermont Youth Conservation Corps in the late 1980s, this trail traverses the spine of the Worcester Range to connect Mt. Hunger in the south with Worcester Mtn. in the north. The trail is marked with blue blazes, or rock cairns in open areas, but can occasionally be obscure in the absence of a well-worn treadway. The Hogback Trail, which connects the Skyline Trail with Stowe Pinnacle, provides a shorter hiking route and access from the west side of the ridge. The trail here is described northbound from the south summit of Mt. Hunger.

DESCRIPTION: From the south summit of Mt. Hunger (0.0 mi., USGS Stowe) at the junction of the Waterbury and Middlesex Trails, the Skyline Trail leaves to the north at a sign, following the exposed rock ridge. After making a brief descent to the east, the trail climbs to regain the ridge (0.1 mi.), soon reaching an unmarked junction where a spur trail to the south reveals views of Mt. Hunger as well as Camel's Hump and Mt. Abraham to the south and southwest. The trail skirts the base of a series of ledges and gradually ascends to the north summit of Mt. Hunger (0.6 mi.). Here, as well as at other points along the ridge, gaps in the canopy of balsam fir can be attributed to the cyclical succession of this species. Known as fir waves, older trees exposed to the wind are blown over, opening up space and light for saplings to take root. These gaps also provide natural vistas to both the east and west, the inspiration for the name of the trail.

Continuing to the north, the trail descends steadily into a saddle and eventually reaches an unmarked junction (1.1 mi.) where the closed Worcester Trail (not to be confused with the Worcester Mountain Trail, page 264) once ascended Mt. Hunger from the east. Bearing to the left, the Skyline Trail continues along moderate grades atop the ridge, winding over puncheon through wet and marshy terrain. The trail then begins an ascent, occasionally scrambling over exposed rocks, to reach a spur trail to the east leading to an impressive vista and an informal trail register (2.4 mi.).

5

From this point the trail quickly climbs through a horseshoe-shaped rock formation and continues along the ridge to reach the highest point in the Worcester Range on the wooded summit of an unnamed mountain (3,642 ft.) (2.8 mi.). After a short descent, the trail reaches a junction (3.0 mi.) where the Hogback Trail departs to the left and descends about 1.0 mi. to the Stowe Pinnacle Trail. Bearing right at the junction and dropping steeply, the Skyline Trail zigzags through interesting rock formations, eventually reaching an outcropping with excellent views to the north (3.7 mi.).

The trail continues atop the ridge, with modest changes in elevation, before finally starting a steady climb, leading first to a false summit (3,278 ft.) (5.4 mi.) and then the true summit (3,477 ft.) (6.0 mi.) of a nameless peak (USGS Mt. Worcester). The trail descends into a saddle (7.7 mi.) and, after another level section, begins a final ascent up the southwest ridge of Mt. Worcester. Gradual climbing soon gives way to a more laborious approach over boulders and rock outcroppings along the west side of the ridge before the trail reaches the exposed rock summit (9.2 mi.). Mt. Worcester is the northern terminus of the Skyline Trail; to the east, the blue-blazed Worcester Mountain Trail descends 2.5 mi. to a public road in the town of Worcester.

WORCESTER MOUNTAIN

Distance: 2.5 mi. (4.0 km)
Elevation Change: 1,970 ft. ascent
Hiking Time: 2¼ hr. (reverse 1¼ hr.)

ABOUT THE TRAIL: Located in the northwest corner of the town of Worcester, the summit (3,293 ft., USGS Mount Worcester) offers good views of the Green Mountains, the Lamoille Valley, and the northern White Mountains.
TO THE TRAIL: From the town hall in Worcester (0.0 mi.), continue north on Vt. 12 a very short distance and take

the first left onto Minister Brook Road. Follow this road west to Hampshire Hill Road (1.5 mi.).

Turn right on Hampshire Hill Road and ascend steadily. After passing Hancock Brook Road, which doubles back to the right (3.8 mi.), veer left into a narrow lane immediately after crossing Hancock Brook (3.9 mi.) and just before a small, red remodeled schoolhouse. Continue up the lane and bear right by a mobile home on the left (4.0 mi.), bypassing a private drive straight ahead. Continue past an overgrown road to the right to a clearing with ample parking (4.1 mi.).

DESCRIPTION: From the clearing (0.0 mi.), the blue-blazed Worcester Mountain Trail begins near the Putnam State Forest sign and follows the course of an old road northwest into the woods. Soon crossing a stream, the trail bears right at a woods road junction as indicated by a small sign, bypassing a more distinct woods road leaving to the left. The trail crosses two small streams, eventually assuming a course parallel to Hancock Brook for some distance. Passing a small unmarked spur to the right and bearing left (0.6 mi.), the trail reaches a level, grassy area. The trail then crosses another stream (0.8 mi.) before beginning a moderate ascent, then makes another stream crossing (1.1 mi.) and then passes between two large boulders (1.3 mi.). The trail then makes three more stream crossings before beginning a steeper ascent towards the ridge crest.

The trail eases its ascent at a shallow sag (2.2 mi.) where it turns sharply back to the left, although a partially obstructed dead-end path continues straight ahead. Now following blue blazes mostly on the rocks, the trail begins a rough, steep ascent, at times following a beautiful quartz vein in the rocks, through thick scrub to the small open summit of Mt. Worcester (2.5 mi.). The view here includes the main range of the Green Mountains to the west with the Stowe Valley in the foreground, the southern Worcester Range, and the White Mountains in the distance to the east. From the summit, the blue-blazed Skyline

5

Trail begins a long traverse of the high ridge of the Worcester Range, eventually ending some 9 mi. to the south atop Mt. Hunger.

MOSS GLEN FALLS

Distance: 0.4 mi. (0.6 km)
Elevation Change: 150 ft. ascent
Hiking Time: 20 min. (reverse ¼ hr.)

ABOUT THE TRAIL: This attractive falls, owned by the state of Vermont, is located in the northeast corner of Stowe. It should not be confused with the spectacular falls of the same name in Granville Gulf in Granville, Vermont.

TO THE TRAIL: From Vt. 100, 3.1 mi. north of the intersection of Vt. 100 and Vt. 108 in Stowe village, turn right onto Randolph Road (0.0 mi.). At the next fork, turn right again (0.4 mi.) onto the gravel Moss Glen Falls Road and continue to a parking lot on the left (0.9 mi.) at a bend in the road before crossing Moss Glen Brook.

DESCRIPTION: From the parking lot, the trail proceeds generally southeast through forest dominated by hemlock trees, then turns to follow the stream. The trail makes a short steep ascent to the first of several viewpoints into the bowl of the falls before continuing its climb and reaching a terminus on an old woods road (0.4 mi.). Note: Extreme caution should be exercised when viewing the falls from the adjacent ledges.

•••••••••••••••••

STERLING FALLS GORGE

Distance: 3.1 mi. (5.0 km)
Elevation Change: 700 ft. ascent
Hiking Time: 2 hr. either direction

ABOUT THE TRAIL: Sterling Falls Gorge (USGS Sterling Mtn.) is located in the northeast corner of the town of

Stowe at the former site of the High Bridge Mill (1860–1920). The gorge lies within the 1,600-acre Watson Forest purchased by the town of Stowe in 1996. Sterling Brook bisects the property, entering it at roughly 3,600 ft. in elevation, and then falling nearly 2,000 ft. A trail system is being developed by the Stowe Conservation Commission; there is currently an interpretive trail to the gorge with a small historical display. A loop around the gorge is possible using two existing trails.

To the Trail: To reach the gorge, follow Vt. 100 north from its junction with Vt. 108 in the village of Stowe (0.0 mi.). Bear left onto Stagecoach Road where Vt. 100 turns right (1.8 mi.), then turn left again onto Sterling Valley Road (3.4 mi.). Bypassing roads to the left and right, follow Sterling Valley Road straight to its end at the gorge parking lot (8.0 mi.).

Description: From the parking lot, the Sterling Gorge Trail follows the course of the brook west, bears left at a junction, crosses the brook, then ascends for a distance before turning sharply right and recrossing the brook. Now becoming the Basin Trail, the path descends north of the brook to reach a junction, where a spur leads back to the Sterling Gorge Trail. The Basin Trail continues east, reaching its terminus at a T-junction on the Catamount Trail. From the right at the junction, it is a short distance back to the parking area.

•••••••••••••••

5

LITTLE RIVER AREA

The Little River area of the Mt. Mansfield State Forest includes more than 10,000 acres of mountainous terrain, bounded on the east by Waterbury Reservoir and on the west by Woodward and Ricker Mtns. (USGS Bolton Mtn., Waterbury). Little River State Park lies within the state forest and straddles Stevenson Brook on the west shore of the reservoir. Established in 1962, the park offers camping facilities but is not open for day-use beyond the hiking trails described below. In season, a fee is charged for day-use of the hiking trails in the park. The park makes a good base camp for hiking in the greater Waterbury-Stowe area. During the summer months, a swim in the reservoir is just the right thing to cool off after a hike. A state-run beach and picnic area is available for day-use off Vt. 100 in Waterbury Center.

The Little River trails generally follow former town roads, some of which are now used for logging roads and snowmobile trails as well as for hiking. The trails are good for walking, cross-country skiing, and snowshoeing. Mountain biking is allowed on some trails. The trails are marked with blue paint blazes. The trail system in the Little River area is accessible from the vicinity of Waterbury Dam on the south side and from Moscow (a settlement on the south side of Stowe) on the north side.

In November 1927, Vermont was inundated by torrential rains, which caused widespread flooding and destruction in almost every major watershed in the state. Waterbury Dam was constructed as a flood control project on the Little River by the Civilian Conservation Corps (CCC) between 1934 and 1938. Below the dam, on the west side of the access road, only a few stone chimneys remain to identify the location of 80 buildings in the camp, which served as the living facilities for the 2,000 men who worked on construction of the dam.

Lying to the west of the reservoir, the Little River area embraces the drainage basins of Stevenson Brook and Cotton Brook. In the late 1700s, settlers began clearing the area for farms, and it became well populated in the nineteenth century. The inhabitants eked out a meager living from subsistence farming and logging, but depletion of the thin soil, the harsh environment, and better economic opportunities elsewhere led to gradual depopulation of the

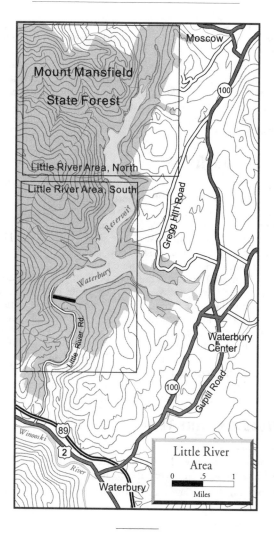

Moscow

100

Mount Mansfield

State Forest

Little River Area, North

Little River Area, South

Reservoir

Waterbury

Gregg Hill Road

Little River Rd

Waterbury
Center

100

Guptil Road

Winooski

89

2

River

Waterbury

Little River
Area

0   .5   1

Miles

5

area. The settlement was almost totally abandoned when the land was acquired for the construction of Waterbury Dam. Stone walls, cellar holes, cemeteries, clearings, apple trees, and lilac bushes remain as reminders of the past.

In 2000, the state of Vermont drew down the Waterbury Reservoir to make critical repairs to the dam. A visit to the reservoir is well worth the trip to view the landscape as it was before the dam was built. The reservoir will be re-filled by 2005.

SOUTHERN ACCESS

TO THE TRAIL: From exit 10 on I-89 near Waterbury (0.0 mi.), go south on Vt. 100 a short distance to the junction with U.S. 2 (0.1 mi.). Turn right onto U.S. 2 and proceed west. Turn right onto Little River Road (1.5 mi.), then pass under I-89. Continue past the unsigned Woodward Hill Trail on the left (3.0 mi.). Then pass a large state parking lot on the left (3.3 mi.) and continue to a parking area by the top of the western dam abutment (4.2 mi.). A formidable gate blocks the access road when the state park is closed (from mid-October to mid-May). The park contact station lies a short distance further along the access road (4.8 mi.).

Parking is available at two lots within the park. From the contact station, bear left, then turn right at an intersection (5.0 mi.) to cross Stevenson Brook on a highway bridge. The Nature Trail parking lot is soon reached on the right (5.3 mi.), shortly before another parking lot on the right signed for history hike parking (5.5 mi.).

WOODWARD HILL TRAIL

Distance: 3.7 mi. (6.0 km)
Elevation Change: 1,270 ft. ascent
Hiking Time: 2½ hrs (reverse 2½ hr.)

ABOUT THE TRAIL: The trail follows a series of gravel roads making it appropriate for early season walks when other trails may be wet and subject to erosion. A loop hike is possible by walking 1.8 mi. along the Little River Road. One end of the trail is accessible from outside the park gate, while the other end is near the park contact station. The trail is described from the Little River Road to the contact station.

TO THE TRAIL: There are two access points for this trail. One is via a class 4 town road that departs Little River Road 1.2 mi. below the state gate at Waterbury Dam (follow the directions on page 270 to the southern access of the Little River area). Parking is available either at a nearby lot on the access road or near the gate itself; both areas are accessible when the park is closed. The other access is in the park near the contact station.

DESCRIPTION: The trail starts at a road junction, by following a woods road, which diverges westerly from Little River Road just beyond the last house. The trail ascends fairly steeply from an initial elevation of 500 ft. It passes a woods road branching to the left (0.6 mi.) and two deer camps (0.7 mi. and 0.8 mi.), which are on private holdings on the left side of the road. A state gate is reached (1.0 mi.), which is locked in the summer. (Cars may be driven to this gate in the summer and parked in a log-loading area on the left.)

Beyond the gate, the trail continues to ascend and reaches a saddle on the east shoulder of Woodward Mtn. (1.8 mi.) at an elevation of 1,770 ft. The trail then descends to a four-way junction (2.4 mi.) where a snowmobile trail goes straight ahead and an improved logging road goes left and right. The trail bears right at the intersection, coinciding with the logging road, and descends to reach another gate (3.5 mi.). Continuing straight ahead, the trail follows the road to reach the park contact station (3.7 mi.), from which point it is an additional 1.8 mi. down the Little River access road to reach the junction at the start of the trail.

5

STEVENSON BROOK TRAIL

Distance: 2.4 mi. (3.9 km)
Elevation Change: 750 ft. ascent
Hiking Time: 1½ hr. (reverse 1¼ hr.)

TO THE TRAIL: The blue-blazed Stevenson Brook Trail starts at a gate at a road junction located 0.2 mi. beyond the contact station where there is a partially hidden trail sign. (This trail begins at the same place as the northern end of the Woodward Hill Trail.) Day-users may inquire at the contact station about parking somewhere between the station and the road junction/trailhead beyond it; otherwise parking is available at the Nature Trail parking lot across Stevenson Brook.

> **WARNING:** This trail is hazardous because Stevenson Brook must be forded twice where bridges are washed out. Bushwhacking on the westerly bank to avoid the two crossings is extremely difficult due to the steepness of the terrain. Do not, under any circumstances, attempt to ford Stevenson Brook when the water is high and flowing rapidly.

DESCRIPTION: The Stevenson Brook Trail follows a long-abandoned road upstream, first paralleling the paved park road through a hemlock grove. Stevenson Brook soon comes into sight. Continuing on easy grades for a short distance, the trail then follows along the western side of Stevenson Brook. The trail crosses the brook (1.0 mi.) and then recrosses it (1.2 mi.) without the benefit of bridges. At the second crossing, the remains of the washed-out footbridge can be seen on the far bank. The trail then crosses a small tributary of Stevenson Brook (1.5 mi.), also without a bridge, which may also prove difficult to cross in times of high water.

The trail then comes to an intersection with the Sawmill Loop Trail, which leads 0.3 mi. north to the Dalley Loop Trail. Immediately after the junction, the Steven-

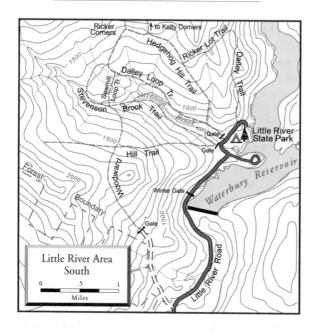

son Brook Trail reaches the site of the former sawmill of the Waterbury Last Block Company (1.6 mi.), which features a locomotive-sized boiler as well as parts of old band saws and a truck chassis. The sawmill was constructed in 1916 and operated until 1922. From the sawmill site, the trail continues northwesterly along the west side of Stevenson Brook. The trail crosses Stevenson Brook (2.0 mi.) on a substantial snowmobile bridge. Proceeding easterly over a rise, the trail passes the farm site (on the north side of the trail) of the first settler to this area, George Kenyon, who arrived in 1790. The trail then reaches its end at the Dalley Loop Trail (2.4 mi.).

5

STEVENSON BROOK NATURE TRAIL

Distance: 0.75 mi. (1.2 km) loop
Elevation Change: minor
Hiking Time: ¾ hr.

ABOUT THE TRAIL: This short trail was developed by the Vermont Department of Forests, Parks, and Recreation to showcase the cultural and natural history of Little River State Park. *Stevenson Brook Nature Trail*, a trail guide describing the botanical, geological, and cultural features of the circuit, is available from the park office. Numbered posts along the trail correspond with the guide; the trail is marked with blue markers.

TO THE TRAIL: To reach the nature trail parking, follow directions to the Little River State Park contact station (page 270). From the office, take the park road toward Camping Area B. After crossing Stevenson Brook on a bridge, park in the parking lot on the right.

DESCRIPTION: Follow signs and the numbered posts. The trail is an out and back with a loop on its end.

HISTORY HIKE LOOP VIA HEDGEHOG HILL TRAIL AND DALLEY LOOP TRAIL

Distance: Loop, 3.8 mi. (6.1 km)
Elevation Change: 650 ft. ascent
Hiking Time: 2½ hr. either direction

ABOUT THE TRAIL: The historic sites along this loop are numbered and described in "History Hike," a pamphlet available at the Little River State Park contact station or from the Barre district office of the Department of Forests, Parks, and Recreation. The hike makes a loop following two trails, the Hedgehog Hill Trail and the Dalley Loop Trail.

TO THE TRAIL: The trail starts opposite the History Hike parking lot, which accommodates a half-dozen cars. Follow directions to the southern access on page 270.

DESCRIPTION: Passing through a gate, the trail shortly reaches a signed junction where it follows the Hedgehog Hill Trail to the right to traverse the loop in a counter-clockwise direction. The trail ascends steadily with a generally moderate grade to reach a parallel detour (0.3 mi.) to the left.

Junction: The parallel detour (from 0.3 mi. to 0.6 mi.) begins with a very steep grade and avoids an eroded portion of the original road.

The detour rejoins the Hedgehog Hill Trail at an unmarked intersection with a road departing to the right.

Junction: This road leads to the Ezra Fuller farm site. While unblazed and unmaintained, the road follows the northerly side of a stone wall until reaching a junction with the presently maintained north side of the Hedgehog Hill Loop Trail. This trail loops back to the park access road near Camping Area B near campsite number 59.

Continuing northwesterly, the Hedgehog Hill Trail soon reaches the Ricker Family Cemetery (0.7 mi.) on the left. (For an instance of nineteenth century longevity, note Phoebe Ricker's tombstone.) The trail then reaches an intersection (0.8 mi.) where the Ricker Lot Trail branches to the right at a sign reading Ezra Fuller Farm.

Continuing to ascend on a northerly and northwesterly course, the Hedgehog Hill Trail ascends to a height of land (1.1 mi.) at an elevation of 1,500 ft., then takes a short detour to the right necessitated by beaver activity and reaches an intersection (1.5 mi.) where a right turn leads to Kelty Corners and Moscow. A schoolhouse was once located at this intersection.

5

Junction: To the right, the Little River Trail ascends to cross over the ridge between the Stevenson Brook and Cotton Brook drainage basins (0.3 mi.), passes an obscure intersection on the left with the Patterson Trail (0.5 mi.), and reaches the signed Kelty Corners (0.6 mi.).

Junction: The Patterson Trail is sparsely blazed and currently unmaintained. It starts opposite two signs pointing in opposite directions to Ricker Corners and Kelty Corners. It goes westerly along the northerly flank of the ridge and then turns to the left, passing over the ridge and descending to the Patterson farm site. It then follows a discernable road to Ricker Corners where there is a sign saying Patterson Trail to Kelty Corners. The trail is about 1.0 mi. long.

From the schoolhouse intersection, the Hedgehog Hill Trail continues straight ahead, descending gradually to Ricker Corners (1.8 mi.) where the so-called upper cemetery is located on the westerly side of the intersection. Here the trail turns left onto Dalley Loop Trail, descending southwesterly to a corner (2.2 mi.) and the intersection with the western end of the Stevenson Brook Trail at a sign saying Sawmill Trail. Turning to the left, the Dalley Loop Trail goes southeasterly, shortly passing another intersection (2.3 mi.) for the Sawmill Loop Trail where another sign says Sawmill Trail.

Junction: The Sawmill Loop Trail makes a fairly direct descent to Stevenson Brook opposite the site of the sawmill of Waterbury Last Block Company. Since there now is no bridge across Stevenson Brook, use of the trail is not recommended. The trail is about 0.5 mi. long.

The Dalley Loop Trail continues southeasterly, passing the Bert Goodell farmhouse, which is the only original building still standing in the Little River Area, and returns to the History Hike parking lot (3.8 mi.).

NORTHERN ACCESS

TO THE TRAIL: From exit 10 on I-89 near Waterbury, go north on Vt. 100. Pass the Cold Hollow Cider Mill (3.3 mi.) in Waterbury Center and the Green Mountain Club headquarters (4.4 mi.) before reaching Moscow

Road on the left (7.3 mi.). Bear left onto Moscow Road, which crosses Little River, and continue through the namesake village. Continuing past Barrows Road and Trapp Hill Road on the right, the Moscow Road reaches a bridge across Miller Brook (9.4 mi.) and an immediate left-hand fork. Bear left onto the gravel Cotton Brook Road where ample parking is available on both sides of the road at a large state lot (9.6 mi.) found immediately after the fork. In the summer it is feasible to drive another 0.5 mi. to reach two small parking lots on the left shortly before a state gate. This area also provides canoe access to Waterbury Reservoir.

COTTON BROOK LOOP VIA KELTY CORNERS

Distance: 11.0 mi. (17.7 km)
Elevation Change: 1,470 ft. ascent
Hiking Time: 6 hrs. either direction

ABOUT THE TRAIL: None of this route is blazed, and there are very few signs; however, it does follow a series of old gravel roads and snowmobile trails. In season, this loop is also open to bicycles. Skiers enjoy this trail in winter, but are careful about snowmobiles. Along the route are sites of the old Little River settlement, including former homes, sawmills, and a school.

DESCRIPTION: From the large state parking lot, the trail coincides with a wide gravel road and follows the westerly shore of Little River and Waterbury Reservoir to the state gate (0.5 mi.). At the gate, a multiuse trail diverges to the left and runs parallel to Cotton Brook Road for a distance before rejoining the road (1.4 mi.). Beyond the gate, the trail coincides with a continuation of Cotton Brook Road which is an improved gravel logging road passable for bicycles as well as hikers. The trail proceeds along the easterly side of Cotton Brook. At an unmarked junction (1.7 mi.) just beyond a utility shed, the return end of the loop joins from the left.

5

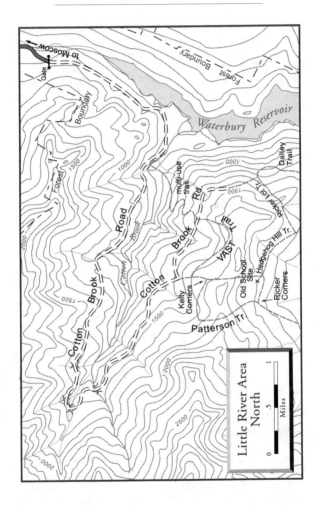

Little River Area
North

0   .5   1
Miles

Continuing to the right, the trail ascends gradually, passing several sites of historic interest. Three streams are crossed, two on concrete bridges (4.1 and 4.5 mi.), and a third on a plank-surfaced bridge, before the trail swings to the south at the crossing of the main branch of Cotton Brook (5.0 mi.) on a large steel culvert. The trail crosses the larger left fork of Cotton Brook (5.4 mi.) on a concrete bridge. On a fairly level course the trail comes to an intersection (6.7 mi.) with an uphill spur to the right where a trail sign points up the spur. The spur is an unmaintained segment of the original road and ascends to Kelty Corners (7.0 mi.).

From the intersection with the spur, the trail gradually descends in a southeasterly direction, offering a 0.8-mi. shortcut to bypass Kelty Corners. Kelty Corners is located on the east side of the ridge separating the Cotton Brook and Stevenson Brook drainage basins. From Kelty Corners, the trail currently takes the sharpest left turn to follow a recently used logging road, which has an uneven surface and is muddy in places. It proceeds southeasterly, descending and ascending gradually to a left turn (7.3 mi.) from which it descends northeasterly on a moderately steep grade to a four-way intersection (7.8 mi.). At this intersection, the shortcut via the road comes in on the left. To the right, the road continues for 0.4 mi. to a log-loading area beyond which is the closed and unmaintained trail connecting to the Hedgehog Hill Trail.

Straight ahead, the trail follows a smooth logging road/snowmobile trail, which zigzags downward to a substantial bridge (8.8 mi.) across Cotton Brook. The trail then follows the easterly side of the brook downstream until it swings away from the brook (9.1 mi.) and makes a very steep ascent to rejoin the easterly side of the loop (9.3 mi.) just beyond the utility shed. The outbound leg is then retraced to the large state parking lot (11.0 mi.).

• • • • • • • • • • • • • • • •

MOUNT NORRIS

Distance: 1.8 mi. (2.9 km)
Elevation Change: 1,320 ft. ascent
Hiking Time: 1½ hr. (reverse 1 hr.)

ABOUT THE TRAIL: Located in the town of Eden, the summit (2,580 ft.) and several lower vantage points on this distinctively shaped peak (USGS Albany) offer good local views to the south and more distant views of the Worcester Range and the Green Mountains. The trail up the mountain is maintained by the campers and staff of the nearby Mount Norris Scout Reservation. (The Larry Dean Trail, named for a dedicated Green Mountain Club member and a veteran boy scout, used to leave from the same trailhead and create a loop hike, but it has not been maintained and is impassable.)

TO THE TRAIL: The trail begins on the west side of Vt. 100, just north of the entrance to the scout reservation, 2.0 mi. north of Eden Mills and 6.1 mi. south of Vt. 58 in Lowell village. The unmarked trailhead is at a gravel pit road, which heads west through an old field. Ample parking is available beside the highway.

DESCRIPTION: This steep and direct route to the summit is blazed with an eclectic mix of faded red and blue paint, green arrows on rocks, and red, blue, or pink flagging. From Vt. 100 (0.0 mi.), the trail follows the gravel pit road west for a short distance, and then angles to the right onto an overgrown old road just before reaching a line of trees and the only trail sign (0.1 mi.). The trail follows the old road to the northwest corner of the field (0.2 mi.) into the trees by a brook where the first blue blazes appear and then follows the badly washed road upstream across a steel culvert bridge (0.3 mi.). The trail continues on the road near the brook on an easy upward winding grade, following the orange and blue tree markings for some distance before coming into the lower end of a large clearing

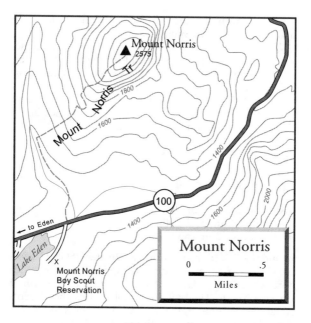

Mount Norris

0 .5

Miles

(0.7 mi.). Crossing to the upper edge of the clearing, the road divides and the Mount Norris Trail enters the woods to the right at a tall red-painted iron pipe and ascends steadily for some distance on an old woods road following blue and orange markings. After a short distance, the road (a narrow path at times) turns right at a big rock. Continuing upward, the trail comes to and then swings to the right of a huge rock at the base of a rock ledge (1.1 mi.) and begins a steep and winding climb around the ledge.

Resuming a northerly direction, the trail continues a steep, difficult upward climb through rocks to a partially open rock area, where there are good views to the south and east (1.3 mi.). Pink ribbons tied on tree branches are

5

used along with the blue and orange flagging to mark the trail from here to the summit.

The trail, now narrow and mostly overgrown, passes several more limited views on and off the trail before ascending to what appears to be a wooded summit. Now only a short distance from the real summit, the trail reaches a 6-ft. drop-off and another short descent before it begins its final ascent to a large rock hogback and a climb to the open summit (1.8 mi.).

•••••••••••••••••

BURNT MOUNTAIN

Distance: 2.0 mi. (3.2 km)
Elevation Change: 1,500 ft. ascent
Hiking Time: 2 hr. (reverse 1¼ hr.)

ABOUT THE TRAIL: Burnt Mtn. (2,626 ft., USGS Hazen's Notch) is the highest point on a spur ridge that trends northwesterly from Haystack Mtn. about 2.0 mi. south of Hazen's Notch. The trail was established by the Hazen's Notch Association and is part of a 30-mi. trail system maintained in association with the Hazen's Notch Cross-Country Ski Area. Most of these trails are for winter use by skiers and snowshoers, but a few trails are open without charge to hikers in the summer season. An area map is available from the association and several stores in the Jay-Montgomery area.

TO THE TRAIL: From Vt. 118 in Montgomery Center, turn east onto Vt. 58 (0.0 mi.), continue past the Hazen's Notch Cross-Country Ski Area, and turn right onto Rossier Road (2.0 mi.). This road is about 9.0 mi. west of Vt. 100 in Lowell. Continue uphill, past a fork to the left, until the road ends at the High Ponds Recreation Area parking lot, near an abandoned farmhouse in a small field (2.5 mi.). Since all trails maintained by the Hazen's Notch

Association are on private property, care should be taken to observe the rules posted nearby.

DESCRIPTION: The Burnt Mountain Trail departs on the left from the Twin Ponds Trail, 0.1 mi. south of the parking lot and a short distance past the two namesake bodies of water. From this signed junction (0.0 mi.), the trail, well-blazed with plastic blue diamonds, soon crosses a small brook and trends southeasterly on an old woods road. Turning sharply right off this road (0.2 mi.) the trail ascends southerly along an old skid road with rough and wet footing and arrives at a junction with the Catamount Trail (0.5 mi.). Bearing left, the trail ascends steadily to the east, continuing through occasional logging debris along the eroded logging road, before bearing right into pleasant woods (0.7 mi.). The trail soon ascends to Window Rock (1.1 mi.) where there are fine views east of Hazen's Notch, Sugarloaf Mtn., and Buchanan Mtn.

At Window Rock, the trail swings to the right and begins a steep and winding climb, eventually reaching and crossing the east side of the ridge (1.5 mi.). The trail continues on easy grades through tall ferns and paper birches to pass near the minor north summit before descending into a sag. The trail then makes a final ascent through spruces to reach the top of a series of ledges, which it follows to its terminus at a cairn on the south summit (2.0 mi.).

From various points along the small, open summit ridge, there are impressive views north to three of the Jay Peaks and east to Hazen's Notch itself. Although the high ridge of the main range of the Green Mountains to the east and the Cold Hollow Mountains to the west preclude views in those directions, there is a good view to the northwest of the Champlain Valley extending into Quebec. The view to the northeast includes the Lake Memphremagog area of the Northeast Kingdom, parts of northern New Hampshire, and several Quebec summits.

5

• • • • • • • • • • • • • • • •

WINOOSKI VALLEY PARK DISTRICT

The Winooski Valley Park District was formed to preserve or acquire natural areas of regional significance and special interest. The park district includes the municipalities of Burlington, Colchester, Essex, Jericho, South Burlington, Williston, and Winooski. The district maintains more than seventeen properties totaling 1,736 acres for passive recreation and environmental protection. Several small, but interesting, locations in Chittenden County providing boat access, picnic areas, or wildlife sanctuaries are described in the district's "Six Easy Walks," a flyer available from the district. Two of the larger district parks that may be of interest to the day hiker are described below. Winooski Valley Park District, Ethan Allen Homestead, Burlington, Vermont 05401; (802) 863-5744; wvpd@together.net.

ETHAN ALLEN HOMESTEAD

ABOUT THE TRAIL: The Ethan Allen Homestead was once the home of Ethan and Fanny Allen. The homestead offers walking trails, guided tours of the restored farmstead, a multimedia show, and museum exhibits as well as picnicking. The trails are open year-round from dawn to dusk. The homestead is open Monday through Saturday, 10:00 A.M. to 5:00 P.M., and Sunday from 1:00 P.M. to 5:00 P.M. during spring, summer, and fall. During winter, the hours are 12:00 P.M. to 4:00 P.M. on weekends, or by appointment Monday through Friday.

TO THE TRAIL: To reach the homestead, take the North Avenue Beaches exit off Vt. 127 (Beltline/Northern Connector) in North Burlington and follow the small green highway signs. The driveway to the homestead begins off this exit ramp. Proceed to the education center where trail maps are available from the nearby information stand or from the office. Ample parking is available.

DESCRIPTION: There are five trails on the property. Two are short wetland trails named Wetlands Walk South and Wetlands Walk North. The three others, each less than a mile long and within easy walking distance of the education center, are the Peninsula Loop, Homestead Loop, and River Loop. Natural features of the Intervale, such as the mature floodplain forests, may be observed from all these trails.

COLCHESTER POND NATURAL AREA

Distance: 2.9 mi. (4.7 km)
Elevation Change: minor
Hiking Time: 1½ hr. (reverse 1½ hr.)

ABOUT THE TRAIL: This 694-acre park, opened by the Winooski Valley Park District in 1997, encircles the mile-long Colchester Pond. This natural area is contiguous with the Indian Brook Reservoir Park (page 286) to the east owned by the town of Essex. No vehicles, motorized boats, or electric motors are permitted in the natural area, which is open dawn to dusk. The one hiking trail in the park nearly circumnavigates Colchester Pond and is marked with yellow blazes and wooden directional signs.

TO THE TRAIL: From the junction of U.S. 2 and U.S. 7 with Vt. 2A in Colchester (0.0 mi.), proceed east on Vt. 2A to the center of Colchester village and turn north (left) onto East Road (1.0 mi.). Turn right at the next intersection (1.2 mi.) onto Depot Road and proceed past the railroad tracks (1.9 mi.) to a fork (2.3 mi.). Bear left onto Colchester Pond Road and proceed past the Curve Hill Road on the right to the parking area on the right (2.6 mi.). The gravel lot contains parking for 20 cars and provides access to both the pond and the hiking trail.

DESCRIPTION: From the parking lot (0.0 mi.), the trail descends along a tree line to reach the western shore of the pond, which it then follows northerly for some distance through three meadows before ascending the shoulder of a small hill. The trail soon meets a junction (0.8 mi.),

5

where it bears right, and then meets another junction, where a spur trail on the right leads to the shore. Continuing left through mature pines, the trail follows the north end of the pond until it intersects the Peninsula Trail (1.2 mi.), which leads 0.1 mi. to the pond's edge.

Continuing straight, the trail crosses a stream on a wooden bridge (1.3 mi.) before meeting and following a logging road (1.6 mi.) along the east side of the pond. The trail follows this road through three hay fields, bisecting each on an indistinct path, before arriving at its terminus near an electrical transmission line at a gate and fence (2.9 mi.). Since there is currently no egress to a public road from this point, the trail remains a long spur, leaving hikers to retrace their steps to the parking lot. Special care should be taken to respect the private property of the residents of this area.

• • • • • • • • • • • • • • • •

INDIAN BROOK RESERVOIR PARK

This 575-acre preserve was formerly used as a municipal water supply and is now managed by the Essex Town Parks and Recreation Department. The 66-acre reservoir was created by damming Indian Brook and is attractive for small nonpowered watercraft. The principal hiking trail in the park circumnavigates the reservoir but is not signed or blazed. A second trail ascends a ridge east of the reservoir, where there is a view to the west.

CIRCUMFERENTIAL TRAIL

Distance: 1.8 mi. (2.9 km)
Elevation Change: none
Hiking Time: 55 min. either direction

To the Trail: From the junction of Vt. 289 and Vt. 15 in the town of Essex (0.0 mi.), proceed east on Vt. 15 and turn left onto Old Stage Road (0.2 mi.). Passing Lost Nation Road on the left, take the next left (0.6 mi.) onto Indian Brook Road and continue into the park at a boundary sign (1.8 mi.). Bear right past two parking lots to reach a third lot located near the boat launch.

DESCRIPTION: From the north end of this parking lot (0.0 mi.), the unmarked and unblazed Circumferential Trail begins its loop around the reservoir by paralleling the east shore. Bearing right at an intersection (0.4 mi.) where a spur leads left to the shore, the trail follows an old road northward to a corner, where a blue arrow on a tree points left. Bearing left, the trail swings to the south and reaches an unmarked intersection (0.8 mi.) where it turns right and crosses Indian Brook on a plank bridge. Bypassing an unmarked trail to the right (1.0 mi.), the trail reaches another intersection (1.2 mi.) marked by a second blue arrow. Bearing left as the arrow indicates, the trail flanks the western edge of the pond, bypassing a spur on the right (1.6 mi.) before reaching a signpost (1.8 mi.) marking the western end of the trail. A short gravel path from this spot leads below the reservoir's dam back to the access road and lower parking lots.

OVERLOOK TRAIL

Distance: 1.0 mi. (1.6 km)
Elevation Change: 300 ft. ascent
Hiking Time: 40 min. (reverse 30 min.)

ABOUT THE TRAIL: The trail leaves the east side of the parking lot for the Circumferential Trail, which was described previously.

DESCRIPTION: The Overlook Trail leaves the parking lot on its east side (0.0 mi.) and proceeds southeast as a mowed path before swinging to the north after being joined by another path from the right. Marked by blue blazes, the trail soon empties into an old road and crosses a stone fence (0.3 mi.). Here the trail makes a sharp left turn off the road as indicated by a blue arrow and follows a narrow path past a sharp right turn (0.4 mi.) to two lookouts (0.7 mi.). From the second of these lookouts the trail makes a sharp turn to the right and continues its northward ascent of the ridge. The end of the trail is reached at a ledge from which there is an excellent view of Colchester Pond (1.0 mi.).

• • • • • • • • • • • • • • • •

RAMBLES

CENTENNIAL WOODS NATURAL AREA

ABOUT THE TRAIL: Centennial Woods is a designated natural area of the University of Vermont (UVM). It consists of 100 acres of mature conifer and mixed hardwood forests, streams, and wetlands used as an ecology laboratory for students. Centennial Woods is notable for its relatively pristine state despite its location along the eastern edge of Burlington, Vermont's largest city. The area is open to the public for foot travel, and a trail loop is maintained by UVM's Environmental Program. Just over 1.0 mi. in length, the trail is blazed sparingly with white paint and some arrows at important turns. For more information, contact University of Vermont Natural Areas, Environmental Program, 153 South Prospect Street, Burlington, Vermont 05405; (802) 656-4055.

TO THE TRAIL: From the jug-handle intersection of Williston Road (U.S. 2), Spear Street, and East Avenue, turn north onto East Avenue and proceed a short distance to the first traffic light. Turn right at the signal, and proceed to the second driveway in front of 280 East Avenue where there are four spaces reserved for natural area visitor parking. The access trail is located across the road near a wooden sign.

DESCRIPTION: At the entrance to the access trail there is a ledger box, which may contain copies of a UVM field guide with descriptions corresponding to numbered stations along the trail. The access trail proceeds to the northeast to cross a wet area on puncheon before reaching a bridge crossing a stream in the bottom of a ravine. The trail then ascends a short distance to a junction, marking the beginning of the trail loop. Following an arrow to the right to make a counterclockwise circuit, the trail ascends steeply to a plateau, then meanders along a ridge covered with giant white pine trees, some 100 ft. tall and 2 ft. in diameter. The trail passes municipal boundary markers, crossing into South Burlington and then back into Burlington, before descending steeply into a ravine and reaching its northernmost point at an electric transmission pole structure. The trail then climbs over a small shoulder to follow a southerly course along the east side of a stream back to the junction with the access trail.

EAST WOODS INTERPRETIVE TRAIL

ABOUT THE TRAIL: Also owned by the University of Vermont, East Woods is a 40-acre woodland in South Burlington exemplary of a mature northern forest. UVM students use the area as an ecology laboratory; it is open to the public for foot travel. An interpretive loop trail, under 1.0 mi. in length, winds through the site's towering pines, hemlocks, and oaks and is sparsely marked with wooden rectangles inscribed with arrows.

TO THE TRAIL: From the jug-handle intersection of Williston Road (U.S. 2), Spear Street, and East Avenue (0.0 mi.), turn south onto Spear Street and continue to a traffic light (2.1 mi.). Turn right onto Swift Street, and

5

proceed west a short distance to the entrance to East Woods Natural Area, which is on the right and marked by a large wooden sign (2.5 mi.). Ample parking is available along the side of the street at the entrance.

DESCRIPTION: From the entrance, the trail leads a few hundred feet to a bulletin board where a ledger box may contain UVM flyers describing the numbered stations along the interpretive trail. The trail continues westerly and shortly reaches a junction with both ends of the loop at Station 3. Bearing right at this junction to make a counterclockwise circuit, the trail descends to approach Potash Brook, which meanders across the property on its way to Lake Champlain. The trail then crosses a slight depression, a remnant of the roadbed of the aborted Burlington and Hinesburg Railroad, which was graded in 1898 but abandoned before any track was laid.

At Station 4 the trail reaches the more obvious roadbed of the Burlington and Lamoille Railroad, which was constructed in 1877, but operated only briefly before being dismantled before the turn of the twentieth century. After following the roadbed for a hundred yards, the trail reaches Station 6, where it turns left off the grade and recrosses the B&L roadbed on a plank bridge. After ascending a small shoulder, the trail then drops to the south shore of Potash Brook, which it follows to the west to reach Station 9. The trail then swings in an arc to the east, with a moderate ascent, to return to Station 3.

RED ROCKS PARK

ABOUT THE TRAIL: Located in South Burlington, Red Rocks Park occupies the former site of a private estate, with interconnected carriage paths that lead through pleasant pine woods to vantage points on the shore of Lake Champlain. The park is maintained by the South Burlington Recreation Department.

To the Trail: From U.S. 7 (Shelburne Road), immediately south of the I-189 interchange, turn west onto Queen City Park Road. After crossing a one-lane bridge, turn left onto Central Avenue and continue a short distance to the park entrance on the right. A parking fee is charged from late June to Labor Day, but pedestrians may enter the park without charge at any time.

Description: From the parking lot designated Parking 1 (0.0 mi.), a trail leads west along the top of a bluff on the north shore of Shelburne Bay, eventually reaching an overlook with a fine view to the south (0.4 mi.). The trail reaches a turnaround loop at the west end of Red Rocks Point, about 50 ft. beyond a turn to the right, where another trail descends to a loop on the east shore of the lake (0.6 mi.). From this latter lookout there is a magnificent vista across the broad lake to the Adirondacks.

North of this main trail are three loops, each 0.6 mi. in length, which may be used to return to the park's entrance. The westernmost loop departs the main path before the turnarounds on Red Rocks Point and circles a 240-ft. knob before returning to the main trail. At this junction, the middle loop leaves to the north to cross the park's 280-ft. wooded summit, passing red rock ledges. This path continues to the east, ending at a junction. To the right, a short path returns to the main trail; while to the left, the easternmost loop heads north to the park boundary before bearing east and ending at the park entrance.

BURLINGTON RECREATION PATH

About the Trail: This 7.6-mi. multipurpose path has many access points along Burlington's scenic waterfront and provides links to other recreation trails in the area. Generally following the former Rutland Railway rail bed, there are striking views across Lake Champlain toward the Adirondack High Peaks.

Local Motion, a nonprofit organization promoting walking and cycling, is working to extend this rail trail northward from Burlington to Canada on the historic Rutland Railroad Island Line. The Island Flyer train ran on these tracks through the Lake Champlain islands from 1901 to 1961.

At this time, the Burlington Recreation Path connects to the South Burlington Recreation Path to the south and recreation paths in Colchester to the north. The South Burlington path is more a spider web of trails than a path. From Oakledge Park, it is roughly 0.5 mi. on Austin Drive to link up with the network.

In 1999, a group of trail advocates established a bike ferry across the Winooski River (the northern terminus of the Burlington Recreation Path) to connect the Burlington Recreation Path with the recreation path in Colchester. On the Colchester side, the recreation path continues 1.0 mi. before connecting with the Mallets Bay Causeway, described on page 293.

The bike ferry is open to walkers, cyclists, and all non-motorized travelers. It runs daily, mid-June through Labor Day and on weekends through October. It operates from 10:00 A.M. to sunset on weekends and from noon to sunset on weekdays. The cost is $1 per person per trip.

To learn more about the ferry and Local Motion's work to unite these existing trails into a regional Island Line Rail Trail, contact Local Motion, 1 Steele Street, Suite 103, Burlington, Vermont 05401; (802) 652-BIKE; info@localmotionvt.org; www.localmotionvt.org.

TO THE TRAIL: To reach the path's southern terminus, from the rotary on U.S. 7 at the head of Shelburne Road, proceed south about 0.7 mi., turn west onto Flynn Avenue, and continue about 0.5 mi. to Oakledge Park where ample parking is available (a fee may be charged). Parking is also available at the Burlington Boat House.

DESCRIPTION: The southern terminus of the paved recreation path is at Austin Drive (0.0 mi.) 0.3 mi. south of

Oakledge Park. The trail continues to the north, reaching the waterfront at Roundhouse Point and Perkins Pier (2.2 mi.), where there is a ferry dock and parking, and continuing north past the foot of College Street, the Lake Champlain Science Center, and Burlington Boat House. The path ascends a tiny hill (3.6 mi.) before reaching North Beach (4.1 mi., parking) and continuing through a wooded area to Leddy Park (5.2 mi., parking). The path becomes less used after crossing Starr Farm Road (6.2 mi.), where it soon passes straight through a junction (7.3 mi.) before reaching its northern terminus at an overlook on the Winooski River (7.6 mi.). See "About the Trail" to learn more about the bike ferry across the Winooski.

Mallets Bay Causeway

About the Trail: At the turn of the twentieth century, the Rutland Railroad constructed a causeway between Mills Point in Colchester and Allen Point in South Hero, commencing rail service through the Champlain Islands in January 1901. Although rail service was discontinued in 1961 and the tracks were removed in 1964, the massive marble blocks of the causeway remain intact, stretching more than three mi. out into the broad lake.

To the Trail: There are two ways to access the causeway, by the Winooski Bike Ferry (see Burlington Recreation Path), or by car.

After crossing the Winooski River on the bike ferry, travel 0.5 mi. on boardwalks and a dirt path through Delta Park (a beautiful lakeshore natural area). Continue 0.5 mi. on bike paths and bike lanes through a small, quiet, residential neighborhood. The bike lanes connect into Airport Park where the causeway path picks up.

Or, to reach the causeway by car (or bike): from Vt. 127, about 1.2 mi. north of the Heineberg Bridge over the Winooski River, follow Porter's Point Road (0.0 mi.) northwest to a four-way intersection (1.9 mi.). Turn left

5

onto Airport Road, and proceed to Airport Park on the right (2.4 mi.), where ample parking is available.

DESCRIPTION: From the park (0.0 mi.), follow a path leading west, which parallels Airport Road at the edge of Colchester Bog. The path joins the old railroad bed, which turns northwesterly to cross the bog, shortly reaching Mills Point Road (1.1 mi.). The trail continues to the edge of the lake (1.5 mi.) before continuing out onto the marble-block causeway. Beyond the first bridge (2.7 mi.), the causeway narrows a bit as the thin ribbon continues out into the broad lake, eventually reaching its end at a gap where the railroad's drawbridge once stood (3.0 mi.). From this point there are fine views in all directions from this unique, low-level perspective. The shore of South Hero lies 0.5 mi. to the north, and to the east the main range of the Green Mountains is clearly visible over the scattered foothills of the Champlain Valley.

Local Motion (see page 292), a nonprofit organization promoting walking and cycling, is developing a bike ferry, replacing the missing turnstile bridge, to link the Colchester side of the causeway with the South Hero side. Once linked, you will be able to walk, run, or cycle through the lake between Vermont's mainland and islands.

GRAND ISLE STATE PARK

ABOUT THE TRAIL: Grand Isle State Park takes its name from, and is located on, the east shore of Lake Champlain's largest island. A short trail opposite the park entrance leads to an observation deck and is the only park facility open for day-use.

TO THE TRAIL: From the intersection of Vt. 314 and U.S. 2 in South Hero (0.0 mi.) near Keeler Bay, proceed north on U.S. 2 to an intersection on the right with State Park Road (1.8 mi.) where there is a large sign for Grand Isle State Park. Turn east onto State Park Road and proceed straight through an intersection with East Shore Road (2.7 mi.) before reaching the contact station (2.8 mi.) where parking is available. A day-use fee is charged in-season.

DESCRIPTION: Opposite the park entrance, on the southwest corner of State Park Road and East Shore Road, is a nature trail sign marking the trailhead of the counterclockwise loop. The trail immediately reaches a junction where a spur to the left leads directly to the observation deck. Continuing straight ahead, the trail crosses several marshy areas on puncheon, then two watercourses. The trail passes from cedar woods into a young hardwood forest as it crosses an open rock knob and the corner of an agricultural field. After ascending a flight of wooden steps, the trail reaches an unmarked four-way intersection. About 70 ft. to the right is a well-constructed, 10-ft.-tall wooden observation deck with good views over the lake to the east. Straight ahead, the trail emerges from the woods to its terminus, 60 ft. south of the trailhead.

ALBURG RECREATION TRAIL

ABOUT THE TRAIL: This nearly 4.0-mi. multiuse trail follows the abandoned East Alburg to Alburg branch of the former Central Vermont Railway. Owned by the state of Vermont and maintained by the Department of Forests, Parks, and Recreation in cooperation with a local snowmobile club, the trail is obvious but unsigned and unblazed.

TO THE TRAIL: The western terminus of the trail is at the easterly end of the Alburg Industrial Park and is reached by the paved Industrial Park Road that leaves U.S. 2 opposite the Alburg Volunteer Fire Department. Ample parking is available at this trailhead.

DESCRIPTION: The trail departs the parking lot (0.0 mi.) and continues easterly along the flat roadbed before entering the Mud Creek Waterfowl Area (0.8 mi.). Managed by the Vermont Department of Fish and Wildlife, the waterfowl

5

area attracts a variety of wildlife, especially in late summer and early fall. The trail continues through areas of marsh and open water before crossing a bridge over Mud Creek (1.6 mi.) and reaching the eastern boundary of the waterfowl area at Vt. 78 (1.7 mi.), about 1.0 mi. east of its junction with U.S. 2. Parking areas are located a short distance east and west.

Continuing across Vt. 78, the trail, now less used, passes intermittently through areas of open farmland before crossing a farm road (2.3 mi.). The trail continues through a narrow band of trees to cross the paved public Blue Rock Road (2.6 mi.) and then the private gravel McGregor Point Road, both within sight of Vt. 78. The trail continues behind a series of private residences and through a wet area to reach an uncertain end in East Alburg, terminating at an active railroad spur track a short distance west of the posted East Alburg trestle (3.6 mi.). Here a road leads a short distance to Vt. 78 at the west end of the Missisquoi Bay Bridge.

BURTON ISLAND STATE PARK

ABOUT THE TRAIL: Burton Island is one of three island state parks located in the northern part of Lake Champlain and accessible from Kill Kare State Park in the town of St. Albans. It is the largest of the state-owned islands (253 acres). Woods Island State Park (125 acres) lies about 2 mi. northwest of Kill Kare and is preserved in a primitive state: no fires are permitted on the island, and camping is allowed only by permit at five designated sites. Knight Island State Park (175 acres) lies about 4.0 mi. west of Kill Kare and offers primitive camping at seven sites. Both islands have hiking trails, but neither has sanitary facilities or potable water supplies. Registration is necessary through the office at Burton Island State Park. The trails described are on Burton Island.

TO THE TRAIL: From I-89 exit 19, follow the signs north to Vt. 36 (0.8 mi.). Proceed west on Vt. 36 through downtown St. Albans (1.5 mi.) to St. Albans Bay (4.5 mi.) and Lake Champlain. Turn right to continue on Vt. 36 (Lake Road), then bear left at an intersection (5.3 mi.) onto Hathaway Point Road. Continue to Kill Kare State Park at the end of the road (8.2 mi.) where parking is available.

A ferry, owned and operated by the state, makes a couple trips daily to Burton Island and Knight Island, starting in late May or early June and continuing through Labor Day. The fee is $3 from port to port, or $6 round trip to Burton Island, or $12 round trip to Knight Island. For information, contact (802) 524-6353 in season, or (802) 879-5686 in the winter months. The state park day-use fee is $2.50.

DESCRIPTION: Three trails may be used to make a counterclockwise circumnavigation of the island. The North Shore Trail starts at the westerly end of the campground (0.0 mi.) at a sign which says nature trail. A descriptive brochure on the geology and ecology to be observed along the trail is available at the Nature Center. The trail runs parallel to the north shore of the island along a mowed grass path through woods and ends at Eagle Bay on the north shore of the island (0.3 mi.). By continuing 0.2 mi. westward along the shore, the northerly end of the West Shore Trail is reached.

The West Shore Trail starts where a defined trail bed (no signage) leaves the shore. The trail, which is poorly maintained, runs parallel to the shoreline and ends on the west shore (0.9 mi.). From this point, it is a 0.2-mi. hike southerly along the shore to reach a clearing on the south end of the island where there are two picnic tables and a park bench.

The Southern Tip Trail leaves the clearing along a wide, mowed path through woods and eventually emerges into another clearing (1.8 mi.). In less than 100 yds., the trail

5

ends at a sign noting the trail to the southern tip, near the maintenance shop on the southerly side of the park facilities.

In addition, the park maintains a 0.75-mi.-long nature trail, which starts and ends behind the Nature Center. A descriptive brochure may be obtained that describes the trail, which follows a partially mowed and narrow path.

MISSISQUOI VALLEY RAIL TRAIL

ABOUT THE TRAIL: Following 26 mi. of the former Central Vermont Railway–Richford Subdivision, this smooth gravel trail generally follows Vt. 105 and the Missisquoi River northeast from the town of St. Albans through Swanton, Fairfield, Sheldon, Enosburg, and Berkshire before ending in Richford. This multipurpose trail, the longest continuous rail trail in Vermont, is owned by the Vermont Transportation Agency and maintained by the Department of Forests, Parks, and Recreation with volunteer assistance. A flyer describing the access, history, and permitted uses of the trail is available from the Northwest Vermont Rail Trail Council, and from register boxes located at major road accesses. Here the trail is described eastbound from St. Albans.

TO THE TRAIL: Although access is available at a number of road crossings, ample parking is available along a designated portion of the old roadbed in St. Albans, at the junction of U.S. 7 and Vt. 105.

DESCRIPTION: From this point (0.0 mi.), the trail bears northeasterly, passing under I-89 and splitting a series of farm fields before crossing Vt. 105 near an old cemetery at the hamlet of Greens Corners (3.0 mi.). The trail soon crosses an interesting marshy area before passing high above the forest floor on the built-up roadbed, and eventually crossing Vt. 105 again near Sheldon Springs. After passing through the village, the trail soon reaches Vt. 105 a third time (8.6 mi.). Due to a missing span in the nearby railroad trestle, a detour east along Vt. 105 is required to cross the Missisquoi River on the road bridge.

Leaving Vt. 105 to the right onto Severance Road (8.9 mi.), the trail soon resumes, departing to the left into the midst of an active grain mill (9.0 mi.). The trail follows the Missisquoi River upstream, eventually making a road crossing in North Sheldon (11.4 mi.) before recrossing Vt. 105 (14.4 mi.) a short distance south of a parking area near a bend in the river.

The trail continues through a series of pastures, crossing Vt. 236 in South Franklin (13.5 mi.) and Vt. 105 twice more (13.9 mi., 15.8 mi.) before crossing a wooden railroad trestle (16.2 mi.) near Enosburg Falls. After passing through the center of town (16.6 mi.), the trail again departs through farm fields and follows the river before making the first of six crossings of Vt. 105 (18.9 mi.). At the last of these crossings, beyond East Berkshire, the trail reaches the east side of Vt. 105 (22.0 mi.) and passes a view up the Trout River to Hazen's Notch and Sugarloaf Mtn. A short distance beyond, the trail crosses the Missisquoi River on a large single-span truss trestle (23.2 mi.), and then continues through rural landscape to reach its terminus on the Troy Road/Vt. 105 (26.1 mi.) in the village of Richford.

MISSISQUOI NATIONAL WILDLIFE REFUGE

ABOUT THE TRAIL: This 6,345-acre area, managed by the U.S. Fish and Wildlife Service, was established in 1943 to provide feeding and resting habitat for migratory waterfowl. Lying in the Atlantic Flyway, the refuge occupies much of the Missisquoi River delta on the eastern shore of Lake Champlain (USGS East Alburg) and consists of marsh, open water, and wooded swamp. Most of the refuge is inaccessible to foot travel.

TO THE TRAIL: The refuge headquarters building is on the

5

south side of Vt. 78, 2.4 mi. west of its junction with U.S. 7 in Swanton village. Parking is available behind the building. About 1.5 mi. of foot trails on a small tongue of land extending southwest between Maquam Creek and Black Creek are open during daylight hours throughout the year. **Description:** The trailhead is at an informational kiosk at the rear of the parking lot. An unblazed but obvious access trail follows a refuge road across the field behind the headquarters building, over the active New England Central Railroad tracks, and past a woodcock management area.

At a signed junction, the Maquam Creek Trail departs to the right and closely follows the shore of the meandering waterway. The trail soon arrives at a signed junction where the Black Creek Trail leaves to the left. Straight ahead, the Maquam Creek Trail continues about 0.5 mi to reach its end at Lookout Point, deep in the heart of the swamp.

Bearing left at the junction, the Black Creek Trail crosses an impressive series of bridges before wandering along the south shore of the peninsula. The trail leaves the water's edge to reach its end on the refuge road at the start of the Maquam Creek Trail, a short distance from the headquarters.

MONTPELIER AREA

Long home to beloved Hubbard Park, the city of Montpelier and nearby East Montpelier now boast an extensive trail network. Walkers and cross-country skiers can enjoy a network connecting trails in Hubbard Park, the North Branch River Park, and East Montpelier.

HUBBARD PARK

ABOUT THE TRAIL: In 1899 John E. Hubbard donated 125 acres to the city of Montpelier. Today the park contains 185 acres and nearly 7.0 mi. of hiking and skiing trails, as well as picnic areas, a soccer and softball field, a sledding hill, and a 54-ft. observation tower with spectacular views of Montpelier and the surrounding mountain ranges. A map of the Hubbard Park Trails is published by the Montpelier Park Commission, and a self-guiding Nature Trail booklet is available at the beginning of the trail. Bikes are not permitted on the trail system. For more information, contact Montpelier Parks Department (802) 223-9512.

A range of habitats are found in the park, including meadows, softwood and hardwood stands, swamps, and thickets. Hubbard Park has several impressive stands of white pine, red pine, and hemlock. The center area is a designated natural area. Near the tower are majestic red oaks, which are at the northern end of their range.

To the Trail: There are several entrances to Hubbard Park. It is easily reached by foot from town or from access roads with parking. A road also passes through the park giving access to many trails as well as to a short hike to the tower. The new Statehouse Trail begins on Court Street 70 yds. east of the statehouse and leads 3,000 ft. to the tower.

Other entrances to the park are on Winter Street, via Court Street, and on Hubbard Park Drive. To reach the Winter Street access, from the intersection of Main and State Streets in downtown Montpelier, head north on Vt. 12. Go three-quarters of the way through the roundabout to take a left. At the stop sign, take a right, staying on Vt. 12. Take the next left onto Winter Street and proceed uphill a short distance to the park entrance and parking.

North Branch River Park

About the Trail: With lands protected by the Montpelier Conservation Commission, the North Branch River Park added 179 acres to Montpelier's parks. Approximately 4.0 mi. of trails are available for walking and skiing. A trail and a new bridge connect Hubbard Park trails with the Vermont Institute of Natural Science's North Branch

Nature Center. The nature center has additional trails including a self-guided nature trail. A trail also leads from the nature center to conserved lands at Sparrow Farm; this trail is open to snowmobiling.

To the Trail: To access the North Branch trails, park at the city pool parking lot on Elm Street and cross the bridge near the tennis courts, or park at the end of Cumming's Street, or at the nature center.

East Montpelier Trails

About the Trail: A nice addition to the Montpelier areas trails, this 8.0-mi. trail network passes through farm fields and forests. The trails give a glimpse into the working landscape of Vermont as they pass through sugar stands, cornfields, and logged areas. The trails allow walking, skiing, snowshoeing, and access to and from hunting areas. Biking, horseback riding, and snowmobile use are also permitted on some sections. The trail system is gradually being expanded and includes a link with the North Branch River Park in Montpelier and the VINS nature center. For access points or a map, contact the East Montpelier town clerk's office.

Stowe Recreation Path

About the Trail: An internationally recognized 5.5-mi. greenway, this scenic, paved, nonmotorized path follows the West Branch of the Littler River from the village of Stowe to the field at Topnotch Resort and Spa. Along the way, there are gorgeous views of Mt. Mansfield, Vermont's highest peak. With seven access points and four designated parking lots, the path is easily accessible for walking, cycling, inline skating, and cross-country skiing. Bikes, skates, and skis may be rented at nearby stores. For more information, contact 800-24STOWE or locally (802) 253-7321.

WEISSNER WOODS

ABOUT THE TRAIL: This 80-acre parcel of woodland was donated to the Stowe Land Trust in 1993 in memory of Fritz Weissner by his family. The trust has established walking trails designed to minimize impact to the site. A map and guide is available from the Stowe Land Trust describing the site and the guidelines for its use; visitors should take care to abide by these rules. Fore more information, contact Stowe Land Trust, P.O. Box 284, Stowe, Vermont 05672; (802) 253-7221.

TO THE TRAIL: From Vt. 100 in Stowe village (0.0 mi.), follow Vt. 108 north and turn right onto Edson Hill Road (3.5 mi.). Continue past the entrance to the Stowhof Inn and take the next drive on the right (3.9 mi.). Parking is available off this private road in a lot on the left.

DESCRIPTION: Two trail loops emanate from a four-corners found about 0.2 mi. from the parking area. To the left, the Meadow Trail, 1.1 mi. in length, offers views of Mt. Mansfield and points south along the main range of the Green Mountains. To the right, the Hardwood Ridge Trail and Sugar House Loop make a 1.6-mi. loop.

LAMOILLE COUNTY NATURE CENTER

ABOUT THE TRAIL: Located in Morristown, this 40-acre nature center is owned by the nonprofit Lamoille County Natural Resources Conservation District. A self-guiding nature trail examines the characteristics of the northern spruce-fir forest and related management practices and land stewardship principles. For more information, call (802) 888-9218.

TO THE TRAIL: From Vt. 100 about 1 mi. south of Vt. 15A in Morrisville, turn west onto the Morristown Corners Road (0.0 mi.). Staying on Morristown Corners Road, bear left at the first intersection (0.1 mi.) and continue

5

straight through the village of Morristown at a four corners (0.7 mi.). Bear left at the next intersection (1.0 mi.)
onto Walton Road and left again onto Cole Hill Road
(1.3 mi.). Continue past the Mud City Loop Road to the
nature center parking area on the right (about 3.7 mi.).

DESCRIPTION: The main nature loop starts to the left of the
signposts and proceeds about 100 yds. to the first station
on the trail, where pamphlets are available. A short trail to
the right of the signposts leads to a wildflower garden,
which attracts many types of butterflies in season. The area
is open from dawn to dusk.

REGION 6

Northeast
Vermont

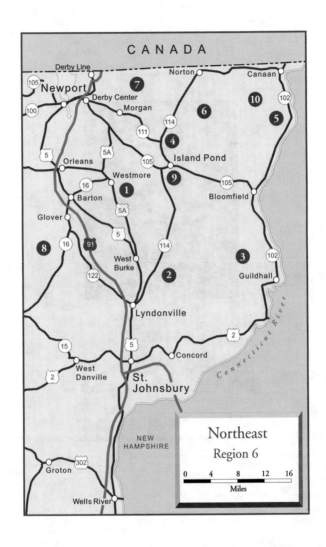

Northeast
Region 6

0 4 8 12 16
Miles

REGION 6
Northeast Vermont

K nown as the Northeast Kingdom, this region is a rugged, heavily forested, and sparsely populated land. Much of the region's interior is accessible only by woods roads, and many people make their living with traditional use of the land. Geologically, the rocks, thin soils, scattered mountains, and dominance of granite make the land more similar to neighboring New Hampshire than most of the Green Mountain state.

This region is east of the major north-south mountain ranges that dominate Vermont and consists of more than 125 randomly scattered mountains and high hills, many of them nameless. Geologists refer to this region as the Northeast Highlands. The area has been subjected to heavy glacial tilling, which has resulted in several large lakes and ponds, among them Maidstone and Averill Lakes. Lake Memphremagog and Lake Willoughby are the best known. In many areas, poor drainage has created extensive areas of swamp and muskeg, making foot travel and route finding difficult.

The classic profile of the Lake Willoughby gateway is the most notable example of the role glaciation has played in creating this landscape.

While these mountains once sported an extensive series of fire towers, used from before the advent of aviation up until the 1970s to protect the area's vast timberland, only a few towers remain. On Bald Mtn. (Westmore) and Burke Mtn., the towers are still publicly accessible. On many other summits, including Gore Mtn., Stone Mtn., Mt. Monadnock (Lemington), and West Pond Mtn. the towers have been closed or removed.

LAKE WILLOUGHBY AREA

Long acclaimed as one of the most scenic areas in Vermont, Lake Willoughby (USGS Sutton, Island Pond, Westmore) has become the center of an extensive trail system. Although the peaks are relatively low, their dramatic cliffs, the deep waters of Lake Willoughby, and scenic views make for excellent and rewarding hiking. Mt. Hor and Mt. Pisgah drop dramatically into Lake Willoughby with some viewpoints looking straight off the mountain to the ice cold waters of the lake 1,000 ft. below. The two mountains form the Lake Willoughby gateway, visible from many mountaintops in northern Vermont.

The Westmore Association and the Vermont Department of Forests, Parks, and Recreation (FPR) have restored old trails and built new trails to reach the major peaks in the area. For guidebook purposes, the trails have been divided into those west and those east of Lake Willoughby. The *Willoughby State Forest Guide*, available from FPR, contains useful information on the western portion of the region. See pages 345 to 348 for contact information.

6

WHEELER MOUNTAIN TRAIL

Distance: 1.3 mi. (2.1 km)
Elevation Change: 690 ft. ascent
Hiking Time: 1 hr. (reverse ¼ hr.)

ABOUT THE TRAIL: Despite its relatively low elevation, Wheeler Mtn. (2,371 ft., USGS Sutton) offers some of the finest and most varied views in the Lake Willoughby area. A white-blazed trail to the summit and Eagle Cliff is maintained by the Westmore Association. An alternate red-blazed route is more steep and creates a loop.

TO THE TRAIL: The trail begins on the Wheeler Mountain Road (Sutton Town Road 15), which leaves the north side of U.S. 5, 8.3 mi. north of Vt. 5A in the village of West Burke and 5.0 mi. south of Vt. 16 in Barton. From the highway, this unpaved road climbs steadily past Wheeler Pond (1.0 mi.) and the beginning of the Wheeler Pond Trail (1.3 mi.) (page 312) before arriving at a parking area on the left, opposite the second of two houses (1.9 mi.). The Wheeler Mountain Road becomes very rough and potentially impassable approximately 1.0 mi. beyond this point, limiting access from the north.

DESCRIPTION: From the parking area, follow the road northerly for 100 yds. to the trailhead on the left (0.0 mi.). Passing through a tree line, the trail quickly reaches an overgrown field and a junction, where an alternate route begins (0.1 mi.).

> **Junction:** To the right, a shorter and more difficult red-blazed route quickly enters the woods, begins a steep and winding climb over the rocks (where there are views of Mt. Norris and Wheeler Pond) and rejoins the main trail in 0.3 mi. The main trail takes the left fork and follows a less demanding route.

From the junction, the main trail soon enters the woods and ascends easily for some distance before beginning a short but stiff climb (0.4 mi.). Soon after turning

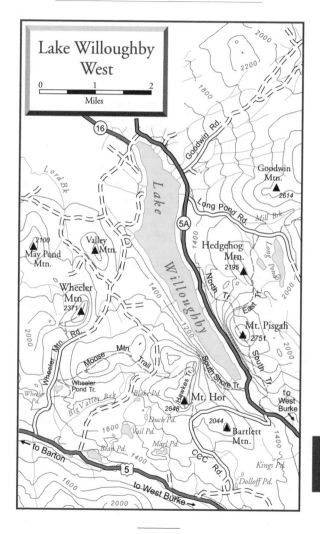

Lake Willoughby
West

0   1   2
Miles

16

Lord Bk

2000

2200

1800

Goodwin Rd.

Goodwin
Mtn.
▲
2614

Long Pond Rd.

Mill Brk.

5A

1400

Lake

Willoughby

Long Pond

2000

2100
▲
May Pond
Mtn.

Valley
▲ Mtn.

Hedgehog
Mtn.
▲
2195

North Tr.

East Tr.

Wheeler
Mtn.
▲
2371

2000

1400

1200

Mt. Pisgah
▲
2751

2000

South Tr.

Wheeler Mtn. Rd.

Moose   Mtn.
        Trail

Wheeler
Pond Tr.

Wheeler
Pd.

Blake Pd.

Big Valley Brk.

Hawkes Tr.

South Shore Tr.

to
West
Burke

◄ to Barton

Mt. Hor
▲
2648

Duck Pd.

2044
▲
Bartlett
Mtn.

1600

Vail Pd.

Marl Pd.

CCC Rd.

Kings Pd.

1400

Bean Pd.

1400

5

to West Burke ►

Dolloff Pd.

1600

2000

6

sharply to the right, the trail continues on easier grades past a view of Wheeler Pond (0.5 mi.) to an open rock area, where the red-blazed alternate route rejoins the main trail (0.7 mi.). A few feet beyond, an unsigned and un-blazed spur to the left ascends 100 ft. to a view, which in-cludes Jay Peak to the northwest.

From the spur junction, the trail winds through spruce and birches for some distance and then returns to open rock (0.9 mi.). Remaining well away from the cliffs com-prising the southeast face of the mountain, the trail climbs steadily in the open past ever-widening views of Lake Willoughby, Mt. Pisgah, Burke Mtn., and Bald Mtn. to an impressive vantage point (1.1 mi.) where the panorama also includes views of Jay Peak, Mt. Mansfield, and many other peaks in the Green Mountain Range.

Beyond the lookout, the trail climbs gradually in the open for some distance, then enters the woods near the summit (1.2 mi.) and descends through spruce and bal-sams to the end of the trail at Eagle Cliff (1.3 mi.). Here, there is an especially grand view of Lake Willoughby, with the open fields in the foreground providing a contrast to the sheer cliffs of Mt. Pisgah and the numerous mountains in the background.

WHEELER POND TRAIL

Distance: 0.5 mi. (0.8 km)
Elevation Change: 80 ft. ascent
Hiking Time: 20 min. either direction

TO THE TRAIL: This trail begins on the Wheeler Mountain Road (follow directions to the Wheeler Mountain Trail, page 310) at a small parking area 1.3 mi. north of U.S. 5.
DESCRIPTION: From the parking lot (0.0 mi.), the trail, marked with yellow-on-blue blazes, immediately crosses a footbridge over Wheeler Brook and reaches a junction

with the Moose Mountain Trail. The Wheeler Pond Trail bears right at the junction and continues through the woods, offering occasional glimpses of Wheeler Pond. The trail meets and joins a woods road (0.3 mi.) that parallels the south shore of the pond, then arrives at a clearing with a limited view of the pond and an old beaver den (0.4 mi.).

Following the road, the trail turns left and begins a gentle climb before departing the woods road to the right and continuing along the south branch of Wheeler Brook. After crossing the brook, the Wheeler Pond Trail ends at the start of the Gnome Stairs Trail (0.5 mi.). Straight ahead are two camps owned and operated by the Appalachian Mountain Club (AMC). The Wheeler Mountain Road lies 0.1 mi. past these camps, and then it is an additional 0.4 mi. north on the road back to the parking area.

GNOME STAIRS TRAIL

Distance: 0.3 mi. (0.5 km)
Elevation Change: 120 ft. descent
Hiking Time: 12 min. (reverse 20 min.)

To the Trail: Follow the Wheeler Pond Trail to Gnome Stairs Trail (0.5 mi.).

About the Trail: The Gnome Stairs Trail leads from the Wheeler Pond Trail a short distance to a series of small waterfalls.

Description: The orange-blazed Gnome Stairs Trail leaves the Wheeler Pond Trail near the AMC camps on Wheeler Pond (see Wheeler Pond Trail, page 312) then follows Wheeler Brook in a southerly direction away from the pond. The trail gently descends and meanders along both sides of the brook before ending at a series of stone benches (0.3 mi.). A unique series of small step waterfalls found here gives the trail its name.

6

MOOSE MOUNTAIN TRAIL

Distance: 3.7 mi. (6.0 km)
Elevation Change: 1,500 ft. ascent
Hiking Time: 2½ hr. (reverse 1¾ hr.)

ABOUT THE TRAIL: This blue-blazed trail provides a route between Wheeler Mountain Road and the east branch of the Hawkes Trail on Mt. Hor. At its eastern terminus, it is identified as the Wheeler Pond Trail. The trail begins on the Wheeler Mountain Road at a small parking area 1.3 mi. north of U.S. 5, which also provides access to the Wheeler Pond Trail.

DESCRIPTION: From the parking lot (0.0 mi.), the trail immediately crosses a footbridge over Wheeler Brook and reaches a junction where the Wheeler Pond Trail departs to the right. Bearing left, the Moose Mountain Trail climbs moderately through a hardwood forest and soon reaches a second junction (0.5 mi.). From this point, a short spur trail departs on the right leading to an outlook with views from southeast to west, including Wheeler Pond.

Bearing left at the junction, the trail climbs more steeply over a series of switchbacks and up a boulder-strewn slope to the west summit. Here the trail descends briefly, then follows a broad ridge to the east, before circling to the south of the east summit and arriving at a another trail junction (2.0 mi.).

Junction: From this point, the Lake Willoughby Vista Trail proceeds straight ahead, and in 0.3 mi. reaches two outlooks with views of the south end of Lake Willoughby.

At the junction, the Moose Mountain Trail bears right and descends, steeply at first, to a forest road in a broad clearing (2.6 mi.). On the south side of the road, the trail enters the woods and soon crosses a small stream. Ascending at an easy grade and keeping to the east of a larger stream, the trail reaches another woods road in a muddy area (3.1 mi.). Turning right onto this road, the trail crosses a small brook on flat stones (3.2 mi.) and narrows to a small path. Then, ascending more steeply, the Moose Mountain Trail reaches its terminus at the east branch of the Hawkes Trail (3.7 mi.).

MOUNT HOR

HAWKES TRAIL

Distance: 1.4 mi. (2.3 km)
Elevation Change: 700 ft. ascent
Hiking Time: 1 hr. (reverse ¾ hr.)

ABOUT THE TRAIL: Mt. Hor (2,648 ft., USGS Sutton), forming the west side of the Lake Willoughby gateway, is notable for the sheer cliffs that rise more than 1,000 ft. above the water. The blue-blazed Hawkes Trail, named in honor of trail-builder Herbert Hawkes, provides access to three lookouts on the mountain. Built and maintained by the Westmore Association, the trail has two branches that lead to two lookouts on the east and a third vantage point just west of the wooded summit.

TO THE TRAIL: To reach the trailhead from Vt. 5A, follow the CCC Road (0.0 mi.) west from the Mt. Pisgah South Trail parking lot. Bear right at a fork, and continue to the trailhead 1.8 mi. from Vt. 5A. There is a small parking area on the right.

DESCRIPTION: From the CCC Road (0.0 mi.), the Hawkes Trail ascends steadily, for the most part on an old woods road. Turning sharply to the left where the road peters out (0.4 mi.), the trail climbs moderately at first and then quite steeply past a piped spring (0.6 mi.) to a junction (0.7 mi.) with the East Branch and West Branch, just below the summit ridge. These two trails each lead to a view point.

> **Junction:** From the junction, the West Branch turns to the left. After ascending steadily for some distance, it continues on easy grades to a point just below the summit, and then quickly descends to the Summit Lookout (1.0

6

mi.). In the foreground are ten small ponds, among them Bean, Wheeler, Blake, Duck, Vail, and Marl. Burke Mtn. is visible on the left, while Hazen's Notch and several of the northern Green Mountain peaks lie to the northwest.

From the junction (0.7 mi.), the East Branch Trail turns to the right and continues just below ridgeline to another junction, with the Moose Mountain Trail (also known as the Wheeler Pond Trail) on the left. The East Branch Trail continues straight through the junction, and then descends for 150 ft. to Willoughby or East Lookout (1.3 mi.), some 1,200 ft. directly above the lake and directly opposite the cliffs on the western face of Mt. Pisgah.

Continuing its descent, the trail soon ends at the North Lookout (1.4 mi.). Here there is a sweeping view of the north end of Lake Willoughby, beyond which can be seen the lower end of Lake Memphremagog, and several peaks along the Vermont-Quebec border. Bald Mtn. lies to the left of Mt. Pisgah.

SOUTH SHORE TRAIL

Distance: 1.3 mi. (2.1 km)
Elevation Change: 150 ft. ascent
Hiking Time: 40 min. either direction

ABOUT THE TRAIL: This short but somewhat rough trail slabs the east side of Mt. Hor 150 ft. above Lake Willoughby, reaching a terminus under the Mt. Hor cliffs.

TO THE TRAIL: The trailhead is at a gated parking area on Vt. 5A, 5.2 mi. south of its junction with Vt. 16 at the north end of Lake Willoughby and 6.2 mi. north of U.S. 5 in the village of West Burke. This lot is 0.5 mi. north of the Mt. Pisgah South Trail parking lot on Vt. 5A.

DESCRIPTION: From the parking area (0.0 mi.), the blue-blazed trail proceeds 150 yds. to a clearing where it bears left onto a woods road for 50 yds. before leaving the road on the right at a small sign. The trail climbs at a moderate pitch in a westerly direction before turning to the north and becoming rougher. With many changes in elevation, the trail ascends to reach its terminus in a large gully under the open cliff face of Mt. Hor (1.3 mi.). From this point, there are limited views through the trees toward the lake.

MOUNT PISGAH

Forming the east side of the classic Lake Willoughby profile, Mt. Pisgah (2,751 ft., USGS Sutton, Westmore) has long been popular with hikers. From the sheer cliffs, which rise more than 1,000 ft. above the lake, there are numerous vantage points with fine local and distant views. Two blue-blazed trails from Vt. 5A, both maintained by the Westmore Association, form a continuous route over the mountain. Completion of the loop, however, requires a scenic 3.0-mi. walk along narrow Vt. 5A. A third Westmore Association trail provides indirect routing to the summit from Long Pond.

The trails near the cliffs may be closed by the state of Vermont during the summer if peregrine falcons are nesting in the area.

SOUTH TRAIL

Distance: 1.7 mi. (2.7 km)
Elevation Change: 1,450 ft. ascent
Hiking Time: 1¾ (reverse 1 hr.)

TO THE TRAIL: This trail begins on the east side of Vt. 5A, opposite a state parking area and the beginning of the CCC Road, 5.8 mi. south of the junction of Vt. 16 at the north end of Lake Willoughby and 5.8 mi. north of U.S. 5 in the village of West Burke.

DESCRIPTION: From the highway (0.0 mi.), the trail descends an embankment and quickly crosses a muddy area on a bridge and then crosses Swampy's Pond, considerably swollen by a beaver dam, on another bridge (0.1 mi.). Turning to the left, the trail follows a hogback to a woods

6

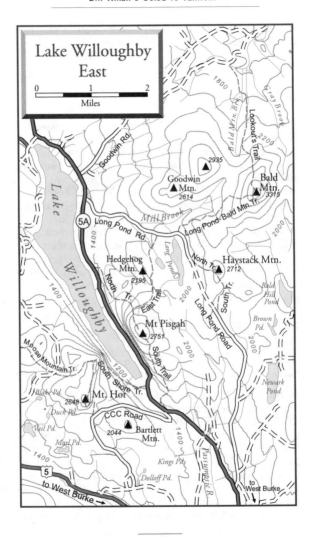

Lake Willoughby
East

0   1   2
Miles

Goodwin Rd.

▲ 2935

Goodwin
▲ Mtn.
2614

Bald
Mtn.
▲ 3315

Bald Mtn. Bk.

Gray Brook

Lookout's Trail

1800

2200

2000

Lake

Willoughby

5A Long Pond Rd.

Mill Brook

Long Pond-Bald Mtn. Tr.

1400

1400

Hedgehog
Mtn.
▲ 2195

Long Pond

North Tr.

Haystack Mtn.
▲ 2712

Bald Hill Pond

North Tr.

East Trail

South Tr.

Brown Pd.

2000

Long Pond Road

Mt Pisgah
▲ 2751

South Trail

2000'

Newark Pond

2000

1200

Moose Mountain Tr.

South Shore Tr.

Blake Pd.

▲ 2648 Mt. Hor

Duck Pd.

CCC Road

▲ 2044 Bartlett
Mtn.

1400

Passumpsic R.

Vail Pd.

Marl Pd.

1400

Kings Pd.

5

Dolloff Pd.

to West Burke →

to
West Burke
↓

road junction (0.2 mi.). Here, the trail turns to the right and ascends for some distance through rocky terrain before again turning sharply to the left (0.4 mi.) and beginning a stiff climb. Soon after negotiating a switchback (0.5 mi.), the trail continues on much easier grades past three lookouts on the left to Pulpit Rock (0.9 mi.). Here, there is an impressive view of Lake Willoughby, some 550 ft. directly below, and Mt. Hor.

From Pulpit Rock, the trail bears to the right, soon begins a steady climb, and eventually reaches an open area (1.7 mi.), where there are views to the south of the White Mountains, Victory Basin, Newark Pond, Burke Mtn., and some of the Green Mountains. From the open area, the trail continues a short distance to the summit and the upper end of the North Trail (1.7 mi.).

> **Junction:** From the summit, a short spur leads to an easterly vista. Straight ahead via the North Trail, it is 0.3 mi. to two lookouts providing outstanding views of Lake Willoughby, Lake Memphremagog, and the Green Mountains, and 2.2 mi. to Vt. 5A, 3.0 mi. north of the beginning of the South Trail.

NORTH TRAIL

Distance: 2.2 mi. (3.5 km)
Elevation Change: 1,530 ft. ascent
Hiking Time: 2 hr. (reverse 1¼ hr.)

ABOUT THE TRAIL: This trail climbs Mt. Pisgah from the north.

TO THE TRAIL: The trail begins on the east side of Vt. 5A, 3.0 mi. south of its junction with Vt. 16 near the north end of Lake Willoughby and 3.0 mi. north of the beginning of the South Trail. Limited parking is available near the trailhead.

DESCRIPTION: From the highway (0.0 mi.), the trail ascends a steep bank and soon enters the woods, following old woods roads on easy grades. After crossing two brooks

(0.6 mi. and 0.8 mi.), the trail follows somewhat steeper grades to a third brook crossing, the last certain water on the trail (1.0 mi.). Beyond the third brook crossing, the trail turns sharply to the left and climbs fairly steeply on an old road. Soon turning to the right off the road (1.2 mi.), the trail climbs steeply on rough footing to a junction (1.5 mi.) with the East Trail (trail description follows), which climbs Mt. Pisgah from the east.

From the junction, the trail climbs somewhat less steeply over rough ground to the first of two spur trails (1.9 mi.), located 150 ft. apart. The lower spur leads 350 ft. northwest to the North Lookout; the upper spur leads west 75 ft. to the West Lookout. Although the views are about the same from each vantage point, the differences in elevation and angle of view provide somewhat different perspectives. From the West Lookout, some 1,400 ft. directly above the lake and the highway, the views include Mt. Hor, Wheeler Mtn., and other local peaks to the west; Lake Memphremagog, Owl's Head, Bear Mtn., and other Quebec summits to the north; many of the Green Mountain peaks from Jay Peak south to Camel's Hump; and Burke Mtn. and a number of New Hampshire peaks to the south, including Mt. Moosilauke.

Past the lookout spurs, the trail continues to the summit of Mt. Pisgah and the north end of the South Trail (2.2 mi.). A short distance beyond, an open area offers views to the south.

Junction: From the summit, the South Trail leads 1.7 mi. down to Vt. 5A. It is 3.0 mi. north along the highway to the North Trail trailhead.

EAST TRAIL

Distance: 1.9 mi. (3.1 km)
Elevation Change: 350 ft. ascent
Hiking Time: 1¼ hr. (reverse 1 hr.)

ABOUT THE TRAIL: Also known as the Long Pond–Mt. Pisgah

Trail, this trail links the Mt. Pisgah trails with the trails to Bald Mtn. and Haystack Mtn. to the east. Maintained by the Westmore Association, most of the route is on a signed but unblazed truck road, while the upper portion is marked with white blazes. The trail joins the North Trail 0.7 mi. below the summit.

TO THE TRAIL: Trailhead parking is on Long Pond Road at a truck road junction 1.8 mi. east of the Millbrook Store on Vt. 5A in Westmore and 0.3 mi. west of the Long Pond Fishing Access.

DESCRIPTION: From Long Pond Road (0.0 mi.), the trail descends southerly on the truck road to a brook crossing (0.3 mi.), and then ascends to a small clearing on the left (1.0 mi.) with views of Bald Mtn. and Haystack Mtn. The trail then continues to a junction in a large clearing (1.4 mi.). Here the trail turns sharply to the right across a tiny stream and a waterbar to enter an older grass-grown woods road. Continuing with minor elevation changes, the trail bears to the left at a fork (1.5 mi.) and follows the road for some distance before turning sharply left off the road into the woods (1.6 mi.). White blazing begins at this point, as the trail climbs easily for some distance, and then ascends more steeply to a junction (1.9 mi.) with the North Trail to Mt. Pisgah. From this point, it is 0.7 mi. south to the summit of Mt. Pisgah or 1.5 mi. north downhill to Vt. 5A.

BALD MOUNTAIN, WESTMORE

Sometimes referred to as Westmore Mtn., Bald Mtn. (3,315 ft., USGS Island Pond) has a summit clearing from which there are good views to the south and east and more extensive views from an abandoned fire tower. The extensive views from the tower include Lake Willoughby, various local peaks, and much of the Green Mountain Range to the west; Lake Seymour, Lake Memphremagog, and several Quebec mountains to the north and northwest; Island Pond, Percy Peaks, the Columbia Range, and

6

northern White Mountain peaks to the east; and Burke Mtn., Umpire Mtn., and the Presidentials to the south.

Two trails lead to the summit. The Westmore Association's trail starts at Long Pond from the southwest, and the original trail to the fire tower, the long-abandoned but still obvious Lookout's Trail, ascends from the north.

In 1921, the Lookout's Trail, a telephone, and a tower line were built on Bald Mtn. This tower atop the summit lasted until 1938, when it was destroyed by a hurricane. It was replaced by the existing steel tower, which was used as a fire lookout until about 1970.

LONG POND–BALD MOUNTAIN TRAIL

Distance: 2.1 mi. (3.4 km)
Elevation Change: 1,450 ft. ascent
Hiking Time: 1¾ hr. (reverse 1 hr.)

TO THE TRAIL: Maintained by the Westmore Association, this trail begins on a truck road that leaves the Long Pond Road 2.1 mi. east from the Millbrook Store on Vt. 5A in Westmore and 0.1 mi. east of the Long Pond fishing access area. Ample parking is available at the trailhead. Except for the unblazed truck road portion, where signs mark critical turns, the trail is marked with yellow blazes.
DESCRIPTION: From the gate at the trailhead (0.0 mi.), the trail ascends northerly on the truck road, bears to the right at a fork (0.2 mi.), and climbs steadily to the northeast into a large clearing (0.5 mi.). The trail turns sharply to the right at the top of the clearing and follows an old woods road for a short distance before turning sharply to the left into the woods (0.6 mi.) where the yellow blazing begins.

Ascending very gradually in an easterly direction through pleasant open woods, the trail eventually reaches an old woods road junction (1.0 mi.). Here, the trail turns sharply to the left, descends gradually to cross a brook (1.1 mi.), and then resumes its ascent, crossing three smaller streams before crossing a larger brook (1.3 mi.)

Beyond the brook crossing, the trail ascends steadily for some distance, and then continues on easier grades to an old woods road junction (1.5 mi.). Here, the trail turns sharply to the right and begins an increasingly steep climb in an easterly direction. After swinging around a large rock outcrop providing limited views to the southwest (1.8 mi.), the trail continues a steady winding ascent for some distance before bearing to the left (2.0 mi.) and continuing on easy grades to the summit and the fire tower (2.1 mi.).

LOOKOUT'S TRAIL

Distance: 2.8 mi. (4.5 km)
Elevation Change: 1,690 ft. ascent
Hiking Time: 2¼ hr. (reverse 1½ hr.)

ABOUT THE TRAIL: Although abandoned for more than 30 years, this unblazed and unsigned route still receives some use and is easily followed in spite of some deterioration from logging activity at the lower end of the trail, as well as some erosion from recent severe storms.

TO THE TRAIL: The trail is reached via town roads leading east from the white church on Vt. 5A in Westmore, 1.0 mi. south of Vt. 16 at the north end of Lake Willoughby and about 11 mi. north of U.S. 5 in the village of West Burke. From the highway and the church (0.0 mi.), follow the paved Hinton Hill Road uphill to the east, take a fork to the right (0.5 mi.), and continue to the next junction (2.0 mi.) where a large glacial boulder is visible in the field to the left. Turn right onto Coles Road, continue past a fork to the right (2.7 mi.), and descend to a fork just beyond a house on the right where an old road goes to the right (3.7 mi.). Although this abandoned road may be passable, with caution, it is recommended that hiking start at this junction. Limited parking is available in the vicinity.

DESCRIPTION: From the road junction (0.0 mi.), the trail ascends in a southerly direction along the old road to a fork and an old trail arrow (0.6 mi.). Here the trail turns to the

6

left, crosses Bald Mountain Brook, and continues on a woods road to the lower end of an extensive logging clearing (0.7 mi.). The trail follows the right edge of the clearing and soon crosses a water bar. Bearing to the right onto an old woods road at this point (0.8 mi.), the trail soon begins an easy climb through pleasant hardwoods and eventually reaches a small piped spring on the left, the last certain source of water on the trail (2.0 mi.). Beyond the spring, the grade increases and soon becomes quite steep. After passing views to the north of Echo Lake and Lake Seymour (2.6 mi.), the trail continues on easier grades to the summit and the fire tower (2.8 mi.).

HAYSTACK MOUNTAIN

Just below the heavily wooded summit of this aptly named mountain (2,712 ft., USGS Sutton, Westmore) are three lookouts providing excellent views to the west, south, and east. Two trails, the North Trail and the South Trail, both established and maintained by the Westmore Association, lead to the summit. The North Trail is the steeper of the two routes. The two trails, with a 1.2-mi. road walk, make a nice loop hike.

NORTH TRAIL

Distance: 1.0 mi. (1.6 km)
Elevation Change: 875 ft. ascent
Hiking Time: 1 hr. (reverse ½ hr.)

To the Trail: This yellow-blazed trail begins at the entrance to a small clearing on Long Pond Road, 2.6 mi. southeast of Vt. 5A at the Millbrook Store in Westmore and 0.6 mi. beyond the Long Pond fishing access area. Parking space is very limited, and care should be taken not to obstruct the narrow public road.

DESCRIPTION: From the road (0.0 mi.), the trail quickly passes through the clearing with its overgrown cellar hole and climbs steadily in an easterly direction on an old woods road. Eventually assuming a southerly direction (0.4 mi.), the trail continues for some distance on easier grades before beginning a moderately steep climb (0.7 mi.) past views of Bald Mtn. and Long Pond (0.8 mi.) to a junction (1.0 mi.).

> **Junction:** To the left, it is 75 ft. to the summit, which is marked by a large cairn. To the right, a spur descends easily for 150 ft. to West Lookout, where there are views of Long Pond, Lake Willoughby, Wheeler Mtn., and Jay Peak. From the summit, South Trail descends 0.1 mi. to East Lookout and 0.2 mi. to South Lookout.

SOUTH TRAIL

Distance: 1.1 mi. (1.8 km)
Elevation Change: 525 ft. ascent
Hiking Time: ¾ hr. (reverse ½ hr.)

TO THE TRAIL: This yellow-blazed trail begins on Long Pond Road, 3.8 mi. southeast of Vt. 5A at the Millbrook Store in Westmore, 1.2 mi. south of the North Trail trailhead. Although ample parking is available at the trailhead, the 1.2-mi. section of the minimally maintained Long Pond Road between the North Trail parking area and the beginning of the South Trail may not be passable for vehicles with low clearance.

DESCRIPTION: From Long Pond Road (0.0 mi.), the trail ascends gradually in a northeasterly direction on an old road to a junction in a large overgrown clearing (0.6 mi.). Here the trail turns to the left, passes the ruins of an old camp, and continues on easy grades through a series of small, overgrown clearings before entering the woods. Soon turning sharply to the left (0.8 mi.), the trail begins a steep and winding ascent around the rocks and ledges to a junction on the east side of the ridge (0.9 mi.). To the left, a spur leads 125 ft. to South Lookout, where there are views of Burke Mtn. and Newark Pond.

From the junction, the trail ascends to East Lookout (1.0 mi.) where there are views of Bald Mtn., Bald Hill Pond, East Haven Mtn., and various White Mountain peaks. From East Lookout, the trail continues to a large cairn marking the summit of Haystack Mtn. (1.1 mi.). A short distance beyond, the trail reaches a junction with the North Trail (page 324) on the right. Continuing straight ahead for 150 ft., the trail ends at the West Lookout.

• • • • • • • • • • • • • • • • •

BURKE MOUNTAIN

Located in East Burke, Burke Mtn. (3,267 ft., USGS Burke Mountain) has a ski area, private campground, toll road, and communications facilities on its west slopes and summit. The mountain's hiking trails offer good views of the surrounding area. The Burke Cross-Country Ski Center offers excellent groomed ski trails.

In recent years, business owners and local people founded the Kingdom Trails Association, which publishes a map and brochure titled "Northeast Kingdom Trails"; it includes hiking trails on Burke Mtn. and a network of mountain bike trails in the area.

The summit of Burke Mtn. was one of the earliest fire tower sites in Vermont. The station was established in 1912 by Elmer A. Darling, who built a camp and tower on the mountaintop. The original tower collapsed in 1932 due to a buildup of ice and snow. A new wooden tower was constructed, but lasted only six years, a victim of the 1938 hurricane, which also destroyed the fire tower atop nearby Bald Mtn. The steel tower with an enclosed cab, currently occupying the summit, was used as a fire lookout until 1984.

TOLL ROAD

Built by the Civilian Conservation Corps, the 2.5-mi. Toll Road leads to a parking area a short distance below the summit. Despite the name, no toll is charged for vehicles or hikers. From the parking area near the summit, the Summit Trail and the Profile Trail lead to the summit and to West Peak; descriptions for these trails follow.

From Vt. 114 in East Burke (0.0 mi.), follow the Mountain Road (the access road leading to Burke Mtn. Ski Area) to where the Toll Road branches to the left (2.2 mi.). The Toll Road is 0.5 mi. below the Burke Mountain Ski Area base lodge parking lot.

SUMMIT TRAIL

From the south end of the parking area at the top of the Toll Road (0.0 mi.), the Summit Trail trends easterly to a junction with the Profile Trail (0.1 mi.). Here the Summit Trail turns to the left and ascends northerly in the woods to the base of the summit fire tower.

PROFILE TRAIL

The Profile Trail (also known as the Under Profile Trail) coincides with the Summit Trail between the parking area and the junction (0.1 mi.), at which point the Profile Trail turns to the right and follows separate routing. After a brief gradual descent, the trail swings to the left into a ravine (0.2 mi.) and ascends along the base of the ledges to an open rock area. It then rejoins the Summit Trail, which it follows for a very short distance to the fire tower (0.4 mi.).

6

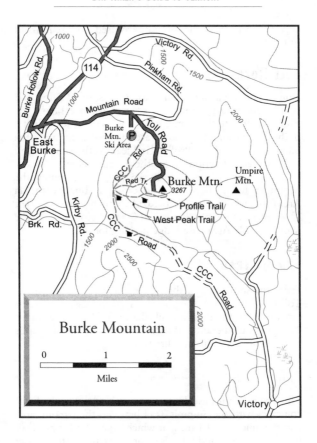

Burke Mountain

0   1   2

Miles

CCC Road

Distance: 3.2 mi. (5.2 km)
Elevation Change: 450 ft. ascent
Hiking Time: 1¾ hr. (reverse 2 hr.)

About the Trail: This is a moderate, multiuse trail built by the Civilian Conservation Corps.

To the Trail: Blazed with blue diamonds, this multiuse trail leaves the Toll Road at a signed junction 0.6 mi. above the ski area access road. Limited parking is available at a small lot 300 ft. below the junction, or alongside the Toll Road a short distance uphill of the junction.

Description: Departing the Toll Road, the CCC Road ascends to the south on easy grades, crossing several ski trails that offer good views to the west. The road continues in the woods to a height of land (1.3 mi.) where the West Peak Trail and Red Trail depart on the left.

From the height of land, the CCC Road descends easily to the southeast into the shallow notch between Burke Mtn. and Kirby Mtn. to the south. Soon after passing a lean-to on the right (2.1 mi.), the trail reaches a junction with a privately maintained snowmobile trail (blazed with orange diamonds), which leaves on the right (2.2 mi.) and heads westerly for about 1.25 mi. to the public East Burke Road between North Kirby and East Burke. Beyond the junction, the CCC Road descends on easy grades past the state forest boundary to a woods road junction (3.2 mi.).

Junction: Straight ahead from the junction, an old road descends on easy grades for about 1.25 mi. to the beginning of a public road which leads south for about 3.5 mi. to the Victory-Granby Road, about 1.0 mi. south of the Mitchell's Landing parking area.

6

WEST PEAK TRAIL

Distance: 1.6 mi. (2.6 km)
Elevation Change: 960 ft. ascent
Hiking Time: 1¼ hr. (reverse ¾ hr.)

ABOUT THE TRAIL: The West Peak Trail (sometimes referred to as the Blue Trail because of its blazing) climbs the western side of Burke Mtn. connecting the CCC Road with the Toll Road. A loop hike is possible using the Red Trail.

TO THE TRAIL: This trail leaves the CCC Road (page 329) at its highest point at an unsigned junction 1.3 mi. south of the Toll Road.

DESCRIPTION: From the unsigned junction (0.0 mi.), the trail ascends 125 ft. to a refurbished lean-to and a junction with the Red Trail, which departs to the left through the rocks on alternate routing to the east slope of West Peak.

The West Peak Trail then climbs steadily through the woods. Soon after passing an excellent view to the west (0.6 mi.), the trail enters an area of open rock and begins easy, circuitous routing past sweeping views of the Passumpsic Valley, the Lake Willoughby area, and the Green Mountains. The trail then continues in the woods to another renovated lean-to on the wooded summit (3,150 ft.) of West Peak (0.7 mi.).

Quickly reaching a good view to the south, the trail circles around the south and east slope to reach the upper terminus of the Red Trail (0.8 mi.), which departs to the left. The West Peak Trail then gradually descends to a ski trail (0.9 mi.), which it follows uphill to the south end of the Toll Road parking area (1.0 mi.).

The West Peak Trail ends at this point, but the blue-blazed Summit and Profile Trails (page 327), which can be combined into an interesting loop, provide routing to the summit fire tower.

RED TRAIL

Distance: 0.7 mi. (1.4 km)
Elevation Change: 700 ft. ascent
Hiking Time: 1 hr. (reverse ¾ hr.)

ABOUT THE TRAIL: Blazed with red paint, this trail provides alternate routing between the CCC Road and the east slope of West Peak.

DESCRIPTION: The Red Trail leaves the West Peak Trail 125 ft. above the CCC Road at a rock outcrop near the left side of a log lean-to (0.0 mi.). The trail makes a steep and winding ascent in the woods and eventually swings around the north slope of West Peak, approaching but generally remaining out of sight of nearby ski trails. The Red Trail terminates at a junction with the West Peak Trail (0.7 mi.), 0.1 mi. east of West Peak and 0.2 mi. below the parking area at the top of the Toll Road.

●●●●●●●●●●●●●●●●

MAIDSTONE STATE FOREST

Distance: 1.8 mi. (2.9 km)
Elevation Change: 270 ft. ascent
Hiking Time: 1 hr. (reverse: 55 min.)

ABOUT THE TRAIL: Lying deep within the Northeast Kingdom, Maidstone Lake was created during the last glacial age, when tremendous forces carved out a deep basin in a preexisting valley. When the glaciers retreated some 12,000 years ago, a clear, cold lake was created, typical of many in the region.

The Vermont Department of Forests, Parks, and Recreation operates two units along the east side of the 796-acre lake. Maidstone State Park offers day-use activities (including a beach), while Maidstone State Forest contains a variety of camping facilities. Three short trails, totaling just

6

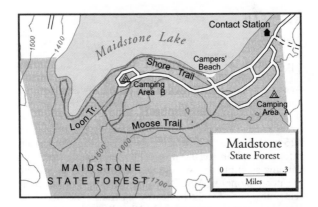

under 2.0 mi., encircle the camping areas in the state forest. A brochure describing the area is available, and a fee is charged in-season.

TO THE TRAIL: From Bloomfield, follow Vt. 102 south for about 5.0 mi., and then turn west onto the gravel Maidstone Lake Road at a Maidstone State Park sign (0.0 mi.). Continue through the state park (5.8 mi.) before reaching the state forest contact station (6.9 mi.). Continue on the access road through Camping Area A to an ample parking lot for the Camper's Beach (7.2 mi.).

DESCRIPTION: The trailhead (0.0 mi.) is at the south end of the Camper's Beach. From this point, the Shore Trail follows the lake's undeveloped south side along flat grades to reach its terminus at a junction (0.6 mi.) with the Loon Trail. From the junction, a spur of the Loon Trail continues straight ahead, passes very close to a beaver lodge (0.7 mi.), and ends in a small loop at the southwest corner of the lake (0.9 mi.).

To the left at the junction, the Loon Trail ascends gently to reach the south side of Camping Area B, where two spur trails leave to the left and enter the campground. The Moose Trail then continues to climb very moderately to three large boulders at the top of a wooded slope, before descending to Camping Area A near the parking lot and trailhead (1.8 mi.).

• • • • • • • • • • • • • • • • •

BLUFF MOUNTAIN

Located in Brighton (USGS Island Pond), Bluff Mtn. rises steeply from the village of Island Pond and extends northeasterly forming the northwestern boundary of the Nulhegan River Basin and overlooking the eastern headwaters of the Clyde River.

BLUFF MOUNTAIN COMMUNITY TRAIL

Distance: 1.7 mi. (2.8 km)
Elevation Change: 1,080 ft. ascent
Hiking Time: 1¼ hr. (reverse ¾ hr.)

ABOUT THE TRAIL: The Bluff Mountain Community Trail climbs to the lower summit and lookout on Bluff Mtn. Although it has existed for many years, portions of the trail have been relocated and stabilized because of recent logging and damage from the 1998 ice storm.

TO THE TRAIL: The blue-blazed trail, built and maintained by the Northeast Kingdom Conservation Service Corps, begins on the north side of Mountain Street in Island Pond, approximately 0.5 mi. beyond the end of the pavement. A trailhead and parking area provide parking space for a small number of vehicles.

DESCRIPTION: From the parking area, the trail climbs moderately to the north through a red pine plantation before bearing west, over two small stream crossings (0.2 mi.), into a mixed forest stand. From here, the trail begins to climb steadily northwest through open mixed hardwoods, crosses an old woods logging road (0.4 mi.), and follows a small ridge until it crosses a game trail and turns sharply to

6

the left (0.6 mi.). The trail soon turns to the right and, climbing more steeply, follows another small ridge before turning left again. Turning westward, the trail descends slightly, crosses a small ravine, and follows a sidehill with young hardwoods where limited views of Island Pond and the Nulhegan Basin are seen to the south. Soon the trail turns sharply to the left and descends a short steep grade before bearing to the right where it continues to follow a sidehill and again descends to the junction with the now-abandoned old trail (0.9 mi.).

From here, the trail turns northward again and, within a few yards, passes a stream crossing and the lower junction of the historic Lookout Trail (1.0 mi.). Continuing north, the main trail passes through a heavily cut area before climbing more steadily north and eastward through an improved section of stone steps and a series of switchbacks. After cresting a small knoll (1.3 mi.), the trail makes a short descent before turning steeply to the left, up a second series of steps and switchbacks, to the summit ridge. To the south and east, several views of the Nulhegan Basin and the surrounding hills are available.

From the top of the steep section (1.5 mi.), the trail continues through a high-elevation gully, winds northward, and drops into a small moose hollow (1.6 mi.) where it crosses a wet area and again climbs up onto the summit ridge. After a few hundred yards, the trail reaches the short summit spur trail on the right and the historic Lookout Trail directly ahead (1.7 mi.). From the summit, Bald Mtn. is evident to the southeast.

LOOKOUT TRAIL

Distance: 0.5 mi. (0.8 km)
Elevation Change: 760 ft. ascent
Hiking Time: 40 min. (reverse 25 min.)

ABOUT THE TRAIL: The yellow-blazed lookout trail is the last remaining portion of the original Bluff Mountain Trail.

From the cliff lookouts near the summit, extensive views of Island Pond, East Mtn., Burke Mtn., and a number of other small peaks are visible to the south and west. Caution: The Lookout Trail is steep and rocky in places and may not be suitable for some hikers!

DESCRIPTION: From the lower junction of the Bluff Mountain Trail, the Lookout Trail crosses a small stream and climbs gently through a large clearcut. At the far edge of the clearcut (0.2 mi.), the trail enters a gradually more mature hardwood forest and bears to the right. Here, the trail climbs steeply at times to the base of the lookout. The trail continues up, with several small switchbacks, over open rock faces to a lower lookout (0.3 mi.). Here, views of the Nulhegan Basin are evident to the south.

From the lower lookout, the trail continues to climb steeply to the main lookout (0.4 mi.) where more extensive views of the surrounding area are available. From the lookout, the trail continues moderately to the summit spur and upper junction of the Bluff Mtn. Trail (0.5 mi.).

• • • • • • • • • • • • • • • •

MOUNT MONADNOCK

Distance: 2.4 mi. (3.9 km)
Elevation Change: 2,108 ft. ascent
Hiking Time: 2.5 hr. (reverse 2 hr.)

ABOUT THE TRAIL: Only slightly lower than its more famous namesake of southern New Hampshire and far less frequently visited, this mountain rises abruptly from the banks of the Connecticut River in the town of Lemington. The mountain is especially impressive when seen from the Mohawk Valley between Colebrook and Dixville Notch, New Hampshire. The abandoned fire tower at the summit (3,148 ft., USGS Monadnock Mtn.) is currently posted against trespass (precluding any views of the surrounding area); climb at your own risk.

6

TO THE TRAIL: The trail begins on the west side of Vt. 102 at a gravel pit 0.2 mi. north of the Lemington-Colebrook bridge. There is designated parking for six cars on the left side of the pit.

DESCRIPTION: From the parking area (0.0 mi.), the trail leaves the rear of the gravel pit and climbs the bank to a sign (0.1 mi.) where it turns to the left and crosses an open field. Proceeding to a white arrow at a fence corner (0.2 mi.), the trail soon crosses a snowmobile trail and enters a young growth forest. Now blazed with yellow parallelogram-shaped markers, the trail emerges into an overgrown field with views north along the Connecticut River Valley and east toward Dixville Notch New Hampshire.

Returning to dense forest for the remainder of the ascent, the trail crosses a brook (0.7 mi.) and joins the old road that originally provided access to the fire tower at the summit. The trail continues to climb with the brook on the right, until crossing it on a small footbridge (1.8 mi.) near a fine waterfall. The trail then follows the brook closely before gradually turning away and beginning a rough and rocky ascent along a shoulder of the mountain. Passing through some wet areas, the grade eases somewhat before reaching the summit (2.4 mi.) in a dense new growth of fir. The summit area is habitat for the rare spruce grouse, commonly known as the fool bird. Near the tower is the foundation of the fire lookout's cabin.

●●●●●●●●●●●●●●●●●

GORE MOUNTAIN

Distance: 3.8 mi. (6.2 km)
Elevation Change: 1,972 ft. ascent
Hiking Time: 3½ hr. (reverse 2 hr.)

ABOUT THE TRAIL: Located in Avery's Gore (USGS Norton Pond), Gore Mtn. (3,332 ft.) forms the northern boundary of the Nulhegan River Basin. The wooded summit offers limited views but is an excellent remote backcountry experience. The recently redeveloped Gore Mountain Trail follows much of the historic fire warden's trail used to access the tower and cabin on the summit.

TO THE TRAIL: The trailhead is in Norton off Vt. 114 across from a pull-off between Lake Station Road and DeVost Road at the north end of Norton Pond. The white-blazed trail, built and maintained by the Northeast Kingdom Conservation Service Corps, enters the woods through a small opening on the east side of the road.

DESCRIPTION: From the trailhead, the trail makes a short climb and follows an unnamed brook for a short way and climbs gradually for the first mile along the old woods road, originally used to access the fire tower and cabin on the summit. After the initial ascent from Norton Pond, the trail levels and crosses several poorly drained areas using bog bridges and step stones. A short spur trail leads left to a beaver meadow (0.6 mi.) where the wooded summit of Gore appears eastward in the distance.

From here, the trail continues gradually, following a series of beaver meadows, and crosses two more small brooks before reaching the most recently abandoned beaver pond (0.9 mi.). The trail skirts the northern edge of the opening and turns eastward, continuing straight for some time through several poorly drained areas and a logged forest.

After passing some abandoned machinery on the right, the trail soon bears left at a signed junction (1.2 mi.) and crests a small knoll (1.3 mi.). From the height of land, the trail descends gradually, winding until it reaches the edge of a wet area and, immediately thereafter, a tributary of Station Brook (1.5 mi.). The trail follows the southern bank of the brook for a short distance and, after crossing it, soon emerges on the edge of an expansive logged area (1.6 mi.). The trail passes through and skirts the logged area, winding through small hardwood stands before turning northeastward and climbing more steeply to the crest

6

of a second knoll. Here, the trail continues for a short distance through a young forest to the edge of a large timber company road (2.0 mi.). The marked trail continues on the opposite side of the clearing.

After crossing the logging road, the trail climbs a short, steep grade and bends right where it soon reaches the junction with the Lookout Trail (2.1 mi.).

Junction: The Lookout Trail leads 300 ft. westward down a gradual grade to the edge of an old sandpit and the timber company road. From here, local views of Middle Mtn. and the Hurricane area are visible to the west.

From the lookout junction, the trail turns left and continues, at a moderate grade, to a second road crossing (2.4 mi.). Here the trail continues opposite the road and after a short distance climbs steeply then moderately through open hardwoods along the northwest ridge of the mountain. Along the way, occasional views are available. To the north are Brousseau and Round Mtns.; Coaticook and the Eastern Townships of Quebec are to the northwest; and to the west are the the the Bill Sladyk (Hurricane) Wildlife Management Area lands in Norton and Holland.

After passing an old skid road (3.0 mi.), the trail turns left and begins a more persistent climb into the higher elevation spruce-fir forests of the summit. The trail bears south and continues steeply over granite bedrock to the shoulder of the mountain. Continuing on, the trail enters the summit forest and turns eastward (3.5 mi.), winding its way until emerging at the edge of the summit clearing (3.8 mi.). Here, the recently repaired fire warden's cabin still stands, and not far away an outhouse is located to the north of the clearing down a short spur trail. From the summit, limited views of the Nulhegan Basin are available to the south.

•••••••••••••••••

BILL SLADYK WILDLIFE MANAGEMENT AREA

Administered by the Vermont Department of Fish and Wildlife, the Bill Sladyk Wildlife Management Area (WMA) consists of about 10,000 acres in the towns of Holland, Norton, Warren's Gore, and Warner's Grant. Although there are no officially marked or maintained hiking trails, most of the area is restricted to travel by foot or snowmobile.

In addition to the many miles of old woods roads, there are several miles of wildlife habitat management access roads and numerous privately maintained snowmobile trails, some of which have signs and orange diamond markers at junction points. The guidebook map shows only a couple trails to small ponds in the area.

Because this is a large area with few conspicuous landmarks, hikers should be especially observant and be familiar with the use of map and compass. The use of a USGS map is highly recommended.

ROUND POND, BEAVER POND, AND LINE POND

Distance: 2.0 mi. (3.2 km)
Elevation Change: 200 ft. ascent
Hiking Time: 1 hr. (reverse 1 hr.)

ABOUT THE TRAIL: Located in the northwest corner of the wildlife management area, these primitive natural ponds are reached from the west side of Holland Pond (USGS Morgan Center).

TO THE TRAIL: From Vt. 111, a short distance west of Morgan Center and just beyond the Seymour Lake fishing access, turn north onto the paved and signed Valley Road (0.0 mi.). After reaching the village of Holland and passing the town garage and a white church, continue straight ahead onto the unsigned and gravel Selby Road (also

6

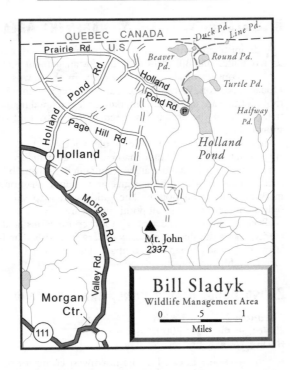

QUEBEC CANADA

Duck Pd.

Line Pd.

Prairie Rd. U.S.

Beaver Pd.

Round Pd.

Holland Pond Rd.

Turtle Pd.

P

Holland Pond Rd.

Halfway Pd.

Holland Pond Rd.

Page Hill Rd.

Holland

Holland Pond

Morgan Rd.

Mt. John 2337

Valley Rd.

Bill Sladyk
Wildlife Management Area

0   .5   1

Miles

Morgan Ctr.

111

known as Holland Pond Road) at a point where the paved road swings sharply to the left (4.8 mi.). After passing straight through a crossroad (6.1 mi.), turn right onto the unsigned and unpaved Holland Pond Road at the next intersection (7.8 mi.). Ignore a road to the left (8.3 mi.), bear left at the next fork (9.9 mi.), and continue to the end of the road at the Holland Pond fishing access area where ample parking is available. From here, the access road leading to the WMA is rough. Vehicles with low clearance should park at the fishing access and walk 0.6 mi. to the gated trailhead. Note: Hikers parking at the Holland Pond fishing access should add 0.6 mi. to all mileages.

From the fishing access (0.0 mi.), follow a narrow private camp road north across Holland Brook. Ignore two forks to the right and continue straight ahead onto a woods road (0.1 mi.) to reach a small clearing, a sign for the WMA, and a gate (0.6 mi.). Vehicles other than snowmobiles are not permitted beyond this point.

DESCRIPTION: From the WMA gate (0.0 mi.), the trail follows the old woods road easterly on high ground above the north shore of Holland Pond to an unmarked trail junction on the left (0.3 mi.).

> **Junction:** From the junction (0.0 mi.), the trail to the left ascends northerly on an old woods road, which is badly washed out in places. After crossing the height of land (0.4 mi.), the trail descends steadily to a small clearing on the southeast shore of Beaver Pond (0.6 mi.). The ridge opposite the pond is in Canada. From the WMA gate to the southeast shore of Beaver Pond it is 0.9 mi.

Continuing straight ahead from the Beaver Pond trail junction, the main trail crosses a small brook on the rocks just below a beaver swamp. A short distance beyond, the trail turns sharply to the left at a junction on the right with an old woods road (0.6 mi.).

After briefly separating and rejoining the road (1.0 mi.), the trail continues to an unmarked spur on the left (1.1 mi.), which descends 100 ft. to the south shore of Duck Pond. The main trail then trends easterly to another unmarked trail junction on the left (1.3 mi.).

> **Junction:** From this junction (0.0 mi.), the trail to the left trends northerly then westerly on high ground above the north side of Duck Pond. After crossing a small inlet brook (0.3 mi.), the spur trail continues on and reaches its terminus at a small open area on the north shore of Beaver Pond opposite a tiny island (0.8 mi.). It is a 2.1-mi. hike from the WMA gate to the north shore of Beaver Pond.

6

Continuing straight ahead from the second Beaver Pond trail junction, the main trail soon reaches another unmarked junction on a patch of exposed bedrock (1.4 mi.). Here a spur trail continues straight ahead for 225 ft. to a log lean-to at the upper end of a large clearing just above the north shore of Round Pond.

The main trail turns to the left at the junction with the Round Pond spur trail and ascends northeasterly in the woods to its final junction, marked by a small birch blowdown and pieces of flagging (1.5 mi.). Hikers should be sure to take the left fork, as the right fork soon swings to the south and continues to the Hurricane Brook area.

Following an old woods road, which is wet in places, the trail reaches its highest point (1.8 mi.) and then gradually descends to its terminus on the west shore of Line Pond, which straddles the U.S.-Canada boundary (2.0 mi.). The boundary, unmarked at this point, is the centerline of the cleared swath around both sides of the pond.

• • • • • • • • • • • • • • • •

RAMBLES

BARR HILL NATURE PRESERVE

ABOUT THE TRAIL: This 256-acre natural area near Greensboro (USGS Caspian Lake) was donated to the Nature Conservancy in 1972 by the Philip Gray family. In 1983, students and staff of Sterling College built a nature trail on the site. An excellent guide is available at the trailhead.

While the summit of Barr Hill is wooded, several vantage points on two short loop trails offer excellent views of four mountain ranges: the main range of the Green Mountains lies to the west, with the Worcester Range slightly south, while south of east is the Presidential Range of the White Mountains, and to the north Mt. Tremblant in the Laurentians in Canada. One loop is 0.3 mi. long and the other is 0.7 mi.

TO THE TRAIL: From Vt. 16 in Greensboro Bend, follow Bend Road northwest for 2.6 mi. to a stop sign in the village of Greensboro. Turn left onto East Street, then right almost immediately onto the East Craftsbury Road (0.0 mi.). Turning right again (0.1 mi.) onto Baker Hill Road (also known as Lauredon Avenue), ignore a fork on the left (0.3 mi.) and continue uphill past the town offices and school. Reaching a junction (0.8 mi.), take the left fork onto Barr Hill Road and continue to the end of the gravel road at a farmhouse, beyond which the Barr Hill sign is visible (1.9 mi.). Continue uphill on the rough and narrow farm road to the signed parking area at the start of the trails (2.5 mi.). Note: It may be necessary to unhook and then rehook the electric fence beyond the farmhouse to enter the access road.

BRIGHTON STATE PARK

ABOUT THE TRAIL: The park has a variety of campsites, as well as developed day-use facilities. An entrance fee is charged in season. A nature trail guide and map of the park's trail system are available at the contact station.

TO THE TRAIL: Located on both the south shore of Island Pond and the west shore of Spectacle Pond, Brighton State Park is reached by following Vt. 105 east from the village of Island Pond for about 2.0 mi., then following the paved Lakeshore Drive/Pleasant Street south for about 0.75 mi. The park entrance and contact station are on the east side of the road.

DESCRIPTION: The park contains four relatively flat interconnecting trails totaling about 2.0 mi. The Shore Trail leads to three scenic vistas of Spectacle Pond, and in con-

6

junction with the Red Pine Trail visits a fine natural stand of mature red pines with an understory of boreal plant species. This plant community, uncommon in Vermont and especially in this region, has been designated a state natural area. Portions of three of the trails are combined into a 0.5-mi. nature trail that focuses on the forests of the Northeast Kingdom.

CHAMPION LANDS

In 1998, roughly 132,000 acres in Essex County that formerly belonged to Champion International were protected for public access through a complex land deal involving the state of Vermont and other parties. About 84,000 acres of the parcel are owned by the Essex Timber Co. and are subject to a public access easement; 22,000 acres are owned by the state of Vermont as the West Mountain Wildlife Management Area; and 26,000 acres have been added to the federal Sylvio O. Conte Wildlife Refuge.

The Champion Lands offer recreational opportunities for hikers, cross-country skiers, nature enthusiasts, hunters, fishermen, and snowmobilers. Although only a limited number of hiking trails cross the property, there are many places to explore in this remote corner of the state. Planning for the use of the Champion Lands is underway. The Green Mountain Club, through its Northeast Kingdom Section, will play an active role as the designated corridor manager for hiking trails. The GMC anticipates providing information about selected hikes in the next edition of the *Day Hiker's Guide to Vermont*.

Useful Addresses

Appalachian Trail Conference, 799 Washington St., P.O. Box 807, Harpers Ferry, WV 25425; (304) 535-6331; general@atconf.org; www.appalachiantrail.org. *Coordinates the work of the organizations and individuals who maintain the Appalachian Trail from Maine to Georgia. Publishes guidebooks to the Appalachian Trail.*

Ascutney Trails Association, P.O. Box 147, Windsor, VT 05089. *Maintains trails and shelters on Mt. Ascutney. Publishes* Mount Ascutney Guide.

Catamount Trail Association, 1 Main St., Suite 308A, Burlington, VT 05401; (802) 864-5794; ctamail@aol.com; www.catamounttrail.org. *Maintains 280-mile Catamount Trail, "The Length of Vermont on Skis." Publishes* Catamount Trail Guide.

Cross Vermont Trail Association, c/o Cross Vermont Trail Coordinator, 81 East Hill Rd., Plainfield, VT 05667; georges@together.net. *The CVT will be Vermont's first east-west, long-distance, multiuse trail extending 75 miles from the Connecticut River to Lake Champlain.*

Equinox Preservation Trust, P.O. Box 46, Manchester Village, VT 05254; (802) 362-4700; ept@sover.net. *Maintains and protects trails on Mt. Equinox and near Equinox Pond.*

Friends of West River Trail, P.O. Box 25, Jamaica, VT 05343. *Maintains West River Trail.*

Green Mountain Club, 4711 Waterbury-Stowe Rd., Waterbury Center, VT 05677; (802) 244-7037; gmc@greenmountainclub.org;www.greenmountain club.org. *Maintains, manages, and protects 445-mile Long Trail System, which extends along the ridge of the Green Mountains from Massachusetts to Canada. Publishes* Long Trail Guide *and quarterly newsletter, the* Long Trail News.

Green Mountain National Forest, Forest Supervisor's Office, Rte. 7, 231 North Main St., Rutland, VT 05701; (802) 747-6700; www.fs.fed.us/r9/gmf/. *Maintains foot trails and multiuse trails as well as camping and other recreation areas. Forest map, day hiking guides, and other publications available. District ranger offices in Manchester, Middlebury, and Rochester.*

Hazen's Notch Association, P.O. Box 478, Montgomery Center, VT 05471; (802) 326-4799; info@hazensnotch. org; www.hazensnotch.org. *Promotes land conservation, environmental education, outdoor recreation, scientific research, and stewardship of natural resources.*

Kingdom Trails Association, P.O. Box 204, East Burke, VT 05832; info@kingdomtrails.org; www.kingdomtrails. org. *Protects, develops, and promotes recreational trail network in Northeast Kingdom.*

Merck Forest and Farmland Trust, Route 315, P.O. Box 86, Rupert, VT 05768; (802) 394-7836; merck@vermont el.net; www.merckforest.com. *More than 2,800 acres devoted to education, conservation, and recreation. Publishes free trail map of 26-mile trail system.*

The Nature Conservancy, 27 State St., Montpelier, VT 05602; (802) 229-4425; kward@tnc.org; www.nature. org/states/vermont. *Preserves plants, animals, and natural communities.*

New England Trail Conference, c/o Forrest House, 33 Knollwood Dr., East Longmeadow, MA 01028; www.wapack.org/netrails/index.htm. *Clearinghouse for organizations and public agencies that maintain and manage trails in New England.*

Putney Mountain Association, P.O. Box 953, Putney, VT 05346; (802) 387-6635. *Protects and maintains trails on Putney Mountain ridge.*

Sterling Falls Gorge Natural Area, 91 Sterling Gorge Rd., Stowe, VT 05672; gander07@realtor.com.

Stowe Land Trust, P.O. Box 284, Stowe, VT 05672; (802) 253-7221; stowelandtrust@pshift.com; www.stowe landtrust.org. *Conserves land in the Stowe area, especially Lamoille Country and the Worcester Range.*

Taconic Hiking Club, c/o Katharine Wolfe, 45 Kakely St., Albany, NY 12208. *Maintains Taconic Crest Trail. Publishes* Taconic Crest Trail Guide.

Vermont Department of Fish and Wildlife, 10 South Building, 103 South Main St., Waterbury, VT 05671-0501; (802) 241-3700; information@fwd.anr.state.vt.us; www.anr.state.vt.us/fw/fwhome/. *Manages state's fisheries and wildlife resources.*

Vermont Department of Forests, Parks, and Recreation, 103 South Main St., 10 South, Waterbury, VT 05671-0601; (802) 241-3655; parks@fpr.anr.state.vt.us; www.vt stateparks.com. *Maintains hiking and multiuse trails, campgrounds, picnic areas, and other recreational facilities in state parks and forests. Publishes maps, brochures. Free trail maps available at many parks or from agency regional offices in Barre, Essex Junction, Pittsford, St. Johnsbury, and Springfield.*

Vermont Department of Tourism & Marketing, 6 Baldwin St., Drawer 33, Montpelier, VT 05633; (800) VERMONT; (802) 828-3237; www.1-800-vermont.com.

Vermont Institute of Natural Science, Montpelier, North Branch Nature Center, 713 Elm St., Rte. 12, Montpelier, VT 05602; (802) 229-6206.

Vermont State Police Headquarters, Waterbury State Complex, 103 South Main St., Waterbury, VT 05676; (802) 244-8727; www.dps.state.vt.us. *In case of emergency, call 911.*

Westmore Association, c/o Paul Moffat, RD 2, Orleans, VT 05860. Maintains trails in the Lake Willoughby area. *Publishes free map and guide of area trails.*

Williams Outing Club, Williams College, Williamstown, MA 01267. *Maintains trails in southwest Vermont and northwest Massachusetts.*

Windmill Hill–Pinnacle Association, 1915 Patch Road, Putney, VT 05346. *Manages trails and protects portions of the Windmill Mountain ridgeline in Westminster.*

Winooski Valley Park District, Ethan Allen Homestead, Burlington, VT 05401; (802) 863-5744; wvpd@together .net. *Protects land and funds recreation and education programs along the lower Winooski River.*

GMC Publications

The Green Mountain Club welcomes inquiries about hiking and backpacking in Vermont. GMC publications are available from the GMC store in Waterbury Center or online at www.greenmountainclub.org. For more information or to order GMC publications, contact:

Green Mountain Club
4711 Waterbury-Stowe Road
Waterbury Center, Vermont 05677
Phone: (802) 244-7037
Fax: (802) 244-5867
E-mail: gmc@greenmountainclub.org
www.greenmountainclub.org

Books

Long Trail Guide (24th edition, fourth revised printing 2000). Describes the Long Trail System and the Appalachian Trail in Vermont. Comprehensive guide with 16 topographical maps, trail summaries, trailhead directions, suggested hikes, and winter hiking suggestions.

The Long Trail End-to-Ender's Guide. A must-have guide for long-distance Long Trail hikers. This supplement to the Long Trail Guide provides up-to-date information on trail conditions, overnight accommodations, equipment sales and repairs, trail towns, mail drops, and transportation.

A Trip Leader's Handbook: Advice for Successful GMC Outings. A handy reference for GMC sections, school groups, outing clubs, and camps. This booklet covers everything a trip leader needs to know to plan and run a successful outdoor trip. Topics include clothing and equipment, emergencies, trail etiquette, and leadership.

Green Mountain Adventure: Vermont's Long Trail. Published in 1989, this illustrated history of the Green Mountain Club, by Jane and Will Curtis and Frank Lieberman, contains 96 pages of rare black-and-white photographs and anecdotes of the club's first 75 years.

Brochures and Newsletters

Long Trail News. GMC's quarterly membership newsletter provides trail and shelter updates, hiking, statewide trail information, club history, and a club activities calendar.

"The Long Trail: A Footpath in the Wilderness." Information about the Long Trail System. Free with self-addressed stamped envelope.

"The Tundra Walk: An Interpretive Guide to the Mount Mansfield Alpine Region." A brochure with illustrations that describes a one-half-mile section of the Long Trail on the ridge of Mount Mansfield.

Additional Reading

These books may make your outings safer and more enjoyable. Shop online at www.greenmountainclub.org.

Natural History and Field Guides

The Nature of Vermont: Introduction and Guide to a New England Environment, Charles W. Johnson, University Press of New England, 1998.

Newcomb's Wildflower Guide, Lawrence Newcomb, Little, Brown & Co., 1989.

The Peterson Field Guides Series, Houghton Mifflin Co. and *The Stokes Nature Guides*, Little Brown & Co.

Reading the Mountains of Home, John Elder, Harvard University Press, 1998.

Tracking and the Art of Seeing: How to Read Animal Tracks and Sign, Paul Rezendes, Harper Resource Books, 1999.

Hiking How-to Books

Backpacking: One Step at a Time, Harvey Manning, Random House, 1986.

The Complete Walker III, Colin Fletcher, Random House, 1984.

Mountaineering First Aid: A Guide to Accident Response and First Aid Care, Jan D. Carline et al., Mountaineers Books, 1996.

The NOLS Cookery: Experience the Art of Outdoor Cooking, 4th edition, National Outdoor Leadership School, Stackpole Books, 1997.

Winter Camping: Wilderness Travel and Adventure in the Cold-Weather Months, Stephen Gorman, AMC Books, 1999.

Winterwise: A Backpacker's Guide, John M. Dunn, Adirondack Mountain Club Books, 1997.

Ethics and History of Outdoor Recreation

Backwoods Ethics: Environmental Issues for Hikers and Campers, Laura and Guy Waterman, Countryman Press, 1993.

Forest and Crag: A History of Hiking, Trail Blazing, and Adventure in the Northeast Mountains, Laura and Guy Waterman, AMC Books, 1989.

Green Mountain Adventure: Vermont's Long Trail, Jane and Will Curtis and Frank Lieberman, Green Mountain Club, 1989.

Wilderness Ethics: Preserving the Spirit of Wildness, Laura and Guy Waterman, Countryman Press, 1993.

Green Mountain Trail Guides and Maps

Appalachian Trail Guide to New Hampshire-Vermont, Appalachian Trail Conference, 2001.

Best Hikes with Children: Vermont, New Hampshire & Maine, Cynthia C. Lewis, Thomas J. Lewis, The Mountaineers, 2000.

Fifty Hikes in Vermont, Green Mountain Club, Backcountry Publications, Countryman Press, 1997.

Guide to the Taconic Crest Trail, Taconic Hiking Club, 1992.

Hiker's Guide to the Mountains of Vermont, Jared Gange, Huntington Graphics, 2001.

Long Trail Guide, GMC Publications, 2000.

Mt. Ascutney Guide, Ascutney Trails Association, 1992.

Index

GMC Membership

B ecome a member — help protect and maintain trails and support outdoor education throughout Vermont. We have two types of membership — section and at-large. See page 20 for information about dues and more details.

GMC Sections

Enjoy year-round outings — hiking, biking, cross-country skiing, canoeing, and more — potlucks, too. Help maintain trails and shelters. Meet people who enjoy outdoor activities in one of these sections:

- Bennington, Vermont
- Brattleboro, Vermont
- Bread Loaf (Middlebury), Vermont
- Burlington, Vermont
- Killington (Rutland), Vermont
- Laraway, Northwestern Vermont
- Manchester, Vermont
- Montpelier, Vermont
- Northeast Kingdom, Vermont
- Northern Frontier (Montgomery), Vermont
- Ottauquechee (Woodstock), Vermont
- Sterling (Stowe-Morrisville), Vermont
- Connecticut
- Worcester, Massachusetts (eastern Massachusetts)

At-large Membership

The club also offers an at-large membership for those who wish to support the GMC but are not interested in affiliating with a section.

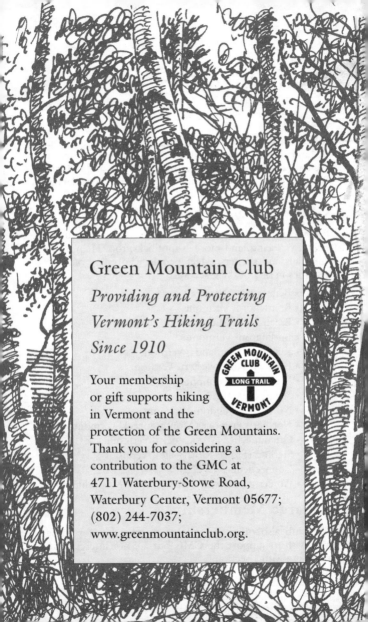

Green Mountain Club

Providing and Protecting Vermont's Hiking Trails Since 1910

Your membership or gift supports hiking in Vermont and the protection of the Green Mountains. Thank you for considering a contribution to the GMC at 4711 Waterbury-Stowe Road, Waterbury Center, Vermont 05677; (802) 244-7037; www.greenmountainclub.org.